Regimented Life

Series Editors: Victoria M. Basham and Sarah Bulmer

The Critical Military Studies series welcomes original thinking on the ways in which military power works within different societies and geopolitical arenas

Militaries are central to the production and dissemination of force globally but the enduring legacies of military intervention are increasingly apparent at the societal and personal bodily levels as well, demonstrating that violence and war-making function on multiple scales. At the same time, the notion that violence is as an appropriate response to wider social and political problems transcends militaries: from private security, to seemingly 'non-military' settings such as fitness training and schooling, the legitimisation and normalisation of authoritarianism and military power occurs in various sites. This series seeks original, high-quality manuscripts and edited volumes that engage with such questions of how militaries, militarism and militarisation assemble and disassemble worlds touched and shaped by violence in these multiple ways. It will showcase innovative and interdisciplinary work that engages critically with the operation and effects of military power and provokes original questions for researchers and students alike.

Available Titles:

Resisting Militarism: Direct Action and the Politics of Subversion
Chris Rossdale

Making War on Bodies: Militarisation, Aesthetics and Embodiment in International Politics
Catherine Baker

Disordered Violence: How Gender, Race and Heteronormativity Structure Terrorism
Caron Gentry

Sex and the Nazi Soldier: Violent, Commercial and Consensual Contacts during the War in the Soviet Union, 1941–1945
Regina Mühlhäuser (translated by Jessica Spengler)

The Military-Peace Complex: Gender and Materiality in Afghanistan
Hannah Partis-Jennings

Politics of Impunity: Torture, The Armed Forces and the Failure of Transitional Justice in Brazil
Henrique Tavares Furtado

Conscientious Objection in Turkey: A Socio-legal Analysis of the Right to Refuse Military Service
Demet Çaltekin

Poetic Prosthetics: Trauma and Language in Contemporary Veteran Writing
Ron Ben-Tovim

The Gendered and Colonial Lives of Gurkhas in Private Security: From Military to Market
Amanda Chisholm

Martialling Peace: How the Peacekeeper Myth Legitimises Warfare
Nicole Wegner

Regimented Life: An Ethnography of Army Wives
Alexandra Hyde

Forthcoming:

Beyond the Wire: The Cultural Politics of Veteran Narratives
Nick Caddick

War and Militarisation: The British, Canadian and Dutch Invasion of Southern Afghanistan
Paul Dixon

Mobilising China's One-Child Generation: Education, Nationalism and Youth Militarisation in the PRC
Orna Naftali

Regimented Life

An Ethnography of Army Wives

ALEXANDRA HYDE

EDINBURGH
University Press

For Lizzy Evison,
in memory of her brother,
Lt Mark Evison

Edinburgh University Press is one of the leading university presses in the UK. We publish academic books and journals in our selected subject areas across the humanities and social sciences, combining cutting-edge scholarship with high editorial and production values to produce academic works of lasting importance. For more information visit our website: edinburghuniversitypress.com

Edinburgh University Press Ltd
13 Infirmary Street,
Edinburgh, EH1 1LT

First published in hardback by Edinburgh University Press 2024

Typeset in 11/13 ITC Giovanni Std by
IDSUK (DataConnection) Ltd, and
printed and bound by CPI Group (UK) Ltd, Croydon, CR0 4YY

A CIP record for this book is available from the British Library

ISBN 978-1-4744-4392-0 (hardback)
ISBN 978-1-4744-4393-7 (paperback)
ISBN 978-1-4744-4394-4 (webready PDF)
ISBN 978-1-4744-4395-1 (epub)

CONTENTS

ACKNOWLEDGEMENTS

Thank you to all those who participated in this research, and the regimental community as a whole for welcoming me so openly. I am particularly grateful to the staff of the Welfare Office at the time my fieldwork took place, for helping to facilitate my research but also for providing advice and their own personal insights and support. I would like to thank the Commanding Officer of the regiment at the time for supporting my project and permitting it to take place. I remain incredibly grateful for the family connection through which I negotiated my access to the regiment, and the trust I relied upon to vouch for my research. Thank you.

Thank you to Marsha Henry and Clare Hemmings at the Department of Gender Studies at the London School of Economics, who supervised the PhD research on which this book is based. Thank you to Cynthia Enloe. Thank you to Rachel Woodward and Vron Ware. Thank you then, and since, to Hazel Johnstone. Thank you to Mary Evans, and to Harriet Gray.

Thank you to the co-editors of the Advances in Critical Military Studies series, Victoria Basham and Sarah Bulmer, for their encouragement with the writing of this book and what it has become, and their own important work to shape the field. Thank you to the reviewers, to Sarah Foyle and all involved in producing the book at Edinburgh University Press.

Thank you, always, to Katie Natanel. Thank you to my mother and father for the motivation to work hard and to the rest of my family for all the support they have given me in so many ways. Thank you to Matthew and the world I couldn't have imagined when this project began.

Introduction: Follow the Cake Stall

On a rainy Saturday afternoon back in March 2012, I found myself standing on a gym mat in the car park of a British Army barracks in Germany, struggling to lift a metre-long tube of plastic piping and manoeuvre it in a figure-of-eight above my head. Two women dressed in camouflage trousers, caps and army boots blew their whistles and everyone moved on to the next exercise in the circuit: flipping truck tyres, lunge-walking with water-filled jerry cans or hitting punch-bags. The regiment's Physical Training Instructor (PTI) strolled among the rag-tag bunch of army wives and a couple of officer-husbands, calling me a 'fanny' as I attempted to run with a wet weighted rope slung over my shoulder. When the 'outdoor caveman circuits' were over and my custom-made, pink '*FIT SQUAD*' vest was soaked with rain and sweat, I followed everyone back inside to the tea urn and cake stall for a homemade fairy cake. This was the 'Fitness Fiesta', a fundraising event organised by women married to servicemen who lived around the army camp. It was, indeed, a landmark event for me during my ethnographic fieldwork. When relaying my experience as an anecdote to amuse friends (who are aware of my general aversion to sport), one of them asked with some consternation why I had chosen to participate in such a ridiculous exercise. I could easily have stayed inside and watched, or at least joined the small number of startled troopers who had been roused from their Saturday-afternoon naps and commanded to make up the numbers in a Zumba class. And it was true, I had observed soldiers setting out their own 'caveman circuits' in the gym several times, finding the format mildly amusing and scribbling field notes about militarised masculinities.

But had I merely observed this event from the side-lines, I would have missed its peculiar duality, its fascinating mixture of militarisation and mimicry. During the exercise the husband of one of the civilian women running the circuits shouted out laughingly to ask if this was proving useful for my PhD. Struggling to speak from beneath a heavy object, I answered that yes, in fact, I was right there and then being *militarised*! Except that I didn't really feel militarised; rather I felt like I was participating in a trend that I had often observed, where humour and irony are used to parody and undercut military ideals of manhood (brute force at the expense of civilisation and sophistication, hence 'caveman'). Yet, at the same time, there was no doubt that by participating in the circuits I was selectively manipulating some of the very same symbolic capital of toughness to mark myself out as someone who was physically strong enough to withstand a 'beasting', which was gratifyingly enforced by the congratulations of some other wives who were spectating, and the wry compliments of the PTI that evening at dinner.

This experience illustrates three important principles at the centre of this book. Firstly, that militarisation is fluid and contradictory. In the instance I describe above, it is the very denigration and undercutting of militarised and masculine ideals of fitness (the 'caveman') that facilitates the compliance of those taking part. Our inevitable failure to reach the standards of caveman fitness was offset by our implicit mockery of those very ideals, at the same time as we were paradoxically underwriting and reproducing them by striving to meet them at least halfway. Had I not been flat on my back on a gym mat 'joking' about being militarised, undertaking a public and personal negotiation with the militarisation of my body and social personhood, I doubt that the double-edged dynamic of the caveman circuits would have registered. The second principle on which this research is founded, therefore, is that it is only by looking at how militarisation is negotiated at a micro-level that we can understand more about its complexities. Catherine Lutz (2002, 725) has argued for the need to connect 'global and national histories' to 'ethnographically understood places and people' to really understand how militarisation operates. It is in order to take the micro-politics of military power seriously that I adopted ethnographic methods for this research. Contrary to studies that conflate militarisation and militarism as shorthand for a monolithic, totalising form of domination, and the military institution as a 'total institution' (Goffman, 1961), paying ethnographic attention to the transformative and co-operative processes through which military power operates on a day-to-day level reveals that it is fluid, emergent and contingent.

Thus, rather than exploring the application of military force as an outcome, or 'being militarised' as the fixed ontological status of the subjects who encounter or are part of military institutions, this study explores militarisation through its imbrication with other vectors of power.

The third and final principle at the core of this book is its attention to the everyday lives and experiences of a group of subjects whose positionality within circuits of military power is deeply ambiguous in relation to what might be called the 'military' and 'civilian' spheres. Simply taking account of women's domestic and reproductive labour as it forms part of the daily life of a military institution, for example, can reveal how gender roles and militarisation intersect to confound and not simply to reproduce the military/civilian divide. At the Fitness Fiesta, the tea urn and fairy cakes set up on a trestle table in the corner of the gym were an incongruous presence that represented more than the irony of doing caveman circuits then gorging on chocolate brownies. In my ethnographic experience, the cake stall (and I frequented or helped out on quite a few of them during my time on camp) is an ubiquitous indicator of gender politics. At the Fitness Fiesta, the cake stall stands for the initiative of the women who, with the support of the PTI, had negotiated British Forces Germany (BFG) red tape to join the regiment's training course, qualify as civilian fitness instructors and run classes for other wives in the gym, which I also attended on a regular basis. In fact, by considering the Fitness Fiesta and its attendant cake stall in terms of women's labour, the event can be viewed as a civilian appropriation of military capital that is both material and symbolic. The Fitness Fiesta culminated in a raffle where the prizes included a week's personal training with the PTI (accompanied by some humorous innuendo about his physical – read sexual – prowess), three baskets of ironing to be undertaken by someone's husband, and free babysitting sessions. As the tombola was wheeled squeakily into a sports hall usually full of soldiers after a run, and the handle cranked by a PTI more accustomed to light artillery, it was women's labour and a familial appropriation of social space that prevailed in demilitarising the gymnasium.

It is over thirty years since Cynthia Enloe (1989, 7) asked 'where are the women?' in international relations, and her work has persistently demonstrated the importance of paying attention to everyday gendered power relations as both a cause and effect of militarisation (see also Enloe 2000, 2007, 2013). There has been a growing critical interest in the impact of military life on civilian women married to servicemen in a British context, much of it working against or to disrupt functionalist frameworks for understanding their role in organisational effectiveness. This includes empirical work on women's experiences of deployment (Long 2019, 2021), as well as domestic abuse (Gray 2017). I embarked upon this research project in order to explore the agency of women married to servicemen and what this might tell us about militarisation; how they actively participate in making and resisting it; are sometimes its agents and sometimes its victims.[1] What this study reveals is that militarisation both maintains and ruptures gendered expectations. It also shows the importance of listening to what people say and feel about military power, how they respond to its everyday forms, and the importance of paying attention to its operation at a micro-scale.

Context and Background

This study is an ethnography of a British Army regiment based overseas, from the perspective of women married to servicemen. It undertakes a gender analysis of the experiences of army wives during a six-month period when most of the regiment's soldiers were deployed on combat duty in Afghanistan. Throughout the book I use a feminist analysis to connect a set of physical, social and political spaces that include Afghanistan as a theatre of war, the UK as sovereign nation, a British military camp in Germany, and the domestic sphere of family homes. The book explores military wives' ambiguous and, I argue, highly mobile positionality between global and local arenas, military and civilian spheres, and public and private domains. In such a way this project sets out to document the everyday mobilities that are subsumed beneath the mass-mobilisation and logistical manoeuvres of the armed forces, less visible but no less significant in terms of their contribution to the configuration of military power at a variety of different levels. These 'military mobilities' include the geographical migrations of the regimental community, from the UK to Germany, for example, as well as the temporal shift from periods of training to deployment and 'normalisation'. They also include the social mobility inscribed in apparently fixed structures of rank as they intersect with gender, race and class. Finally, these mobilities extend to the fluctuations in human relations produced by real and imagined violence and absence and separation during an operational tour. Ultimately, I use an assessment of military wives' power as both subjects and agents of military mobilities to illustrate how militarisation is a process that is always in flux: spatially and temporally contingent, socially constructed, non-linear and negotiable rather than fixed and absolute. These are the conceptual ideas that emerge from the qualitative, in-depth and nuanced portrait this research aims to provide on an empirical level. In contrast to the study of military-institutional power as a top-down structure of control, I look to its more diffuse operation at a micro-scale, in everyday life.

It was ten years ago that I spent six months living in the barracks of the regiment whose culture I explore here, a period that now requires contextualising briefly in terms of the institutional, political and scholarly context of the time. The necessity for a brief retrospective in this book itself underlines the wax and wane of military power, which is a form of state control that comes in codenamed surges. There are peaks and flashes, 'hot' periods, global and national fluctuations where the Armed Forces are more visible, before they go to ground again. This includes foreign wars but also domestic crisis points such as the COVID-19 pandemic more recently, or, in a slightly different vein, the deployment of the regiment I was with in 2012 to support security for the London Olympics. Then there is the sense in which military power again recedes, lies dormant, camouflaged.

When I began my fieldwork, in January 2012, the regiment in question was deployed on front-line operations in Afghanistan, one of three operational tours that it conducted between 2008 and 2014, following three operational tours in Iraq between 2003 and 2007. The official withdrawal of five hundred British troops from Afghanistan had been announced by Prime Minister David Cameron in 2011, so the tour was already weighted with the hope that it could, or should, be the last one the regiment would have to bear. Even at the time of the 2012 deployment, less than a year after US Special Forces killed Osama Bin Laden, Afghanistan itself was slipping in and out of public consciousness in Britain. Domestic productions of recognition and remembrance became gradually less visible,[2] though the rehabilitation of the British Army continued through a range of new charities harnessing consumer demand for a particular brand of national nostalgia (Basham 2016; Tidy 2017). The war in Afghanistan so easily slipped into history, it seemed, that the chaotic fall of Kabul and Helmand Province to the Taliban in August 2021 came as a shocking recall,[3] like an opening of old wounds, with radio and television commentary focusing either on the sense of futility and waste or a desperate revival of discourses of honour in national service, global security and twenty years' worth of terrorist threat successfully defused.

In academic research in the UK and elsewhere, the wars in Iraq and Afghanistan that followed the events of 11 September 2001 brought about a renewed interest in the role and visibility of military power and its function in everyday life in the West. In many ways, this critical reappraisal of military power in countries like the USA and the UK picked up where formulations of Cold War military power left off (see, e.g., Der Derian 2001). There was a new wave of critical interest in war and military institutions, heralding theories and frameworks for understanding gender in relation to 'New Wars' (Chinkin and Kaldor 2013), for example, and anti-militarism movements against 'empires' of military bases (Lutz 2009). Scholarship on military families can be located within policy-oriented research often funded by the US Department of Defense (Castaneda and Harrell 2007; Hogan and Seifert 2009; Little and Hisnanick 2007; Westhuis et al. 2006), though more recent bodies of work have provided insights into military family experience in a wider range of international contexts such as Argentina, Estonia and Israel, and from different disciplinary perspectives (Moelker et al. 2015 and 2019). In the UK the British government began publishing its own yearly survey on military family welfare contemporaneously with the beginning of my research, in 2010.[4] In 2011, then Prime Minister David Cameron launched the Armed Forces Covenant as a pledge to provide support for active and former service personnel and the 'spouses, civil partners, and children for whom they are responsible' (Ministry of Defence 2011a, 4). Using progressive, inclusive terms such as 'spouse' and 'partner' to include military husbands and same-sex relationships, the Covenant remains in place today as a channel for financial aid and assistance.[5] Meanwhile, the symbolic visibility of the 'military wife' in British political and cultural life reached its peak around the same time with the BBC television series *The Choir: Military Wives*,[6] a reality show that focused on the establishment of a choir as a way of bringing women together for mutual support during deployment (for a feminist analysis, see Cree 2020). It is my contention in this book that the complexity and contradictory nature of the experiences and identities of women married to servicemen remain largely obscured by the easy stereotypes perpetuated by the British media and populist accounts that uphold the value systems of the military institution (see, e.g., Stanford 2011 and, for a critique, Gray 2022)

Against this backdrop, my ethnographic research can be framed as a contribution to the growing number of empirical studies of specific communities 'living with' military institutions in particular places and at a particular times, which are also informed by feminist and queer scholarship and the critical turn in military studies (e.g. Baaz and Verweijen 2017; Basham and Cantigani 2018; MacLeish 2013; Silva 2017; Wool 2015). Like many of these studies, my wider aim is to explore the link between people's everyday experiences and what these might tell us about military power as a national and global apparatus of state power. Research within the multidisciplinary field of gender studies, and feminist research in particular, provides the critical framework for my approach. Work by feminist scholars such as Cynthia Enloe (2000), Vron Ware (2012) and Rachel Woodward (2004) have been my inspiration here for the careful attention they pay to the complex reliance of military power on all kinds of intersecting power relations in everyday life. Gender as an analytic has been well used in scholarship within the field of critical military studies to explore the social construction of military masculinities among service personnel, for example (Belkin 2012; Higate 2003; Razack 2000), but also questions of gendered forms of labour among men and women peacekeepers (Henry 2012) and within organisations such as NATO (Bastick and Duncanson 2018; Hurley 2018), in addition to private security companies (Chisholm 2013; Higate 2012). Such research is invaluable for highlighting the politics of militarised identities. However, the analytic of military femininities as at least co-constitutive of masculinities, let alone in their own right and for their own sake, has not achieved the same epistemic resonance. It is not that women and occasionally femininity as a lens (see Titunik 2008) are entirely absent from studies of military power, war and the production of violence, where feminist scholars have explored the construction of gendered identities largely with respect to the question of women's participation in armed forces or organisations (Basham 2016a; Chua 2022; Duncanson and Woodward 2016; Holland 2009; Holyfield et al. 2019; Lobasz 2008; Sjoberg 2007; Taber 2011; Wilcox 2013). There is an enduring interest in, and need for, debates around women's participation in military institutions, the case for which has been strengthened by debates around the participation of gay and lesbian personnel in various state contexts (e.g. Bulmer 2013; Kaplan and Ben-Ari 2000), and transgender politics (e.g. Okros and Scott 2015). This has provided rich terrain for theorising the dependence of military discourses on normalising ideas about gender and sexuality. Yet, within this, less empirical attention has been paid to the question of exactly how that reliance on heteronormative ideals is produced in everyday life. Examining how the military control of gender and sexuality has and continues to be deeply embedded in the twinned heteronormative institutions of marriage and the family, as I do here,[7] provides valuable insights into the social change that this new wave of critical sociological research seeks to potentiate.

Research Setting

The community at the heart of this study includes a cohort of families who experienced what was considered by many as a culturally and historically significant change in soldiers' exposure to war and physical violence. The post-9/11 wars in Iraq and Afghanistan, in particular the 2003 invasion of Iraq, were frequently framed as landmark events with respect to understandings and approaches to soldiers' risk of death or disability and family separation or bereavement, as well as the media visibility and political economy of the British military institution within the UK and globally. The geographical setting for this study, however, is a location that is neither on 'the home front' nor in a faraway combat zone. Rather, this study was conducted among a community of British Army families living within a garrison on the outskirts of a provincial German city, with the regimental camp and barracks as its administrative centre. Already, at the time of my fieldwork, the setting for this study was slipping quietly into history, with the draw-down of all British Army regiments permanently based in Germany announced in the 2010 Strategic Defence and Security Review (UK HM Government 2010), to be completed by 2020 (ibid., 28). The trend towards base closures in certain locations has been increasing over the past twenty years, mirrored in the literature by an acknowledgement of the consolidation or rundown of large, long-term installations of the US or British military domestically and overseas (Sandars 2000, 303; Woodward 2004, 153), which includes 'Closing Communities' (Hawkins 2001, 257) in Germany.

The UK military maintained a large and continuous presence in Germany post-1945, when the British Army of the Rhine (BAOR) was formed to control the British zone of Allied-occupied Germany (Chrystal 2018). Along with other NATO allies such as the US Army (Hawkins 2001), British Armed Forces maintained an active defence presence in Germany throughout the Cold War. The reduction of forces as part of UK defence cuts in 1993 saw the creation of British Forces Germany (BFG) with several garrisons closing and the role of the UK military shifting to operations based on training and readiness, as well as combat service support after 1994. The withdrawal of the British Army's permanent presence in Germany (the last facility was handed over to the German Bundeswehr in February 2020[8]) has entailed the relocation of twenty thousand military personnel and their families to the UK since this research began. The most recent policy on adapting the British Army for the 'generational and societal changes' (Ministry of Defence 2021, 11) of the twenty-first century addresses the increasing demand for long-term home-ownership and stability among service families, which was already a key factor in many people's ambitions during my fieldwork. In 2012 regiments based in Germany for decades were already being moved to new headquarters in the UK. With speculation rife as to which unit would be relocated next, the feeling was overwhelmingly of a community on the cusp of change, holding out in an increasingly archaic setting with its World War II–era barracks and parade grounds, Cold War bunkers and 1960s housing estates, so long the province of drab training exercises and waiting for action that never came. Remnants of Cold War (even World War II) conditions still defined some quirks of everyday life in the garrison: if I wanted to buy coffee or cigarettes, it was explained to me when I arrived, there was a ration card through which my purchase of these goods would be taxed in the correct way. For petrol, there were fuel tokens. This, despite the global repositioning of threat according to the post-9/11 'axis of evil' such that, since 2003, troops had been returning to their German headquarters in desert camouflage from a tour of duty with 'Op Telic' in Iraq or 'Op Herrick' in Afghanistan, via a two-week stop in Cyprus for warm weather 'decompression'.[9] In this sense, and as portrayed in a photographic retrospective of BFG published to mark the withdrawal (Johnston 2019), my fieldwork sometimes felt like a final opportunity to capture the experiences of a community already slipping into history, living out their final months in a Cold War time warp.

One of the risks of undertaking research on a community that might be said to represent the end of an era is that it fixes them further into a particular place in history.[10] But the legacy of these historical features of British Army life in Germany are part of the point of this study. While it is important to pay attention to what is new in the processes of social change experienced by the regimental community in Germany – new wars, changing demands and expectations around diversity along with shifts in societal norms, including equal opportunities for women married to servicemen to fulfil their own career needs or aspirations, for example – it is also essential to question what has been blindly carried over from the past, ingrained in social orders and spatial arrangements, or adapted in order to endure. The archaic stereotypes that adhere to the figure of the army wife, a deeply heteronormative sexual division of labour, and questions of women's paid labour are all still relevant here. Celebrating the supposed modernisation of the present-day role of military spouses within the British Armed Forces, for example, Annabel Venning (2005, 320) quotes an officer who declares:

> If the [Commanding Officer] comes into the mess nowadays and asks an officer if his wife can arrange the flowers on a particular day, he's likely to get the response, 'sorry, she can't, she's a barrister and she's in court that day', or 'she's a surgeon and is needed at the hospital' – or she may be in the Army herself.

Such an optimistic view of women's labour power is still defined by substitutable and tokenistic archetypes that inhere in class and economic background correlating with particular ideas about rank, as I explore in Chapter 3. As such, the military institution has been characterised as suffering from a kind of cultural lag (Higate and Cameron 2004). The timeliness of this research, therefore, is less about capturing the end of an era. Rather, I am interested in the convergence of multiple processes of social, institutional and political change, not all of which were perceived by everyone as going in the same forward direction. The experiences of women married to servicemen are particularly relevant precisely because of their mobile position at the points where many of those conduits of change – family life, social norms, multiple generations, basing policies and combat operations – intersect.

The British Army Regiment as a Unit of Analysis

Between January and July 2012 I lived in the barracks of a regiment whose headquarters had been located in Germany for well over fifteen years. When I was first introduced to the regiment, it was at a briefing in the UK for the families of single, junior soldiers, designed to prepare them for the upcoming operational tour in Afghanistan.

I met the Welfare Officer, who would be my main point of contact for everything during my stay, where I would have a desk in the welfare office. During this meeting I was given a plastic wristband of the kind that had recently become popular through charities like Help for Heroes. Bearing the colours and insignia of the regiment, the wristband was an instant signifier of its localised patterns of support and belonging. Most of the family members at the briefing wore one. Sold by soldiers sent out to shopping malls and supermarkets in local areas around the regiment's UK headquarters, the wristbands tag the geographical catchment area of its regional affiliation, signalling its visible presence as an institution – and an employer – for multiple generations of local families as well as for young recruits from farther afield, who might be attracted to its reputation and image as a front-line, action-oriented regiment. The wristbands are sold to raise money for the regiment's own charitable fund, through which it provides financial aid for families on a loosely defined, informal basis at its own discretion.

When I was given a wristband during my first formal meeting with the regiment, before my fieldwork had been agreed, it seemed like an invitation to declare my loyalty; an initiation. Standing awkwardly in an office with the Welfare Officer, I wasn't quite sure what to do with it. I slipped it into my bag. Unworn, the wristband soon assumed the status of an anthropological artefact: it travelled home with me and sat on my desk for a while, one of those objects one cannot use but cannot throw away. It wasn't just that I felt queasy about displaying this instant token of support for the military and, presumably, its aims and methods in current operations. More than this, I didn't quite feel I had earned the right to become part of the regimental network so swiftly and casually. In other words, I didn't feel that I belonged.

I explore the social patterning of regimental belonging further in Chapter 4 of this book. Given what my research shows about the centrality of the regiment as a cultural production to modes of military belonging, it is perhaps inevitable that the regiment came to define my own social, cultural, geographic and administrative boundaries during fieldwork. My starting point for gaining access to the British Army was a member of my extended family, who vouched for me personally and facilitated the submission of my project proposal to the appropriate personnel within his own network. As my relative joined this particular regiment as a junior soldier and stayed with it for over twenty-five years, reaching a senior position, there was never a question of me being placed anywhere else. From the very beginning, therefore, my research was bound by the kind of family loyalties that, as I show, are fundamental to its will to belong.

With my relative's continued support and advice, I was able to liaise directly with the regiment's senior personnel to gain permission to carry out my research, communicate its aims and objectives, and clarify the practical and ethical conditions under which it would be conducted. My independent, small-scale project was classified as 'informal' in a meeting with a representative from the PR department of the UK Ministry of Defence (MOD), where the consent I had been granted from the regiment was upheld in acknowledgement of the autonomy of its commanding officer. This is testament to the regiment's control over its minor, everyday administrative affairs, but also to its surprising informality. As a living, working organisation – an organisation for which people work, yes, but also an organisation with which they live – there were many processes and practices that allowed the regiment to function iteratively, with a kind of informal power that took an interpretative approach to top-down institutional policies. As I discuss in my conclusion to this book, the regimental welfare office that hosted me during my research is an aspect of the unit's support structure that more than anything perhaps, encapsulates the blurriness of boundaries between 'working for' and 'living with' the regiment, and therefore the informal and the formal, the private and the public, the institution and the domestic sphere. For me, as well as many of the women I talked to during my fieldwork, the welfare office and its personnel fulfilled the role of what ethnographic study guides call the 'gatekeepers' to research (O'Reilly 2005, 91).

In this technical sense, the regiment and its camp in Germany constituted my geographical research setting and an accessible institutional and social structure through which to meet participants. I was offered accommodation and meals in the sergeants' mess, which was also home to a handful of soldiers who were divorced and 'living in' or separated and living 'married unaccompanied'. Married personnel lived with their families in Ministry of Defence– owned estates of service family accommodation (SFA) nearby. In many ways, the regiment provided a practical cut-off point for a reasonably sized group of research participants. While there were many different units and regiments stationed around the garrison town, I restricted my research sample to women married to personnel in or attached to the host regiment. I conducted over fifty interviews in total, which included several follow-up interviews that were conducted towards the end of my stay with women whom I had first interviewed earlier in my fieldwork period. The sample also includes two servicewomen from among the very small number of female personnel serving in the regiment, two servicewomen from other units who were married to male members of the regiment, and ten interviews with servicemen.

The centrality of the regiment as a social unit here underlines the particularity of my project in time and space, as well as its particularity within the reified organisational structure of the UK military. I draw on a range of literature relating to military institutions around the world for my analysis in this book, yet my data derives from one single branch of the British military, the British Army (the others being the Royal Navy and the Royal Air Force [RAF]), and one single regiment of a specific type within that. My choice to retain the general terms 'military wives' and 'women married to servicemen' alongside 'army wives' reinforces the analytical connection I seek to make between the everyday experiences of the women I encountered and the broader workings of military power writ large. At the same time, it must be stressed that 'the military', even within the UK, constitutes myriad sites, times and types of service. The experiences I document here are forged in specific conditions that might be argued to complicate the idea of any kind of unitary 'military culture' at all (Murray 1999; Soeters et al. 2006; Winslow 1999), with an interrogation of regimental culture at its heart. My fieldwork also coincided with a period when particular regiments within the British Army were under consideration for amalgamation. The importance of regimental history, culture and belonging was vociferously defended during this time. As I discuss in Chapter 4 of this book, however, 'regimental culture' – its basic forms and practices replicated with granular variation across many regiments in the British Army, materialised by all of them in objects such as mugs, ties and insignia such as cap badges, 'colours' (flags) and even animal mascots – is an acquired, and indeed a fallible, form of belonging, far less absolute than such visibility might suggest.

The rarefied cultural identity of British Army regiments in all the minutiae of their internal variation must also be acknowledged for the constraints it imposes upon my own analysis. One condition of my research, in line with standard ethical practices, was that the identity of the regiment and those who were part of its community at the time should be anonymised. Not only does this mean that all names have been changed, but also that some have been changed multiple times from one chapter to another, and I have not included extensive biographical details to contextualise each contributor's particular personal or professional situation. This reflects the fragility of confidentiality within such a close community and the difficulty of maintaining anonymity when representing it. It is also symptomatic of an organisation that relies for its social order on so many structures of difference and distinction, and so many potential modes of identification, that anonymity is strikingly difficult to achieve. In terms of regimental identifiers, these include its national identity and regional affiliation within the UK (e.g. in relation to Scotland, Northern Ireland, Wales or England), its location as part of a particular garrison in Germany, and the kind of regiment it is (e.g. infantry, cavalry, artillery). Any combination of these immediately narrows down the criteria for identifying the regiment I was with. Therefore, particular aspects of its institutional identity (aspects that many within the regiment would describe as fundamental to the particular subculture that it represents) are referred to in the abstract (e.g. the nature of its operations in Afghanistan and its national and regional affiliations). In terms of identifying particular people within the regiment and its social circuits, even relatively bureaucratic details (such as the precise role or rank of a particular woman's husband or details about her employment status) very soon narrow down the criteria for identifying individual members of that community. This presented a challenge for writing up my research, and there is no doubt that some of the subtleties and nuances of the women's narratives and my own analysis have become lost in translation from fieldwork into a document that must remain accountable to those whom it represents.

It is at this point, however, that I have supplemented the analysis I can offer of other people's experiences with some analysis of my own experiences during fieldwork. A reflexive approach to ethnography as supported by theories and examples from feminist scholarship (Alcoff 1991; Brah 2012; Thomas 2012) was a fundamental element in how I planned, conducted and wrote up my fieldwork (Hyde 2014). Ethnography as a mode of studying culture and subcultures in particular places at particular times facilitates proximity, duration and depth of exposure for an insight into the everyday lives of research participants. Working close-up and in situ, it thrives on the kind of detailed annotations (often in different forms – see Michael Taussig's [2011] consideration of drawings in his own fieldwork notebooks) that make up the most mundane aspects of everyday life yet frequently offer startling insights into the local textures of social relations. Ethnography yields particularly interesting insights into institutions such as the military because of its capacity to get beneath the surface of a deceptively formal social order and uncover the messier, informal and more ambiguous power relations that work both with and against its apparently rigid structure. Critical ethnography (Abu-Lughod 1991; Madison 2005), moreover, provides a range of tools and a deconstructive capacity to question the apparent sanctity and exceptionality of 'regimes of knowledge and social practices' (Madison 2005, 5).

Participant observation, facilitated by the opportunity to live on and around the regimental camp and exemplified by my experience of the Fitness Fiesta, was a foundational part of my ethnographic methods. While there was never any question that I would, somehow, 'become' a member of the regiment in any formal way, I also felt the disciplinary effects – and appeal – of its will to cohesion and belonging at certain points. Many of my fieldwork notes track the various processes through which I strived to both blend in with, and keep myself apart from, regimental belonging. They are a queasy record of my own attempts to navigate the fraught gender and sexual politics of military belonging that I explore throughout this book, as well as a record of my ambivalence as to their effects on me personally, and on others whom I observed. Work on the significance of reflexivity when researching the military specifically has revealed the complex web of power produced by the intersection of multiple power dynamics such as gender, rank and class, such that researchers have theorised the impact of navigating an insider/outsider status (Higate and Cameron 2006). Ethnographic methods, particularly the obligation to blend in and adopt local customs when doing participant observation, have not always made it easy to keep track of the place of the researcher in the research, the traditional aim being to merge with one's surroundings to the degree that full acceptance by a community is believed to reduce the 'reactivity' (Davies 1999, 73) of one's findings. Feminist scholars have advocated for a reflexive approach to the ways in which research is written up as well (Page 2017; Stanley 1992), and emphasise the need to resist 'mastery' (Alcoff 1991, 22) over the stories that research is used to tell. Such approaches embrace the messier ties of everyday social relations as the object of sociological enquiry themselves, without the impulse to tidy up loose ends and set social relations into twinned pairings of binary opposites (Smart 2009).

In response to the call for a kind of reflexivity that exposes the many contradictions of doing ethnographic research, therefore, I offer four interstitial chapters that link to, but also grasp at something beyond, the more formal elements of my analysis in each main chapter. These interstitials are not intended to offer concrete answers or conclusions that round off or tie up the data analysed elsewhere. If anything, they are designed to mess with the neatness to which this conventional analysis aspires; they leave loose ends hanging, feel their way, are unmediated and, as such, expose faults and errors in my own judgement and behaviours. They offer alternative or additional insights that complicate, trouble or challenge. These interstitials are the best I can make of the mess of my fieldwork and the personal undertaking that it entailed. They represent remnants of my own experience back then, at the same time as they are, of course, filtered through all that has passed since: layers of scholarship, lessons from students and teaching, academic conventions, but also personal change. In the ten years since I conducted this fieldwork, for example, I have had children of my own (though I have resisted the institution of marriage). This is something that has doubtless put the experiences I explore here around reproductive labour, heteronormativity and the centrality of the family into a new perspective, but it has also strengthened my conviction in my critical approach. I offer some of my personal experiences in this book so that readers may judge for themselves.

Organisation of this Book

The book is organised around three central empirical chapters that describe different but interlinked aspects of women's day-to-day negotiations with the military institution. In the first, 'Military Mobilities', I consider women's international migration with the military institution, as well as other overlapping and internal circuits of mobility that shape their lives. I explore a number of discourses through which this mobility and its effect on women's labour and social personhood is normalised. While one set of discourses relies on the sexual division of labour, the family and women's role as wives and mothers, another relies on women's conversion of geographical mobility into a kind of social mobility. I argue that social hierarchies within these overlapping circuits of mobility serve to produce women's simultaneous feelings of 'moving on' and being 'held back'. While most women migrating with the regiment might not transcend the boundaries of the national military institution, their knowing manoeuvres in relation to militarised hierarchies – including their 'dual citizenship' as both military and civilian subjects – offers an alternative measure for women as agents of those mobilities.

In the second empirical chapter, 'Ranking Difference and Distinction', I consider the multiple hierarchies through which women negotiate their social personhood. One of the most significant foils for the construction of women's identities is rank, which I argue intersects with gender, class and other vectors of power to shape women's identities in particularly complex ways. I document a number of social and material conditions that constitute the disciplinary effects of rank in women's everyday lives. These include the circulation of social stereotypes as well as expectations surrounding women's voluntary labour, patterns of mobility, the spatial organisation of the community and the chain of command. I explore the productive power of rank in ways that extend far beyond these conditions and produce effects through other vectors of power that call into question the exceptionality of rank as a military technology of control and normalisation. Despite the scope and depth of rank as a multivalent form of power, women's everyday negotiations with rank demonstrate its relational nature and thus, opportunities for dissent and disassociation. While hierarchies of rank undoubtedly produce compliance based on recognition and assimilation therefore, they are also subject to disavowal and disidentification, or can be strategically adapted by women to define and appropriate their particular place within the regimental social order.

In the final empirical chapter, 'Regimented Life', I consider the meanings of military service as they are understood and appropriated by women married to servicemen. Exploring notions such as duty and sacrifice as they are produced through the affective ties that the military promotes, I look at the production of regimental belonging and its significance during the particular period of my fieldwork, when the regiment's troops were deployed on combat duty in Afghanistan. My analysis takes account of the multiple modes through which women participate in, opt out of and translate the terms of their involvement in regimental belonging. This reveals the central role of the heterosexual family as a twinned institution through which regimental belonging gains its meaning and impact. The messy imbrication of personal and political, public and private, that this represents reaches its apotheosis in the hybrid form of the 'regimental family', a cultural production that, I argue, is fraught with desire and disappointment. The social bonds that tie the community together, however tenuously, are further explored in the rest of the chapter by looking at various permutations in relation to war.

It is here that I add a further dimension to the socio-spatial analysis I use throughout the book, moving on to consider the temporality of the operational tour. I explore women's experiences of a period of deployment, and a range of continuities between the combat zone and the home, such that 'Afghanistan' constitutes a kind of presence that women married to servicemen also inhabit. By paying attention to a temporal register (everyday, routine time) and a spatial zone (the domestic sphere) that rarely figure in assessments of violent military force, I show how women married to servicemen work to absorb its effects. The spectres of violence that haunt the domestic times and spaces of the operational tour reveal the fragility of any divide between the combat zone and the home, war and peace. What this underlines is the role of the sexual division of labour, and a host of false binaries within it, in sustaining military power.

Throughout this book I ask what might be revealed about military presence if we question it from the perspective of a population who occupy a deeply ambiguous and hybrid position in relation to that presence – simultaneously outside and within, occupying multiple and mobile positionalities that transcend the so-called divide between military and civilian, public and private, what is political and what is personal. I pay attention to the multiple mobilities of women married to servicemen living overseas because they trouble the boundaries intended to keep military power contained, and which have also served to construct the limits of scholarship that defines where military presence is, whose labour sustains it, and what it does. In this book I trace the mobilities of women married to servicemen as they interact with, acquiesce to and resist military presence and its influence over their lives. What is at stake in these investigations is no more and no less than the question of people's agency in relation to a range of structures through which that agency appears to be foreclosed. The chapters that follow push and pull in a range of different directions around this question,[11] which after all is concerned with the very ambiguity of women's position not at the margins of the military institution, but at the centre of anything called the military/civilian divide.

Notes

1. Similar to the proposition of Maria Eriksson Baaz and Judith Verweijen (2017) in their work on army wives in the Democratic Republic of Congo, my starting point works against the assumption of women's automatic militarisation through association with its many forms, though my focus is on their mobilities rather than their liminality.

2. Where cultural productions such as the patronage granted to 'Royal' Wootton Bassett had previously served as a prominent and visual reminder of soldiers' national service and sacrifice. Royal Wootton Bassett is a small town in Wiltshire whose residents came to play a voluntary role of collective witness to the repatriation of soldiers killed in Afghanistan (Jenkings et al. 2012).

3. For a timeline, see: https://www.theguardian.com/world/2021/aug/16/timeline-the-talibans-sweeping-offensive-in-afghanistan; and for geopolitical context: https://theconversation.com/afghanistan-taliban-victory-inevitable-despite-the-trillions-the-us-poured-in-166060

4. The Tri-Service Families Continuous Attitude Survey (FAMCAS) (Ministry of Defence 2011b, 15) did not at the time disaggregate its data according to the gender of military spouses, underlining the assumption that women still constitute the majority of civilian partners of service personnel. Quantitative findings were divided into technical categories relating to accommodation, living conditions, health and dental care, childcare and education, deployment and employment (ibid.).

5. https://www.armedforcescovenant.gov.uk/about/, last accessed 27 July 2022.

6. http://www.bbc.co.uk/programmes/b0178gcj, last accessed 27 July 2022.

7. Following scholars such as Zoe Wool (2015) in a US context, who has explored the queer potential of thinking through embodied vulnerability, intimacy, affect and the politics of care, for example.

8. https://www.forces.net/news/british-military-base-handed-back-germany, last accessed 23 September 2021.

9. The Armed Forces Covenant (MoD 2011a, 38–9) states that: 'In order to ensure that Service personnel returning from operational theatres are given time to re-adjust, a period of decompression is provided as part of their deployment, immediately after leaving the operational theatre and prior to their return to the UK. The aim of a period of decompression is to reduce the potential for maladaptive psychological adjustment. Decompression is one element of a complete Post-Operational Stress Management cycle which fulfils three functions designed to improve the quality of homecoming. This is achieved by giving personnel the opportunity to rationalise, contextualise and talk through operational experiences. During this period of decompression Service personnel will receive mandatory health, safety, and welfare briefings and be given the opportunity to unwind together wherever possible, all of which combine to facilitate adjustment to a non-operational routine and the management of expectation concerning returning to the home unit. Importantly, decompression also provides an opportunity for mental health readjustment for those who need it.'

10. https://www.theguardian.com/uk-news/2020/feb/22/british-army-hands-back-last-headquarters-germany, last accessed 23 September 2021.

11. My thanks to Katherine Natanel for this helpful way of thinking about the experiences I have attempted to describe, and the ways in which my writing came to mirror them.

Bicycle

I climb onto my bike and pedal in a broad sweep across the parade ground. I approach the guardroom at the gates of the camp. I'm reluctant to slow down for the speedbumps and even more reluctant to slow down for the squaddie to come out and lift the barrier.

No.

Fuck this.

I sweep out through the footpath instead. I push down on the pedals then stand, knees locked, swooping in a wide arc across the empty road and out, down through a side-lilt, now gliding along the faultless tarmac of the cycle path, then pedalling away.

More distance now behind me and the camp, my whole body sensing the smooth motion of the bike. I sit down on the saddle, relax my arms, lean this way and that. The wind makes my clothes flap about. I breathe in a palpable feeling of relief, verging on escape.

My bike was a steel-framed, German-engineered upright bicycle with back-pedal brakes and the name 'Alpina' stencilled on the crossbar. I bought it for fifty euros from the second-hand bike shop at the station. The Alpina was a good-looking bike. Heavy and solid in gleaming, unpainted metal. It swooped like a starling, held me aloft. It transformed the grey tarmac behind the barracks, an open square of empty car park, into a place of looping play on my way back into camp. Just a few swerves, a few balletic tilts. Nobody would see.

The fact that it was called 'the Alpina' lent the bike a certain anthropomorphised character – my companionate object.[1] It was tempting to use the pronoun 'she', as when people gender nations, ships or cars. But that kind of possessive or paternalistic sentiment doesn't really reflect my attachment to the bike, nor is it relevant to the way in which the bike became attached to me, which was gendered in more complex ways.

I knew I needed a bike as soon as I arrived on camp. Based in the welfare office, I soon came to know the gripes and complaints of a group of duty drivers tasked with providing occasional lifts for women married to servicemen: another fraught intersection of dependency and entitlement. Sometimes, the welfare office had the air of a taxi rank, with drivers sitting round on plastic chairs, sent while they were waiting to clear up the family room or hose down the regimental bouncy castle; playing practical jokes like covering every surface with yellow Post-it notes.

No. I needed to get out.

A bicycle would be the most convenient mode of transport for getting around and travelling between interviews.[2] The geography was ideal, the city being largely flat with a pleasant historic centre. German state provision for cyclists also made for optimum conditions, with an extensive cycle network consisting partly of separate routes as well as smaller paths integrated into wide pavements.

Someone from the sergeants' mess offered me an old mountain bike. He adjusted the seat, pumped up the tyres. But I wasn't used to riding a mountain bike and found it clunky and uncomfortable. Thanks, I said, returning it sheepishly to the camp's hangar-like workshop where he also repaired larger, more menacing vehicles.

A few weeks later, a local woman I met at the 'Anglo-German coffee morning' advised me to try the city's central station, where they restored and sold unclaimed or abandoned bicycles. The Alpina soon became fundamental to my mobility within and beyond the military community in a way that far exceeded its literal, mechanical function.[3] As a technology of the self, the constitution of the Alpina – of its social meaning, as well as what the Alpina meant to me as my possession – entailed a relational processes of recognition: of being, and being perceived.

Sometimes the Alpina made me more visible, sometimes it helped me blend in. Cycling was a popular and safe mode of local transport that was integral to civilian life in the town. Cyclists have right of way over cars, and I became accustomed to riding across junctions with straight-backed speed. Beyond the camp, there were many bicycles like the Alpina, including one used by a German woman married to a serviceman in the regiment. As well as travelling to interviews, the Alpina opened up a touristic itinerary of places to visit. There was a small café where I wrote my field diary in the afternoons, a time warp of 1980s fitted furniture where local retirees went for *Kaffee und Kuchen* in the afternoons. I took meals out in a restaurant by the canal and disciplined myself in cultural assimilation, eating pork that was a little pink in the middle; I attended a cycling show in the grounds of a castle where I ate *Bratwurst* and browsed collapsible baskets.

Consciously or not, my choice to buy an old-fashioned, Continental-style bicycle from a non-army source was a mode of distinction – a matter of taste – through which I sought to establish my own brand of cycling as a culturally 'German' thing to do. The Alpina signalled (to myself as much as anyone) a sometimes desperate aspiration to integrate, or at least to appear to integrate, into local German life.

I was 'going native', people joked. Although this does not account for the irony (and the flaw in anthropological methods) that to blend into the local German population would be in contradistinction to, rather than assimilation with, my target population: the British. I am of fair complexion and have short hair, characteristics that, it was also asserted, made me appear to be German. I owned a pair of Birkenstock sandals. Obviously, people laughed, German!

And yet. Riding German bicycles and wearing German shoes do not a German person make. We all knew that. And I knew, as I did of the many props and narratives I relied on emotionally throughout my fieldwork, that my bicycle and rudimentary list of local tourist activities were of entirely superficial value for exploring what it is to experience life in Germany. They have even less value – are at best distracting, at worst misleading – as any measure here, in a book, of what it is to 'be' German.

The question isn't really the degree to which I might or might not have 'passed' as German, therefore. It's about how these boundaries and borders function, the dynamics they reveal. And the traces of gender and ethnicity that stick to them. For example, the stereotype of German identity that it appeared I embodied is lazily negligent of the heterogeneity of contemporary German multiculture. My 'passing' for a German woman by dint of being fair skinned, short-haired and cycling upright on my bicycle in Birkenstock sandals reveals how dominant and unquestioned whiteness is as a frame for the perception of both sameness and difference around British Forces Germany.

While the Alpina might have helped me blend in as a vicarious consumer of German culture beyond the camp, back on camp or around the MoD housing estates, the Alpina made me visible in ways that stood out from particular norms. Even when I wasn't on it, the

Alpina called attention to where I was, whether it was locked up next to the sergeants' mess or the welfare office such that people knew if I was 'in'; or outside someone's house, such that people mentioned that they saw my bike and knew that I had been there. This element of visibility was perhaps the least helpful, being impractical for my ethnographic methods in terms of the maintenance of anonymity when conducting interviews. In a community that is inward-looking and self-surveilling, small details stand out.

In the same way that the Alpina became a vehicle for simplistic national or ethnic stereotypes, it was also significant in upholding or subverting other social orders and value systems. In a masculinised context where 'vehicles' were tanks, and soldiers owned mountain or racing bikes as accessories to low-end sports cars, the Alpina was eminently mockable, at best quirky and alternative, at worst infantilising and ridiculous. It was a novelty vehicle, feminised by its step-through frame and an oversized yellow basket that I bought for the front, which was unwieldy and made me wobble clownishly when pushing off.

In its antiquarian visibility, its laughable nostalgia, the Alpina also exposed me to the accusation of seeking to make an obvious distinction of myself. Perhaps, even, I was *attention-seeking*, that much maligned, feminised trait. A senior soldier told me that he had seen me on my bike and pointed me out to his wife. She did mention, he said, that she could see right down my top.

It seems necessary, at this point, to try to rescue the Alpina from the kind of critical deconstruction that leaves me with a pile of broken parts that are difficult to reassemble back into the thing I loved.

Because I really loved that bike.

It's not just that I loved my bike as a thing that I owned, an aesthetic object that I admired, or even as a technology of the self. I loved the way the Alpina made me *look*. Not the way it made me appear, but in terms of what it enabled me to *see*, and how. More of the town and its surroundings, but also how I saw things from a particular vantage point. It's not that these are always noble practices either – they cannot be detached from the dynamics of distinction and differentiation that I have already outlined. The Alpina facilitated a kind of looking-down, lofty and aloof, speeding past slow-moving mothers and pushchairs with a friendly but nonchalant wave, overtaking soldier hatchbacks at traffic lights, asserting my right of way.

I loved how the Alpina made me *feel* (superior? detached? as though I wasn't a part of the community; that I was, in fact, *different*).

But the question of how the Alpina made me feel is not just about a desperate grab for my sense of self during one of the most destabilising social experiences of my life. On a related but far more visceral and embodied level, the bicycle was also – perhaps primarily – the conduit for a distinctive kind of mental and physical release. This was different from just going for a walk or a run when I wanted to get out of my barrack room. The Alpina enabled the feeling of turning my back, pedalling fast like a child-thief,[4] *let's get out of here.* The connection was deeply corporeal, instinctive yet mediated.[5] Being an object outside of myself, a machine, a technology, the Alpina became a catalyst or cipher for my nervous or frustrated energy, a kind of prosthetic mechanism that converted my feelings into kinetic force such as fast-pedalled speed or playful swerves. This final level of control and release that the Alpina permitted returns it to its use as a pleasingly literal, physical tool: a mechanism (one that you can feel) for converting intentional bodily strength into movement in the form of an enhanced capacity for speed and smooth motion.

Relatedly, the Alpina was also the conduit for a distinct kind of embodied knowledge of the physical geography of my fieldwork setting. It enabled the act of becoming a proficient cyclist on the Continent, established my navigational knowledge of cycle routes and short cuts, but also a physical sense of my body in synergy with the city, as filtered through clicks and gear changes – twig-breaking and sliding through the woods, gliding around the smooth roads of housing estates, glistening in the sun or rain, getting lost or finding my way.

Only a pushbike (only the Alpina?) could have facilitated this kind of simple and direct mechanisation of bodily mobility – foot to pedal push and *go* – the motion deriving so palpably from bodily power and the discipline required to pedal and keep pedalling; the sense of control produced by the response of the bike to one's every pitch and turn; the satisfaction of an expertly pre-empted gear change. It is this embodied sense of converting feeling into motion that translated both into a much-needed sense of control, and a much-needed sense of escape.

The Alpina was the vehicle that carried me out of and away from camp. It helped me to experience my body as a form of power and release, to make movements away from or out of a place not in a solitary way, but via a piece of companionate machinery that took my own raw feelings and converted them into a greater capacity to act.

The Alpina was empowering.

Notes

1. Perhaps this is something like Sara Ahmed's (2017) 'survival kit'.
2. David Valentine (2007) has documented similar dynamics in his own mobility between locations in an ethnography of gay and transgender communities in New York City.
3. Again to acknowledge the work of Sara Ahmed (2019), the Alpina swiftly exceeded the literal or self-evident terms of its 'use'.
4. The metaphoric and embodied function of the bike I'm looking for here is evoked in tracking shots in the Dardenne brothers' film *Le Gamin au vélo* [The Boy on a Bicycle] (2011).
5. Such as Karen Throsby (2013) has explored in relation to swimming.

CHAPTER 1

Military Mobilities

Introduction

In this chapter I want to explore a range of overlapping mobilities that shape the everyday experiences of women married to servicemen living overseas. This first tier of mobility – moving with the British Army to a country other than the UK – might be viewed as the most fundamental in terms of material impact. From this flow many of the social and structural conditions that constrain women's choices, as well as creating opportunities for them to leverage the social and cultural capital of living 'overseas'. The geographic mobility of Armed Forces communities also implicates military power in the making and remaking of the nation state. From the historical legacies of colonialism with its outposts and encampments,[1] through to the post–World War II formation of a chain of garrison towns in places such as Germany and Cyprus (Higate and Henry 2011), the military assertion of British sovereignty overseas has always relied on the cultural reproduction of national boundaries. While these boundaries are manifest in the physical space of military installations, the reproduction of national identity, community and belonging through these spaces works through complex processes of exchange between 'host' and 'home' nations.[2] Less observed, are the fault lines of belonging among people *within* the camp community on a domestic scale, in other words the internal variation of hierarchies, modes of difference and distinction, that people navigate in ways that complicate simplistic ideas of a homogenous nation defining itself in relation to an external 'other'. My interest in this chapter, therefore, is in how gender, class and ethnicity shift and are reconfigured within and among the camp community in response to these complex notions of both 'host' and 'home'. What this reveals is that military mobilities are as much about social mobility as geographic mobility.

Thinking of military mobilities as plural in this way – as being about geographical relocation, yes, but also about relocation within domestic or institutionalised social relations – helps to reveal the complex dynamics on which military power depends. The military mobilities I explore in this chapter are distinct from traditional conceptions that inhere in the use of 'military technologies, ordnance and their logistics' (Merriman et al. 2017, 46), though they are, of course, determined by a multitude of political and geographic imperatives that shape relations between the nation state and multiple 'others' in relation to a camp's location overseas and a distant theatre of war. The profusion of social media that scholars have argued also constitute contemporary military mobilities (ibid.), and increasingly support and distort relations of intimacy, proximity and distance in military life, was emergent in the community among whom I conducted my fieldwork in 2012. Networks such as Facebook, for example, were lauded and resented in equal measure by the welfare office as an extension of some of the more problematic aspects of close-knit community dynamics. As much as people made clear the value of having simultaneous contact with distant friends and loved ones in real time through mobile communications, the use of new technologies – and new social practices – was also seen as an increasing threat to military control of information, or as potentially harmful to the social fabric of the community through issues like online gambling, for example. While these public and private online networks were salient in people's everyday interactions, my attention in the field was very much on the embodied and inhabited inscriptions of military mobilities as they were produced by people's interactions with and across the local spaces of the camp. It is this particular focus on the routes that women married to servicemen articulate which reveals the connection between geographic and social mobility and expands the terrain of military mobilities in significant ways. For military mobilities are also part of an institutionalised lifecycle that includes all the domestic landmarks of reproductive and productive labour: marriage, births and deaths as well as deployment, promotion and postings. Tracing the movements of gendered subjects as they produce and are produced by these mobilities reveals an altogether different sense of how military structures are navigated on a daily basis, as well as people's losses and gains along the way.

I begin my analysis of military mobilities by looking at the internal economy of exchange – both material and cultural – between the institution of the military and the institution of marriage,[3] where women's labour, I argue, is the principal currency in a militarised value system. It is at this point that the mobilities entailed in army life emerge as deeply contradictory and ambiguous in relation to contemporary expectations around gender equality and women's empowerment through participation in the workforce. The effects can be confusing and hard to articulate, as Joanne, a woman who had lived with the British Army in multiple locations throughout the duration of her husband's career, articulated:

> How can I explain? – like when I go back [home] my sisters who have lived there all their lives, grown up, got jobs, gone to school, had kids but still in the same . . . like, no one's moved on if that makes sense and I feel like sort of I have if that makes sense? But I also feel it's held me back because I haven't really done anything – that's an awful thing to say but career-wise I haven't really done anything with my life.

Visiting Joanne during the day and at home, I was struck by her singular, neat and contained presence, a fashionably dressed woman in her mid-forties sitting alone in a spacious and immaculate family-sized house. Joanne's husband joined the military as a teenager, a junior soldier from a working-class background, and had worked through the ranks to become a commissioned officer reaching a position of responsibility within the regiment. As she explains it here, Joanne's geographic mobility has culminated in a far more expansive sense of mobility expressed in the idea of having 'moved on'. It is worth pausing to think about the value system expressed by the notion of 'moving on' as more than simply a matter-of-fact description of physical or geographical relocation, or the accumulation of material resources. Rather, the idea of 'moving on' suggests an added value accruing to Joanne as the mobile subject who has changed places but also some element of herself, necessarily posed in relation to people or conditions that she has left behind. The precise terms of this value system (class? socio-economic advancement? education and empowerment?) are left unsaid. Joanne does not define what has changed for or about her in terms of status or wealth, though she was undoubtedly in a position of relative privilege in terms of material resources linked to her husband's rank (the messy imbrications of which I explore further in Chapter 3). Instead, her conceptualisation of how she has 'moved on' inheres in the notion of 'back home' being fixed and inert, with a sense of regression and stasis folded into it. Yet if Joanne's view of herself does articulate a trajectory of upward mobility, it is clear that she does not attribute this to her own actions or identity ('I haven't really done anything'). Hence, the ambivalent, contradictory sense of also being 'held back', in terms of neoliberal discourses of women's empowerment, 'career-wise'.

Such are the subtle and ambiguous effects of military mobilities experienced by many of the women I met during my research. Their recollections of various postings within the UK and overseas made clear the impact of the institutional requirement for geographic mobility upon their careers and employment opportunities in a material sense. In addition to the rigid structures implied by military hierarchies and bureaucratic processes, however, women's narratives of living 'abroad' also shed light on the kind of *social* mobilities entailed in moving with the military institution. Ironically, it is within these overlapping circuits of geographic and social mobility that feelings of fixity and stasis are generated, like the kind of regression expressed in Joanne's sense of being 'held back'. This begs the question of which social structures are held down or maintained by the military institution – or who is kept in their place – so that other forms of mobility can function according to the demands of institutional efficiency and the fluctuations of global politics.[4]

To return briefly to Joanne, sitting on a pale, new-looking sofa in her empty family home, her husband in Afghanistan, her older children at boarding school in the UK, her younger child at the MoD-run garrison school. If she constitutes her own mobility through a feeling of having 'moved on', her current position is also shaped by modes of separation and loss through which she might be argued to have been left behind.

> I knew Steven was in the Army when I married him [. . .] but I didn't know what it would entail [. . .]. People say, 'I hate it', if you maybe have a conversation about them being away or in Afghan. And people say, 'Well, you knew that when you married him.' Well, I'm sorry you don't know that, you really do not have a clue. But I think it's the old cliché: a lot changes when you have children and they do come first. And obviously because they're away [at boarding school] – that is another thing that wouldn't have happened if we weren't in the Army. I'm not particularly happy about the fact that half their childhood I've not seen them if that's how you look at it, but that was better and they'll even say now that was better for them.

If marriage to a soldier is a kind of choice – the original choice that sets the terms for all choices to follow – then it is a choice that Joanne qualifies as being largely uninformed. Any agency that Joanne salvages from marriage and its mutual imbrication with the military here comes from taking responsibility for its consequences, living with its repercussions, and focusing on the benefits accrued by others.

The narratives I explore in this chapter reveal a deep ambivalence that I think is fundamental to the meanings women make out of their encounters with the military institution. These are narratives that are fraught with the deliberation of compromise, of being pushed and pulled in multiple directions, of making the most of circumstances that are less than ideal. In a sense, the ambivalence that patterns women's ways of narrating their choices, their sense of self and their relationship to the institutions of marriage and the military, is as fundamental a feature of military discipline as any other formal discourse that is naturalised and internalised by its subjects. As I explore in Chapter 3, military discipline as it extends to women married to servicemen shares many of the confusing dynamics of what Aaron Belkin has called 'discipline-as-collapse' (Belkin 2012, 40). Civilian wives' options for making sense of the impact of military power on their everyday lives falls back in a similar way upon the explanatory power of militarised logics – hierarchies of rank and class, implicit assumptions about whiteness and ethnic continuity, heteronormative ideas of family and wifehood. I want to look further at these structures as they are experienced and adapted by women married to servicemen here, at the same time as I explore how the ambivalence that is also a crucial part of their power allows women to articulate feelings of unease and dissatisfaction as well as resignation and acquiescence. In its sheer prevalence as a mode of articulation, its repeated, almost stylised expression of what comes to signify an essential condition of life with the military, ambivalence itself might be described as a particularly gendered tool of militarised logic. It is gendered because it is produced by, and produces, a liminal subjecthood (Long 2022) characterised as perpetually caught between one institution and another: the subjecthood of 'the military wife'.

Paying attention to women's sense- and self-making practices through their encounters with the regiment reveals the sedimented layers of heteronormativity on which the military institution depends. It also shows how these are deeply engrained in the reproduction of class hierarchies, and implicitly connected to colonial legacies of race and ethnic homogeneity. In this chapter I look at some examples of these foundational elements of military power, beginning by setting out some initial terms through which women make sense of their geographic mobility. I then consider the incorporation of their productive as well as reproductive labour in migration, revealing the less visible economy of exchange between the military institution and wives of personnel as a reserve army of labour. Finally, I explore some of the more complex imbrications between bureaucracies of nationality, citizenship, labour and leisure around the military camp overseas, as experienced by Foreign and Commonwealth (F&C) personnel, among others. Throughout, the institution of marriage and the gendered, heteronormative assumptions that go with it emerge as fundamental to the military's highly localised formations of national sovereignty overseas. Finally, I look at the limits of notions of travel and cosmopolitanism as a way of framing women's understanding of their own creativity, self-making and choice in privileged migration.

Married and Mobile

Military mobilities are messy and multiple. If they take women one step forward, they can also take them two steps back. The pathways women articulate are convoluted and circuitous; at other times they are as linear and direct as the chain of command. The bureaucracy that manages military careers is likewise complex and testifies to the relative lack of autonomy with which military personnel themselves can determine the location of their postings. The degree of geographical mobility undertaken by personnel and their families varies considerably depending on a soldier's job role and membership of particular units within the Army. Members of 'attached arms' units, for example, typically rotate to a new posting every two years, as opposed to a regiment being based in one location – which could be domestic or overseas – for much longer periods of time. Rob, a senior soldier posted to the regiment from an attached arms unit, described some of the strategies he deployed when navigating posting procedures:

> Most soldiers have the opportunity to put in a PPP [Preferential Posting Proforma]. Which has a first, a second or a third choice [. . .] So you can elect to go somewhere and usually they try and hit the first, second or third choice. However sometimes they can't. [. . .] I seem to be slightly out of kilter by one posting every time. [. . .] What I try and do is take it as a bit of a puzzle, and every different post or position that you hold is a jigsaw piece, so as you've done these, the [full] picture starts to pull together [. . .] So that's what it's been about, it's piecing it all together.

The resources and discourses available to soldiers for rationalising their mobility allow for a professionalised, albeit perhaps illusory, sense of control. Rob's full description of the gradual and piecemeal construction of his career trajectory was peppered with acronyms pertaining to the very specific structures and skillsets he has negotiated (units, battalions, job type). It is interesting to compare Rob's rationalisation of his mobility to Annie's, which was characteristic of many wives' accounts. Annie was married to an officer who did not belong to the regiment 'by trade', but had been appointed to a particular post for a two-year period. The rotation of officers above a certain rank on postings to different regiments is common, once they have served an initial period with their 'home' regiment, which they select or are selected to join when they graduate from officer training at the Royal Military Academy, Sandhurst. For Annie and her family, this would be another temporary posting with a new regimental host, lasting for roughly two years. The family arrived in Germany shortly before the deployment to Afghanistan began. Like Rob, Annie's account of her working life and career priorities are responsive and adaptive to military prerogatives:

> Yeah, well I sort of fumbled around a bit, which is why it's quite nice to come to a new place where people didn't know us, again, getting away, put our identity on who we are now. As I said I've dabbled a bit with working again but it's very limited so I've kind of resigned myself to the fact that at the moment, until we get back to the UK, my identity is Henry's wife, John and Hannah's mum and that's fine actually, I'm not struggling with that at the moment. I have moments when I think 'Ugh, bit unfulfilled' but that's where you go and plug the gaps with the volunteering thing. Next week I'm starting volunteering in a nursery! [Laughs] Not my bag at all! Somebody said, 'Oh we're crying out for volunteers', and I thought, you know what, it might just make the next five or six weeks [of the tour] go quicker, and it's again something to put on a very pickled CV [. . .] You can finesse a bit of time out for child rearing but now it's like, right I need to have a few things on there. So if there's not going to be a serious job on there at least I need to . . . so again, selfish motive, you know actually this has got to work for me as well.

In comparison to Rob's strategic 'puzzle', wives' narratives of migrating with the military were often characterized by ideas of fluidity and flux that were informal, emergent and responsive rather than proactive and bureaucratised. The necessity to respond to the changing demands of her husband's career places Annie's emphasis on contingency in the present ('put our identity on who we are now'). There is a sense in which the trajectory of Annie's own career is suspended both in time and place, waiting until the family returns to the UK, a suspension that is rationalised as coinciding with a career break mandated by motherhood. Compared with Rob's rationalisation of military mobilities, Annie's description of 'fumbling around' and 'filling the gaps' underlines their differential sense of autonomy over their circumstances. While both might be argued to be operating under a kind of forced flexibility in respect of their career choices, Rob constitutes himself as the agent of his mobility ('piecing it all together'), while Annie appears to be the object of hers.

I often began interviews by asking women about their family or career histories, asking them to trace the trajectory of their arrival at the here and now. We would be sitting in the garden while the children were at school or after they had gone to bed. They'd make me a drink, pop a mug down on a coaster, offer a biscuit. Once I asked questions while someone apologetically rested on the sofa with her eyes closed. The initial recounting of steps in each woman's journey to Germany would be convoluted, often lengthy. There would be much counting on fingers, tracing back – *let me think* – to produce narratives that were often strikingly logistical. I interviewed Carol, for example, in her garden in the first flush of early summer. Her husband was part of the rear operations group that had stayed behind in Germany to help run the operation from HQ. It was early evening and he was inside putting the children to bed while Carol and I sat with a glass of wine. Carol's story about getting married and starting a family was somewhat hard to follow, a journey I've edited to streamline here but which twists and turns through multiple upheavals of relocation and mobilisation, the intricacies of which sometimes become conflated and confused.

> No, what happened: the regiment went to Catterick in, I think, 199—. So while Simon was in the UK I met him. We got married in 2000. We'd been unaccompanied all that time in between. Got married, remained unaccompanied. I had [our first child] and at that point – because I had a career, a job I loved, and only when I had [our child] went on maternity leave and then resigned – never went back – I then joined Simon in a quarter in Catterick and then shortly after we moved to [Germany] in the summer of '0—.

Initially, Carol and her husband chose to live separately ('married unaccompanied' is the official designation for a soldier who elects to live in a single room in barracks, rather than with his family on an MoD housing estate) due to Carol's career, which kept her in another part of the UK when the regiment moved to a new barracks in the north of England. It was the birth of their first child that represented Carol's absorption into the military community, whereupon she joined her husband in service family accommodation. Shortly afterwards, the whole regiment was relocated to Germany. Logged according to the formal categories of housing provision ('married unaccompanied', 'in quarters'), Carol tracks her moves according to the milestones of a militarised lifecycle – marriage and births but also regimental relocation, promotions and, occasionally, invasions. As a result, these formal pathways for mobility – postings, training, deployment – are woven through with an alternative set of mobilities that are instinctive, responsive, *reproductive.*

> That was the massive regimental move in '0—. That's right [. . .] It was massive [. . .] I'd given up my job. [. . .] I had a four-week-old baby. I'd left home. Simon [had an important job within the regiment], there were expectations on me as his wife, which I was a little bit resistant to. [. . .] I got [there] in January, I'd only been there six weeks and they deployed to the Gulf. To the [Iraq] War [. . .] It was a big, big thing back then. You know. They were front line, we knew that. We knew the roles that they were doing. [. . .] And I, I literally hot-footed it home. I just – Simon left and I got in the car. And I remember [the baby] in the back of the car, [they] slept from Catterick down to [my home town], and I cried all the way.

Carol's experience provides a counterpoint to discourses of rationalised, strategic mobilisation in a military sense, articulating instead a set of messy family ties and multiple connections. These are manifest in impulsive decisions and haphazard car journeys, pushed and pulled by contradictory notions of belonging and obligation. Importantly, there is resistance in Carol's movements and for a while she runs counter to the expected direction of travel, resistant to an ideology of wifehood and reacting to the twin unknowns of war and new motherhood. Yet institutionalised ideals of duty and support soon pull her back:

> And I stayed for three, four weeks and then I felt an obligation to go back. And I dragged myself back to Catterick and I hated it. [. . .] But I just – I think my obligation to go back was definitely not to let Simon down. To be his wife and to be that dutiful army wife which you hear all the time. [. . .] I suppose I wanted to help where I could. And once I got back – and I think Simon must have had a word with

the Welfare Officer – and they came knocking on my door and said,
'Would you like to come and do the food parcels?' And I went in and
I found a purpose. And I loved packing up these shoeboxes for the
soldiers. And it became a lot easier.

Carol is an experienced military wife, she narrates the different
mobilisations she has managed with hindsight and years of accumulated knowledge. Yet her narrative demonstrates the absolute centrality of the sexual division of labour as a way of rationalising, and
depoliticising, the effects of military mobilities. Like the reassuring
comfort of packing empty shoeboxes with everyday objects of care
and concern, her story finds its resolution in the explanatory power
of reproductive labour:

> But I think a lot of my issue wasn't maybe . . . it was [having a baby],
> it was just being a new mum. [. . .] I didn't know what to do and here
> I was in the middle of nowhere, I didn't really know anybody, stuck
> in Catterick, no husband, with a five, six week-old baby that I wasn't
> quite sure what to do.

Despite the material ways in which military structures, state and
global politics can be argued to have caused the conditions that
shaped Carol's experience, their effects are explained in terms that
are explicitly domestic. Carol's rationalisation of her circumstances
is not based, as it might legitimately be, on being swept up in the
implementation of institutional or government policy pertaining to
national strategic defence – regimental relocation, the invasion of
Iraq – but works instead through a heteronormative logic of gender
that encompasses reproductive labour and notions of wifely duty.
In this, Carol actively domesticates responsibility for those experiences and internalises them at the same time, in that responsibility
is shifted away from the public military institution and onto the new
mother. Annie, likewise, describes her desire to make each deployment work for her professional aspirations as well as her husband's
as 'selfishness', though this selfishness seems to be based on taking a
job that she described just a moment earlier as '[n]ot my bag at all!'
How has military power come to work so seamlessly with marriage,
the family and reproductive labour that it can conceal its own workings so effectively?

These are not the kind of mechanisms that speak to military power
as a rational, strategic deployment of productive labour, bureaucratised through the formal structures of an institution and deployed

strategically according to state control. What Carol's and Annie's narratives demonstrate is that military mobilities are in practice chaotic, messy and leaky, as each move is redrawn on a domestic scale and accrues more and more emotional baggage. It is these messier, affective imbrications of geographic and social mobility that require particular ideologies and practices in order to be brought under control and rationalised. The impact of military mobilities on women married to servicemen might be thought of as a kind of mission creep, where military prerogatives overspill the bounds of the institutional structures designed to limit collateral damage and maintain a targeted approach. Yet, thinking of the effects of military power as 'spillover' (Gillem 2004, 40) in this way would be to ignore the degree to which it is the structures themselves, not simply their effects, that are woven much more expansively – subtly yet decisively – through a far broader infrastructure than the tightly bounded spaces and esoteric practices of the military institution imply.

Internal mobility – flexibility but also replicability – might be argued to be a fundamental characteristic of military power. Take, for example, the organisational structure of the regiment itself, and the soldiering activities designed to reproduce it. When the regiment returned from Afghanistan towards the end of my fieldwork, the hitherto sleepy camp was transformed by the inimitable presence of soldiers. Troops gathered for inspection in the morning or hung around smoking cigarettes after lunch, squadrons of them sweated in the gym, and there was the sound of boots marching across the parade ground. At such times, whoever was in the Welfare Office might look out and watch the soldiers marching past on drill. It was funny and endearing, their marching round and round, wives trying to spot their husbands among the identically dressed lines of men and a few women. The ritualised activity of drill, designed to prepare 'individuals to act as components of a larger machine' (Ware 2012, 106), is one of the military institution's defining vehicles for social cohesion. Anthony King (2006, 495) has argued that collective tasks such as drill (and the hierarchies of command as well as cooperation they promote) are central to unit cohesion. The drill imposed upon the regiment's troops on return from Afghanistan was in preparation for a series of ceremonial homecoming parades, which included a trip to the UK to march through its home city. With all the buzz of the return from deployment I decided to follow the regiment back to the UK to watch the parade. To drive into the regiment's UK barracks and see the same soldiers in the same uniforms doing the same PT routine was indeed to witness a kind of mechanical replication, a double-take moment in which the regiment, captured in duplicate from the soldiers' sit-ups to the same faces at desks in a different office, appeared to be a machine made of composite parts that could be picked up and reassembled with striking continuity.

Yet this is only a partial, cropped image of the logistical movements of the regiment at that time. In one sense, this functional picture privileges what Kirke and York (2005, 308) have characterised as 'enlightenment' paradigms of British military doctrine founded on concrete and coherent patterns and structures. Accounting for the human mechanics of regimental logistics, however, omits the messy attachments and informalities of a postmodernist command (Kirke and York 2006, 313). A more experiential picture of the regiment's syncretic movements might include, for example, its inefficiencies (something I frequently heard about at dinner in the sergeants' mess) as well as soldiers' insubordination (Kirke 2010; see also Hockey 1986). But to further interrogate the function and coherence of regimental logistics, it is necessary to widen the frame even further beyond these considerations to reveal the itineraries of those 'following' the regiment back to the UK for the parades. For a fuller picture of regimental logistics in this case, one must look beyond the well-rehearsed illusion of straight lines and tight turns in drill, and beyond the commercial coaches and ageing minibuses that transported squadrons of hungover soldiers to the homecoming parade in the UK. The informal, messier mobilities at the margins include the women married to servicemen and the majority of the regiment's families, who travelled independently back to the UK in order to take up their role as spectators of the parade. There was no formal requirement for families to attend the homecoming parades in the UK. However, the regiment timed its 'harmony leave', a period when the whole regiment is given time off in one block, for the week following the parade, which also happened to coincide with half term in the British school calendar (to which MOD schools in Germany conform). It therefore made practical sense for families to stay on to visit relatives in the UK after a long period of operational duty. Though families' attendance at the parade was not mandated, therefore, it was certainly anticipated or expected. In this sense, the formal structures of regimental life were managed to combine rather than compete with family life, and, as such, compel their integration (Bourg and Segal 1999, 648).

For my purposes here, the temporary relocation of the entire regiment back to the UK also provides an example of what might be described as military wives' own 'task cohesion' (MacCoun 1993 in Basham 2009, 732). Unlike the formal provision of transport to take soldiers back to the UK barracks, there was no formal provision of transport for their families. For many couples, the regiment's provision of transport for soldiers to travel en masse disrupted a marital division of labour, whereby the journey back to the UK was usually undertaken by husband and wife together in order to share driving and childcare responsibilities. The subtraction of husbands' labour from this equation resulted in an alternative form of collective organising, comprising a flurry of lift-sharing between wives, who teamed up so that one woman could drive back to the UK and the other could feed, entertain or cajole children in the back seat. These lift shares created new, female-headed units in cars buzzing with sat-nav, iPads, I-spy and directions given over mobile phones, connecting the nuclear family based in Germany to extended families in the UK, meeting mothers-in-law at service stations or staying at grandparents' houses on the way. While the soldiers were transplanted from the Germany to the UK barracks as a single unit, their wives ensured the family stayed together and fell in behind.

This snapshot – the regiment travelling in convoy by coach and the family estate cars weaving behind – reveals an additional form of regimental logistics, and the shared journeys to the UK by car emerged as a source of stress and inconvenience but also pride and achievement in many women's narratives. In the weeks leading up to the parades and in casual chit-chat in the welfare office, regimental shop and at social events, different women's plans for the journey were often discussed, frequently construed as a challenge of everyday resilience for which women planned carefully in advance. In many conversations, the journey seemed to take on the status of a rite of passage. Women who had done it before had tips and knowledge to pass on about the infamous interchange at Antwerp under misdirection from sat-nav systems; women who were doing it for the first time surprised themselves; there was collective organising, the provision of packed lunches and often a sense of empowerment summed up by the necessity to 'crack on'. The idiom of the need to 'crack on' despite circumstances that were inadequate or frustrating was widely and frequently asserted during the operational tour. Wives' own appropriation of this term illustrates a degree of cultural assimilation at the same time as it indicates their appropriation of ideas about resilience and resourcefulness. It is in such ways that stereotypes of the 'model military wife' (Enloe 2000, 162) become sanctioned and gain their disciplinary power. However, if the assertion that one must 'crack on' with a task comes at the end of an extended conversation about how troublesome, challenging and unreasonable that task is, it also serves as a permissible way to register a good deal of complaint as well as, ultimately, compliance.

In such ways, women participated in the collective and vociferous assertion of the value of their own labour as part of regimental logistics. It is important to note, however, that none of this – the hours of planning, the lift-shares, the packed lunches, the stressful motorway interchange at Antwerp, nor the soldiers napping in the kind of touring coaches more generally associated with groups of pensioners or schoolchildren – was visible to the passers-by who eventually watched the parade pass through the regiment's home city. It is also necessary to point out that, without the dedicated spectatorship through which wives and children, dressed in their best clothes, also took up the role of public witnesses and supporters of the parade,[5] it would have been diminished as a vehicle for the projection of national and regional pride that was given extra emotional weight by the return of soldiers to the bosom of their families from a faraway war. Yet the public performance of the parade shows little sign of the domestic labour it took to produce.

In the narratives of military mobilities that I have explored so far on a domestic scale, it is hard to avoid echoes with historical archetypes such as 'camp followers' (Venning 2005) or categorisations such as 'tied movers' (Little and Hisnanick 2007, 547) or 'tied migrants' (Cooke and Speirs 2005, 343). More recently, ideas about the British Army's geographic mobility, global reach and flexibility are being reframed as part of the MoD's conceptualisations of 'a more lethal, agile and more expeditionary' army (MoD 2021, 3). This includes a recognition of the 'generational and societal change' (ibid., 11) that is shaping the wider military community of families, to which the MoD has responded with a new emphasis on 'individual lifestyle choice' alongside the demands of 'unit cohesion' and 'workforce mobility' (ibid.).[6] Trends in military basing policies alone, however, are not enough to explain the complexities of civilian women's mobilities upon marriage to a soldier in the British Army. What requires attention as well is the intimate connection between marriage and the military as twinned institutions and the sexual division of labour it underlines. As Enloe (2000, 182) has argued, military family policy relies at its core on the patriarchal assumption that the location of families should be determined according to (men's) productive labour, with the status of reproductive labour expressed by the classification of a soldier's spouse and children as 'dependants'. In all the accounts above, gendered expectations carry with them a distinct feeling of inevitability that each woman finds it hard to escape, and professes to have accepted. The tropes that these women use, and to which they knowingly acquiesce, expose gendered wifehood as a ready-made set of practices and identities that, like a tool or a support, can be taken off the shelf and dusted down when required. In this sense, gender is an object of use, a technology, but a limited one. It must be noted that the different components of this formula are shifting with increasing numbers of women soldiers and joint career couples in the UK armed forces, some aspects of which I explore in Chapter 3. While it would be interesting and relevant to look at the differential experiences of civilian men married to and migrating with servicewomen, or at same-sex couples as well as joint-career couples juggling army careers and family life, the experiences of civilian women married to servicemen remain highly significant as something of a baseline in terms of the enduring heteronormativity of institutional structures, and an underused starting point from which to assess a multitude of broader questions about women's place 'in' the military. In the next part of my analysis, I look further at the value of women's labour to the British Army overseas, addressing questions raised by feminist scholars Shirley Ardener and Hilary Callan in their 1984 study, *The Incorporated Wife* (Callan and Ardener, 1984). These are questions that remain tellingly relevant regarding 'the nature of institutional boundaries, mechanisms of inclusion and exclusion, and the structural dilemma that arises when, because of marriage, women have to be given a location in, on or outside the boundary of an organisation' (ibid., 1).

The Incorporation of Women's Paid Labour

Many of the women with whom I spoke during fieldwork asserted the value of their role as wives, mothers and (for some) members of the Armed Forces community for their sense of self. But that is not to say that many of them did not also want or need to find paid employment while living overseas. Indeed, the prominence that women gave to their experiences and identities as wives and mothers in their own accounts should not obscure their material contribution to both the military institution and family income via participation in the local labour force around the camp. In fact, British Forces Germany (BFG) relied heavily upon the paid labour of women married to servicemen, who were often employed directly by the institution with the status of a Locally Employed Civilian (LEC). As such, dependants of personnel, including children of working age as well as spouses, formed part of a huge, flexible workforce employed on short-term, local contracts in the garrison. The Garrison Labour Support Unit (GLSU) was the dedicated human resources facility that supported the particular requirements of this labour market. While providing this support, the Ministry of Defence acknowledged the constraints, as well as the mutual potential, of employing the civilian family members of personnel:

> Family members, posted to Germany, have a number of concerns regarding employment. For some, the concern is the potential loss of a second income through lack of employment opportunities whilst for others it is the unwanted and forced career break, which could, in extreme cases, jeopardise the currency of professional qualifications. The result is that people who are qualified, experienced and willing to work fail to find appropriate work whilst too many jobs, many providing support in key community services, are left vacant or suffer from excessive turnover of staff due to incorrect matching. Strategic Command Germany Enabling Office (2023)

As was pointed out to me several times by different men and women within the community, and as research in other military contexts has shown (Castaneda and Harrell 2008; Cooke and Speirs 2005), military spouses' motivations to work vary according to class, educational background and household income. This variation in need and motivation are acknowledged in the policy discourse above. Less explicit is the causal link by which military mobilities create a surplus of labour that the institution then incorporates for its own use. If women are forced to leave their positions in skilled or unskilled jobs in the UK to migrate with the military community, it is the military institution that benefits directly from the redeployment of their labour as a material resource. This sets up a rather limited formula for opportunities to offset some of the disadvantages of moving with the military, and more broadly for women's freedom and independence from overbearing military structures or culture. If, by seeking paid employment, women married to servicemen wish to counter some of the negative impact of military mobilities on their everyday lives – loss of financial independence, increased confinement to the domestic sphere, disruption to their own career trajectories – they do so at the ironic cost of the direct incorporation of their labour (back) into the military institution, increased exposure to its social and bureaucratic structures, and the circumscription of opportunities for cultural exchange beyond the British Army.

For women whose motivations to work combined career aspirations larger than or in addition to economic need, it is telling that the most salient measure of the adaptability of their skills was not the capacity to find a job that worked for them 'in' Germany, but one that worked 'in' the military. Thus, a London-based events manager working for a luxury chain of hotels becomes a journalist for the BFG newspaper; a public-sector PA becomes a 'leave and movements clerk'; a project manager for the National Trust of Fiji becomes the garrison family liaison representative working out of the garrison's information centre for service communities; and a marketing executive is employed as a consultant careers trainer for personnel about to leave the army. It is striking that, rather than the conversion of these women's skills and qualifications into another language, culture or state structure, what is required instead is the translation of their labour power into something of value for military-institutional prerogatives. While the GLSU promotes flexibility and adaptability in the local labour market (helping women move on), it is possible to see how these roles can also be constraining for them (holding women back). Military mobilities promote flexibility only as far as one is able to fit in: any equivalence they offer is an approximation, a kind of proxy role whereby spouses attempt to find a military version of the civilian job they did before. This is not cultural adaptation; this is the militarisation of women's labour power.

The GLSU is a key example of how the cultural specificity of the community's location in a particular national and local space – a provincial town in Germany – is elided by military-institutional belonging. What it also shows is that, in material terms at least, military-institutional belonging is difficult to separate from its basis in national belonging, a kind of replication that replaces local cultures and structures with imported systems, remaking bounded territories as it goes. The experience of Käthe, one of several German women married to British soldiers and living within the community, is testament to this. Käthe might initially be assumed to be more mobile in her capacity to negotiate the sovereign terms of her relationship to her husband's employer; to be able to forge opportunities based on access to resources from both British and German state structures. Käthe was born and educated in Germany, with German as her first language. And yet, the extent to which the military provides for its community overseas leaves little room for her to manoeuvre:

> K: I trained as a geriatric nurse in Germany, but that doesn't count in the UK so I can't really transfer much of that to life in Britain, and now I'm a childminder.
>
> A: But you're in Germany, so could you . . .?
>
> K: I could but it's just the fact that my husband is a soldier and my kids go to an English school, so if I were to get a job with the Germans I would have to explain to them well no our school holidays are slightly different, that's why I need holidays there and no I can't work weekends because [. . .] I can't interfere with [my husband's] work enough for me to get a decent shift pattern out of it, so that's why I can't work as a nurse in Germany anymore. [. . .] I know lots of German women that have got the same problem 'cause it's just so different. I don't know why but the German employers don't really like it when you're married to a soldier because they know, 'Oh she's probably only going to be here for a year or year and a half and then they're going to go again and if the husband's deployed she might have to stop working and . . .' They know that we're not as reliable as a German family with Mum and Dad living next door so . . . [. . .] me living here as a German doing my job in Germany, it doesn't work with me being married to a soldier.

Although in an arguably privileged position with respect to working and living in Germany – speaking the language, having German citizenship and qualifications – Käthe has chosen to import a British framework for her career options to match the 'British' way of life imported by the British Army for its families living overseas. Here the structures and cultures of military mobilities operate so comprehensively that any opportunity for a kind of 'flexible accumulation' (Ong 1999, 136), so often heralded as a source of liberation for skilled migrants in the era of globalisation, is foreclosed.

Given the militarisation of women's paid labour in the ways I have shown, it is deeply ironic that, when spouses are employed through the GLSU, they are contracted not through the UK tax system but as Locally Engaged Civilians (LECs) (Ministry of Defence 2012). Unlike service personnel, whose employment is centrally managed, taxed and remunerated through the MOD in the UK, the jobs available to women married to servicemen do not qualify them as 'civil servants',[7] nor are they accompanied by the same UK tax structures or benefits such as pensions. LECs are paid in euros and benefit instead from tax exemptions in both the UK and Germany. These tax breaks and the flexibility of many of the employment opportunities are supposed to compensate wives for their more precarious employment status in relation to both civil servants and service personnel paid through the British Army in the UK. However, LEC status was also seen as justification for the institution to pay them less in the first place, leading to a two-tier job market. This economic localisation of what essentially becomes a feminised job market reflects the political economy of military households (Chisholm and Eichler 2018), namely the relegation of their labour to the flexibilised, part-time, undervalued 'local' sphere.

As Enloe (1989, 72) has argued, it is the 'largely unpaid work' of women married to servicemen upon which the military relies to 'transform an overseas base into a 'community' (ibid.). This was materially evident during my time on camp, though in a way that demonstrates the blurred line between women's voluntary labour and the economic – even commercial – interests of the regiment. The beginning of my fieldwork coincided with work to transform the President of the Regimental Institute (PRI) shop on camp from a cave of regimental souvenirs and dusty penknives to a high-quality gift shop. The new PRI was an initiative run on a voluntary basis by three women from the regimental community, with financial backing from the regiment. Any profits made supported the regiment's own charitable fund, but the women's stated aim was based on demand: to provide a better range of products than those supplied by the Navy Army Air Force Families Institute supermarket (NAAFI), a low-rise complex of shops offering UK produce and some tax-free luxury goods exclusively to the garrison community. The monopoly that the NAAFI held over consumer produce in the garrison was subject to much complaint. Since part of the NAAFI's operations in BFG had been taken over by private contractors, a perceived decline in the quality of goods and services it offered, as well as its monopoly over local enterprise, had triggered some discontent. As an example, Anne, who was in all but official title (this being 'voluntary' work) the manager of the regiment's new PRI, complained that since the NAAFI canteen had been replaced by a franchise of Costa Coffee it had stopped doing a full English breakfast. This had been popular at weekends, and it was indeed a complaint that I had already heard from some of the soldiers, for whom pre-packaged sandwiches, salads or pastries were not a viable alternative.

Anne, who was married to a senior NCO in the regiment, brought vision, professional experience in retail and full-time commitment to drive the shop's impressive transformation forward. She was assisted by a few other women working on stock management and service. Abby, who was employed as an administrative assistant with the regiment, was informally seconded to the PRI for some of her time and popped down from HQ to help with deliveries, as well as being trained on the till. The shop occupied a large space next to the welfare office along the corridor from the family room. I watched in fascination as the room was gradually transformed. It was freshly painted and then display units, made from MDF and painted white by a trooper who was a trained carpenter, were installed around the walls, as well as a large, free-standing, multi-tiered shelving and a display structure in the middle. The cash register was set up near the door, plus several rotating racks for greetings cards. The vision for the shop was unambiguously feminised and somewhat aspirational, directing consumer tastes towards new and established brands in women's fashion accessories and home decor that one might find in any quaint provincial gift shop. The shoulder-height, multi-tiered structure at the centre of the shop evolved like a timelapse of consumer taste. It amassed accessories and house-hold items like a giant magnet – scarves, scatter cushions, mugs and coasters, photo frames. Several frilly umbrellas were suspended from the ceiling above the till, creating a kind of pavilion effect. There were high-street favourites – multicoloured spotted Emma Bridgewater tableware, tasteful prints on greetings cards blank for your own message — as well as a large range of jingoistically nostalgic 'Keep calm and carry on' merchandise. There was a selection of floppy-eared soft toys of a particular brand and semi-precious Pandora jewellery that was much admired, in addition to a range of Hunter wellies. One morning, two soldiers from the post bunk come down to help with the boxes. They comment on the jewellery on offer – 'Too colourful for my missus,' says one – but both agree the shop is a good idea.

As the new PRI evolves, its effect – and success – is marked. It attracts more custom, drawing in wives who come for coffee mornings in the family room down the corridor. Some officers' wives call in to buy gifts for another woman's new baby. This requires some coordination of who will buy which item and card, so as not to duplicate. Much later, when the regiment's soldiers return from Afghanistan, one of the women's husbands comes in and states that he can point to all the items that he recognises from their house, which his wife has been buying on what Abby says should be her PRI 'gold card'.

News of the PRI spread, as did the sense of growing domestication around what had hitherto been a sleepy and scruffy corridor where the welfare office and old PRI were based. You could almost feel the force of it rippling out from the central display unit, a tidal wave of pure aesthetic power. The adjoining kitchen, used as a staffroom by the welfare office, fell under the spell. First there was a tablecloth, then a slightly impractical rug on the floor. There were new coffee and sugar containers (though no tea towels, due to the difficult question of who would wash them). Finally, a special, individual sugar container was brought in to prevent Sergeant Wilson from putting his dripping teaspoon into the sugar bowl and making the sugar crystallise into hard brown lumps. Sergeant Wilson ran the other, 'old', PRI, the one that sold hip flasks bearing the regimental crest, outdoor camping accessories and, at the top end, a few mountain bikes. His shop had been moved to a room next door, further down the block and accessible through the new PRI. It was about half the size and badly lit, though the murkiness could have been due to the overriding presence of the colour khaki. The most striking feature of the new PRI was the prevalence of the colour pink.

The transformation continued. I returned to the camp after a two-week break over Easter, and the new PRI had expanded into a further room to sell clothing through a contract negotiated with adventure brand, The North Face. They would also be stocking riding-style boots as worn by the Commanding Officer's wife, Anne told me. I noted that the monotone wave of pink had been broken up a little with lime-green spotty paper and by moving some of the pink goods into the other room. Yes, said Abby. When they came in and took photos they realised how pink it was and decided it might put some of the soldiers off. It is the soldiers, they say, who they are aiming at. I express surprise, but Anne explains that they're the ones buying gifts for their wives. Better-quality gifts. They are now all wearing polo shirts with a regimental crest on the front and 'The Gift Box' in pink quirky font on the back.

What is clear from the scale, vision, skill and ambition invested in the PRI is that women's voluntary labour as a resource is far from merely an informal or incidental by-product of the sexual division of labour around a military base overseas. And its deployment is far from limited to unquantifiable aspects of social reproduction. What the example of the PRI makes clear is the material as well as the social value of women's labour to the local economy. That the PRI was run for profit as an economic investment on the part of the regiment was never in doubt, the necessity for sound financial returns frequently emphasised by the officer who had lobbied for the investment of regimental funds in the first place, reinforced by the complaints of the clerk tasked with maintaining the shop's accounts. That the shop was a commercial enterprise was further underlined by an incident when, due to its growing reputation within the garrison, the regiment received notice from the NAAFI that it was in contravention of contractual agreements around competition to supply, and rumours circulated that the new PRI might have to shut down. The issue was greetings cards, one of the main areas where the shop had carved out a successful distinction for itself, because, as Abby explained, German cards were all in German and the NAAFI selection was 'rubbish'. It wasn't until much later in my fieldwork when I was due to leave, after the dispute with the NAAFI had been resolved (and the PRI had stopped selling greetings cards), that the regiment began a somewhat complex contractual process to formally employ Anne and another woman on a paid basis.

The quasi-professional status of the women responsible – and only eventually remunerated – for their work in setting up the regimental shop is one decisive example of the degree to which the *productive* labour and professional skills of military wives are directly harnessed by BFG as a material resource. Although the PRI might be dismissed as a trivial corner of trinkets and scented candles, it is testament to the forms of gendered and *productive* labour that are fundamental to the garrison and its capacity to socially reproduce itself as a working, cohesive community. In this sense, women married to servicemen sustain an internal employment market where both demand and supply is determined by military prerogatives. Once one becomes aware of the material significance of military wives' paid labour to the garrison overseas, its presence is everywhere. Women in tabards in canteens or dressed all in black to serve dinner in the officers' mess; writing for garrison magazines or running information and advice services; teaching assistants or childminders; cleaners, shopworkers, bartenders, cooks, clerks, admin assistants and PAs. Once one knows they are there, one sees an army of workers keeping things going, servicing the military institution and its relentless needs: a reserve army of wives. What underlines the sheer incorporating will of the military organisation in this case is its selective renegotiation of the terms of its sovereign status in Germany in order to create a localised, flexibilised and feminised workforce, whose members, instead of being classed as civil servants with structures of remuneration such as pensions, are classed as Locally Employed Civilians and paid in euros. In the section that follows, I will further explore the imprint of British sovereignty as it is maintained in Germany or adapted to fit the peculiarities of local conditions, through military geographies (Woodward 2004) and women's interactions across local space.

The Spatialisation of Sovereign Power

While military bases can be read as a juridical and territorial imprint of sovereign power according to their Status of Forces Agreements with host nations (see, e.g., Cooley 2008), it is the productive, social and cultural effects of their presence that I am interested in here. My analysis focuses on the ways in which the spaces and structures of the military institution are sensed, lived and inhabited in situ. It is this question of military presence and, importantly, how it is felt that reveals the diffusion of military power through its effects. Critical geographers such as Rachel Woodward (2004) have shown how the boundaries of military power extend far beyond 'the fact of physical presence' (Woodward 2004, 35), while scholarship on sovereignty and security has likewise focused on the ways in which national boundaries and borders of control are understood, felt and reproduced in far more socially complex, even intimate ways, for example in liminal spaces such as international airports and by subjects such as customs officials as sovereign actors (Chalfin 2008). The military control of space is likewise 'a discursive as well as a material practice' (Woodward 2004, 36), in addition to being carried out by and through embodied subjects and their interactions. This view of security and securitisation un-sites sovereign power from state apparatus to place it in the hands of those people – such as the military community overseas – who are subject to its rules and limitations but also responsible for its implementation and adaption. This offers insights into the ways in which the proscriptions and protections of sovereignty are navigated by subjects in their everyday lives.

In the analysis that follows, I ask what kind of processes produce and maintain people's sense of military power and presence through the spaces of British Forces Germany. My aim is to go beyond the physical buildings and boundaries of the army camp where I stayed, beyond the garrison's shooting ranges, or questions of its environmental 'spillover' (Gillem 2004, 40). More specifically and sometimes literally, this means tracing people's alternative routes *around* military presence: diversions around obstacles, shortcuts or the exploitation of administrative loopholes; people's interactions in and across space, their reinterpretation, through alternative uses and meanings, of material culture and resources. This more adaptive reading of military power is attuned to questions of how people *sense* and *make sense of* its presence in their everyday lives; in other words, it looks at how military presence is *inhabited*. This means following the mobilities of military wives to the places where military power takes shape in alternative forms and structures, beyond the wire. It means attending to the places where military presence is camouflaged and concealed, or, indeed, 'civilianised'; where it is kept out, actively converted or kept at bay. It means tracing circuitous routes that skirt around military presence, that subvert or mock its authority, confronting dead ends or getting stuck; paying attention to places where borders are muddied or pathways merge and dissolve.[8] Following military wives – themselves traditionally the ones posited as 'following the drum' (Venning 2005), it is often hard to tell where 'military' ends, and 'civilian' begins. And that is the very point. My first exploration in this section attends to some of the sovereign spaces around the camp as they are spatialised through the garrison's extraordinary fleet of civilian vehicles, before detailing some of the peculiarities of sovereign law and citizenship produced by the nexus of marriage, the military and migration.

The spaces I illuminate in this section are unremarkable in many ways, yet they reveal a great deal about the mutual constitution of military and civilian zones around a garrison town overseas. One prime example is the visibility of the BFG community as manifest in the cars people drive and the routes they articulate. The BFG workforce is arguably one of the most asset-rich in terms of brand-new people carriers, SUVs or souped-up saloon cars. Rob explains the economic potential of this historical arrangement as part of the British Army's package of tax breaks and overseas allowances for those posted abroad:

> They used to have two cars you could buy a year, tax free: one for you, one for your spouse. So you could buy a car, have it for a year, trade it back in, get a brand-new car because your trading value is about the same or higher as a brand-new tax-free car. So you could actually keep going throughout your time over here, changing every six months and end up with a brand-new car which is all paid for.

Tax breaks on the import of British-registered vehicles for service personnel overseas underline the material necessity for continuity as a counterbalance to military mobilities. This is similar to the ways in which the MoD provides British-run schools and commercial facilities to serve military communities overseas. The import of British taxed and registered cars is an example of military exceptionalism at an everyday level, renegotiating European trade regulations as part of the Status of Forces Agreements brokered between Germany and the UK. In material terms, the cars can be seen literally and figuratively as a mobile asset that is transferable across national borders, designed to smooth over the inconvenience of relocation (where families might otherwise have to buy cars in Germany only to have to sell them again in order to move home). Given the principles of continuity that undergird this provision, it is ironic that the scheme was put to *use* according to quite a different set of priorities, involving the frequent exchange and upgrading of vehicles in the way Rob describes.

The continuity provided by the import of British-registered and taxed vehicles also ensures continuity in the regulation and policing of driving practices. This again highlights the foreclosure of what might otherwise, for some members of the community at least, be an opportunity for a more flexible or selective – even transnational – manipulation of sovereign power. A particular nexus for the study of citizenship and militarisation in a British Army context is the status of Foreign and Commonwealth (F&C) personnel. The regiment with which I conducted my fieldwork included only a small number of F&C families, the majority of them from Fiji, one of them from South Africa. The British Army has an established history of recruiting soldiers from among Commonwealth populations, the cultural implications of which has been explored in depth, including from the perspective of women married to F&C personnel, by Vron Ware (2010, 2012). Fijian nationals have been one of the largest ethnic groups to fill the junior ranks of regiments struggling to recruit their full quotas from local regional catchment areas in the UK. One of two interviews I was able to secure with Fijian women married to F&C soldiers in the regiment here was Jacquelyn. Jacquelyn was married to a soldier who had responded to British Army recruitment campaigns in Fiji, and together they had moved to the UK and then to Germany with the regiment. It is Jacquelyn's experience of driving in Germany that throws some of the new, transnational dynamics of migration with the military into relief. And it is these messier effects of multiple levels of migration and mobility that must be brought under control – nationalised – as the British Army puts in place the administrative processes and categories to accommodate a group of soldiers and families whose status overspills conventional bounds of military-bureaucratic and national belonging. As Jacquelyn explains, driving licences for military personnel overseas are regulated by BFG on the basis of the UK government's Driver and Vehicle Licensing Agency (DVLA) regulations. Jacquelyn holds a Fijian licence, but, according to BFG/DVLA rules, this will become invalid after an initial period of six months, after which she will be unable to continue driving her British-registered car. Faced with the prospect of having to pay for lessons and a test to obtain a DVLA driving licence, Jacquelyn found out that, by German law, her Fijian licence was still considered valid:

> I went to the German guy that was doing my driving and he goes, 'With a Fiji licence do you realise that you can drive in Germany?' And I said well I was told that [. . .] you can only drive a BFG car for six months with a Fiji licence. But under German law, you [can] use your Fiji licence. So [. . .] I actually wrote to the master driver in Garrison Headquarters but he said, 'No, [you have to abide by] British Forces Germany law.' I thought he was supposed to make things easy for me! I could have got a German car to drive but that's the thing, if I get involved with an accident, I have to go through the German authorities and I need translation for that.

On this occasion, circumventing British law and its proxy application through BFG was not considered a viable trade-off with other conditions of security and citizenship that come with it – the fact that British citizens in the military community in Germany are subject to prosecution but also a kind of *protection* under the British legal system as enforced in Germany by the Royal Military Police.

In addition to the continuity of sovereign rule, the garrison's fleet of brand-new, British-registered cars was also productive of socially and culturally visible effects through their everyday use. While the cars were in many ways indistinguishable from others among the German population in that they featured the same range of familiar global brands and popular models, they all shared one defining feature: the letterbox-shaped British registration plates featuring a combination of clear, unfussy letters and numbers, white at the front of the car, yellow at the rear. These contrast markedly with the smaller, boxier shape of German registration plates, which contain letters and numbers in a different formation over two lines as well pictorial elements of state insignia. Whenever I was cycling between interviews and approached an area where the MOD had built or rented housing to accommodate service personnel, the sudden profusion of cars marked out by their clear, rectangular plates with large font produced a strong impression of entering a kind of British zone. In this way, British number plates came to function as a reassuring indication that I was nearing my destination, in the right place: a spatial boundary marker. A further effect of this outdated clause of Britain's Status of Forces agreement with Germany, then, is the *familiarity* these cars inscribe as they are parked, or weave their way around the garrison. For me, wherever I happened to be, seeing a car with a British number plate provoked the secondary response of looking closer at the driver to see if I knew them and then, potentially, giving a wave. As well as a national boundary marker, then, the British cars became productive of practices of internal (e.g. regimental) familiarity and recognition, whereupon one is hailed and hails the other as simultaneously a British and an army subject.

The zones articulated by the British cars are also productive of an alternative version of the German city in much the same way that scholars of everyday life, after geographers such as Henri Lefebvre ([1961] 2008), have shown how 'the users of the city, in their daily circulation, create a second, metaphorical city within the first [. . .]' (Sheringham 2006, 224). The routes traversed by the BFG community inscribe a circuit that connects a string of British-run facilities, including schools overseen by the MOD and named after English poets, the NAAFI and the camp. This reconfigures the map of the city, bypassing local landmarks, defining what is considered 'near' or 'far' and reshuffling centre–periphery relations, as one woman concedes in response to my questions about the centrality of the regimental camp to the community: 'Well, I think it's where it all happens, so I mean if you're someone who's been posted out in [another small town roughly 3 km away], you may as well be living on Mars.' Thus the community's sense of place is constituted by the centrality of the camp, more so than the German city centre with its cathedral, rail station or regular Saturday farmers' market (one of the places I regularly went and very rarely saw anybody I knew, for example).

The reordering of local geographies produce competing and overlapping circuits of distance and proximity, familiarity and otherness, British and German nationality, military and civilian identity around the camp. And they are further intersected by gender. This is revealed if one considers the cultural meanings and identities ascribed to the particular *kinds* of British-registered cars that are imported to Germany, as well as their drivers and the routes they take. These distinctions are narrated self-knowingly by Pippa, for example, who was in her early thirties and had been in Germany with the regiment since marrying a junior officer. She was keenly aware of the discursive mechanisms, articulated most frequently through a brand of collective humour that she appeared to share, through which family life is separated from life at the centre of the regiment, on camp:

> There's lots of different terminologies I'm still finding out about. Like for example we're called 'DABS',[9] I can't remember what that stands for but it's basically you know, families, army families. All the single soldiers living on camp call the ones with families [. . .] DABS, with their DAB-wagons, which is the Ford S-MAX or the people carriers all driving around [laughs].

To the young unmarried officers or junior soldiers on camp, the 'DAB-wagon' is an overt signifier of family life, the butt of jokes and the marker of a low-adrenaline zone characterised by the herdlike circulation of sensible people carriers from school run to supermarket and home. This kind of discourse is actively invested in naturalising the boundary between military and civilian, as well as further distinctions between junior and senior or younger and older personnel, and gendered ideas of productive action versus reproductive domesticity that feminise the camp's external zones.

In such ways, military mobilities produce a host of structural and social conditions that are contested, adapted, diverted and converted by military subjects living overseas under sovereign rule. At the same time, these conditions serve to limit and circumscribe people's material and social resources, often through the regulation or overdetermination of their mobilities. The dynamic that might be argued to best express the ambivalence and contradictory nature of military mobilities is the double-bind. From women's work and the incorporation of their labour back into the military institution, to Jacqulyn's driving licence: if one of the features of military mobilities is to be sent round in circles, bringing one constantly back to be reincorporated, is there ever a way out? In the next part of this chapter I want to explore in more detail some of the moves women make to try to evade or at least maximise the benefits of their encapsulation, specifically the processes of exchange – the bargains with militarisation – that this entails. Moving on from some of the structural, material conditions of military mobilities, I want to engage with some alternative currencies of value that are made possible by women's ambiguous position with respect to military belonging. I begin with an exploration of some of the motivations and meanings with which sovereign structures such as citizenship are invested, particularly as these are inhabited, sensed and made sense of through cycles of migration and mobility bound up in family life and the futurity of the next generation. I then go on to explore women's crossing of multiple boundaries and the potential this represents for the transformation of social and material resources around a military base, particularly through classed and gendered modes of consumption. Questioning the relevance of migration as a model for military mobilities, I am interested in the tensions, contradictions and, ultimately, the failure of this comparison in many ways. Wherever there is potential to transcend the territorialisations of military power, women are encapsulated by a multivalent set of mobilities that are so overdetermined as to put them straight back in their place.

Military Migration?

Women married to servicemen living overseas are not usually included in non-military or mainstream research and statistics around global migration, or in the broader context of migration studies. Nor, must it be said, are service personnel. The state-sponsored global mobility experienced by members of the Armed Forces and their families is distinct in many important ways from the experiences of those more conventionally classified as migrant workers, for example. One of the most obviously jarring aspects of configuring the experiences of women here as a form of migration is the question of relative social and economic privilege. Because migration with the military is institutionalised (as with global corporate or diplomatic mobility), it is both formal and collective. As well as providing a high degree of security and material support, migration with an institution also produces a degree of ethnic and cultural homogeneity – a bubble or enclave (Fechter 2007) – that comes with its own culturally productive power. Kristin Atwood (2013, 6) has argued that military families exist in a 'grey area' between migrant and expatriate categories (ibid., 19). It hardly needs stating that this is in stark and inequitable contrast to the experiences of other gendered subjects whose experience of global mobility is characterised by enormous risk and insecurity.

This significant qualification having been made, in the rest of this chapter I want to persist with the question of what *kind* of mobility military wives might be argued to experience in a couple of different ways. The first follows recent scholarship on military migration and multiculture led by Vron Ware's (2012) book *Military Migrants: Fighting for YOUR Country*, by paying further attention to the experiences of F&C personnel. Given the variety of experiences of relocation that might be classified under the term 'military mobilities', from regional and regularised moves within the UK, to the decision by couples or families from Fiji, in the case of this regiment, to serve in Britain and then beyond, it is important to persist with the question of what different – often inequitable – migratory obstacles are encountered by different women married to servicemen, and the practices they adopt in response. The second kind of mobility I explore in the rest of this chapter is inspired by scholarship on gender and privileged migration (e.g. Coles and Fechter 2008) to examine the particular ideas about gender that help to construct and maintain the boundaries of belonging within and beyond the military base overseas. This entails thinking about collective identities founded on ideas about nation, culture and ethnicity as well as institutional belonging in relation to a 'host' nation or community, and can be broadly aligned with scholarship that has focused for example on colonial, diplomatic and corporate mobility (Coles 2008; Fechter 2010; Fechter and Walsh 2010). I want to question the construction of privilege and belonging in ways that complicate the terms of that privilege and show how it is nevertheless unevenly distributed and experienced in ways that are not always liberatory.

Much of what is assumed to produce stability, familiarity and continuity (and, therefore, ease) in the migrations of military wives might be argued to be based on conditions of citizenship. Namely, an alignment of wives' citizenship and national identity with the nation that their husbands serve and the extension of sovereign protection (and regulation) accordingly. I have already shown some of the disciplinary effects of sovereign rule as they are complicated by the status of women whose own national affiliations might not align so neatly with the British state. In the analysis that follows, I want to explore the investments that some women make in citizenship and sovereignty by return, and what these ties tell us about how military power is sensed and made sense of.

Unsurprisingly perhaps, the main formal negotiations that the Fijian women I met were invested in related to questions of citizenship and freedom of movement within Europe and back to the UK. These were questions that were rarely if ever raised by the other majority-white, British women with whom I spoke, illustrating the taken-for-granted status of the citizenship upon which many of the practicalities as well as discourses of national service are based. This is borne out in Jacquelyn's reflection upon the lack of awareness on the part of military welfare services.

> I was the first [Fijian] wife to come over and join the regiment. What was difficult for me was [that] the Welfare kind of had no knowledge at all of what covers me [. . .] I feel that even though they came to do the recruitment, they got so many Fijian boys, I still feel that the Army lacks that bit. The unit welfare doesn't do that bit [of] homework. Or probably they haven't got the people that informs [*sic*] them what covers Foreign and Commonwealth.

Issues around visas and citizenship were a focal point for local organising and targeted advocacy among F&C personnel in the garrison. They were the primary subjects of debate among attendees of a Fijian Support Network briefing that I attended towards the end of my fieldwork, which attracted a large group of Fijian women to air their views and ask questions of military welfare and F&C representatives. It is not possible to offer a comprehensive survey of F&C experiences based on the limited number of personnel in the regiment in question here, and the limited sample I was able to interview. What did emerge from my interviews with two Fijian women were some of the administrative hurdles entailed in migrating to the UK, then Germany, as part of the first wave of recruits from Fiji. Their encounters with bureaucratised borders were complicated from the micro- to the macro-level, from battles with the regimental welfare office to the direct experience of the spaces and processes of UK border control. Jacquelyn continues:

> So I don't know if it's supposed to be my job or [the welfare office's] job to do that bit for me. My visa was six months' visitor's visa from Fiji. By April it was due so I had to get a renewal. I walked into the welfare and they just looked at me point blank – 'You've got to call immigration. As far as [we] know you've got to sort it out.' So I've got to call immigration, [. . .] get the forms, fill it in. While [my husband is] away [fighting in Iraq]. So I fill in the forms [and] I can remember I called [UK immigration] every second day to find out what's happening – I don't want to be deported by April because my visa's due. So [I'm] sitting at home waiting for my passport to be returned, next thing I know I call the welfare and they go 'Oh it's been sitting here.' Really? Great. How come? 'Well, they recognise us, the Army, they don't recognise the individual doing the [application].' It's not on! Come on, I did that out of my own effort and you need to be recognised?

Jacquelyn's account here underlines the tension between ideas about collective and individual responsibility for migration processes. Here, as in many other women's accounts of everyday administrative hurdles, the military institution, together with the all-encompassing regulatory power it represents, establishes the expectation that it can override or bypass state structures, being an exceptional part of the state apparatus itself. It is at such moments and in such places that the myth of military exceptionality is confounded or undone.

This failure of military-administrative promise has its implications for how women married to servicemen perceive their own exceptionality as mobile subjects. Patti, who was thirty-one years old and worked in one of the garrison retail outlets, arrived in Germany in 2003 to join her husband Manasa when he was posted to the regiment. She offers a more sympathetic interpretation of the Army's best efforts to cater to Fijian families like her own: 'I think the Army are trying so hard in terms of the Commonwealth and the Foreign.' Patti and Manasa, whom I interviewed together, had known each other during school in Suva but were married only after he had joined the British Army and returned to Fiji on summer leave ('And then things started – yeah, it heated off again. I think because he was yeah, in the British Army'). While largely forgiving of the Army's internal practices surrounding F&C citizenship and visas, Patti had experienced the securitisation of national borders in ways that she didn't expect. She described the administrative system that regulates her leave to remain in Germany in vague terms, processed through the MoD, but is clear about her distaste for the depersonalised yet embodied experience of UK immigration and border control:

> P: For me, I have to apply for my status – that's a status to live here. That's for the four of us, we have to have that. And normally it gets renewed. If I was to travel to UK, [. . .] we have to apply for visa. We do it ourself [*sic*].
>
> A: Totally outside of the military?
>
> P: Yeah.
>
> A: Do you go to the UK very often?
>
> M: [No] – the only reason why it's stopping us is because of the visa. If not, we would have been travelling to—
>
> P: Yeah. Because it's really annoying. I get really fed up. Last time I went to UK was in 2009, and normally we have to [go] through the agents here, border agents here. And then I was telling [Manasa], the day I walked in there it made me feel like a . . . a refugee. Because you just felt so – the atmosphere there was just – you

> know, it's wrong that you are there because your husband is fight-
> ing for Queen and country and then you have – you're waiting like
> the rest of the people trying to get into the UK. It really – I wasn't
> happy when I was there and that just peed me off.

Patti's anger and disappointment at having to join 'the rest of the
people trying to get into the UK' indicates the degree to which she
conceives of her own geographic mobility in military terms as an
exceptional mode of migration-within-migration; a fast-track or special service. It is interesting that the grounds for Patti's expectations
of border control are conveyed first and foremost through the idea of
national service – 'fighting for Queen and country', a colloquialism
that is shorthand for ideas about duty and sacrifice. If Patti expects
to transcend normal civilian restrictions on freedom of movement,
however, her experience serves only to highlight the inequity of the
terms through which her bargain with the British Army is made,
hence the unfortunate irony through which she is restricted from
freely entering the country that her husband serves.

Both Patti's and Jacquelyn's experiences offer a sense of the lived
complexities that arise from the bureaucratic structures through which
the British Army's recruitment of F&C personnel is managed. Their
military mobilities encompass multiple layers or rings of migration-
within-migration: their geographic relocation to Germany *within*
their migration from Fiji to the UK, but also the tensions between
collective and individual responsibility for visas and citizenship, and
the collapse of military exceptionality in the face of UK border control. These are mobilities fraught with irony and absurdity, the only
response to which, perhaps, is to try and maximise resources. While
'Queen/King and country' are the ready-made, discursive terms upon
which people are called to 'serve' in the British Army, the *meaning* of
this form of militarised citizenship is distinct for different groups. In
her paper. 'Not for Queen and Country or any of that shit . . .': Reflections on Citizenship and Military Participation in Contemporary
British Soldier Narratives', Rachel Woodward has explored soldiers'
interpretations of citizenship as 'mateship' (2008, 377) through the
ways in which ideas of national belonging are performed, personalised and, to some degree, rejected in everyday life. Citizenship in
the case of the majority of white British personnel is implicitly produced by race as a foundational aspect of national identity and the
white cultural homogeneity onto which it is mapped. It is only here,
perhaps, where citizenship is secure and can be taken for granted,

that it is open to playful subversion in terms of the titular rejection of 'Queen and country and any of that shit' (Woodward 2008). The complex meanings of British citizenship warrant further exploration on the part F&C personnel, whose place in terms of the social, cultural and material conditions of belonging is far less secure, and shaped by nationhood and race as alterity and otherness. Any rejection of the notion of 'Queen and country' that women married to F&C personnel might make, therefore, hinges less on the privilege of a secure basis for that citizenship than on their precarious position in relation to multiple and often contradictory social and bureaucratic processes. Jacquelyn's response is pragmatic, translating the meaning of citizenship into terms that are individual rather than collective, and instrumental:

> A: What is the military about for you? Is it serving the British nation or Queen – do you view yourself as part of British Army life?
>
> J: I think that's far away from my head. For me, being in the Army I would say is an opening of opportunity [. . .] for me and my family. That's what I'm grateful for. And I always tell myself every time I get hindrances and frustrated I tell myself 'Come on, it's an opening door, [. . .] this is just a foundation for me to do better to go on to something else.' And whatever privileges is opening to us and whatever that we are able to grab from it, grasp as much as you can [. . .] and move on from there. That's why I thought it's an opening door last year with the boys could get naturalised. And this year, this is opening up, *Life in the UK* test has come this far to Germany, that's an opening door. So I'm always telling myself [. . .] with all these things that's barriers, I try to look beyond the barriers and see what I can grasp.

For Jacquelyn, the capacity to 'grasp' what one can from limited, even deleterious, circumstances comes with attendant ideas of sacrifice in the present and the implication of deferred benefits in the future. Thus the struggles and frustrations that Jacquelyn encounters are transformed – converted like currency – into a kind of investment in the future that is personalised and domesticated, framed explicitly in terms of the benefits accruing to the nuclear family and, within this, the next generation.

In terms of these practices of domestication and personalisation, it is essential to note that the ideals that shape people's bargains with militarisation are produced not only through the structure of the military as a state institution, but also by the contract of marriage.

This is framed by Patti in the more intimate terms of how visa and citizenship status bind families together, shaping the power relations between wife and husband:

> A: Would you ever swap to a British passport?
> M: She would.
> P: I would. He won't. He's got attitude [laughs].
> M: No, it's because – because not only—
> P: He has this vision that if he changes his passport and if I change I'm going to leave him.
> M: No it's not that.
> P: Yes it is, that's what you tell me [laughing].

This exchange hints at the more intimate power relations bound up in couples' decisions to migrate, Patti's jokes indicating the private negotiations couples make between themselves, and the potential insecurities that arise as a result. While it is not appropriate or possible to assess Patti and Manasa's own personal bargain with one another here, Patti's humour brings into the open the possibility that citizenship for some might be a tool of emotional control, of dependency or freedom negotiated between spouses; of the power that one spouse may wield over another to grant or restrict movement and independence.

Citizenship, in all these examples, is loaded with multiple and complex meanings, many of which represent deeply personal as well as practical investments in the promise of a military career. This is a kind of promise linked to people's most intimate or personal desires, their insecurities and ideals, their past mistakes and corrected futures. Military power in this sense might be argued to work through aspiration and projection on a personal scale, as it does through the projection of power and anticipation of threat on the global stage. Like the hierarchy of rank providing a visible pathway for self-improvement and status, as I will explore in Chapter 3, military power is deeply aspirational. In this light, it is possible to see the speculative investment that Jacquelyn and others make in British citizenship as based on the potential to convert geographic mobility into social mobility. It is the next generation – not the first but the second – who are cast as future inheritors of dividends paid in return for their parents' sacrifice. This was already manifest for both families I spoke to, as, for example, both sets of parents prioritised applying for dual Fijian and British citizenship for their children before themselves. For Patti and Manasa, this decision relates to the social and cultural opportunities open to their children already. While Patti and Manasa highlight the importance of their children's geographic mobility as newly made British citizens, the cultural capital their children accrue is still very much formed by the interlocking cycles of migration that have determined their current location in Germany:

> M: The reason why we want [our children] to get their passport is because they are in school now. And then most children will be having trips [. . .] I'm lucky I've got a British Army ID card. I still find it hard sometimes they will stop me and keep asking me questions, you know? But for them it'll be hard because they still don't . . . That's the reason why we want to try and get their passport done: we don't want them to be questioned or stuck at the airport when we're not there. Especially with these trips going on. They have skiing in Austria, all these other places. Switzerland. [. . .] Yeah, they're so lucky.

Manasa's motivations in applying for British citizenship for his children are bound up with his experience of restrictions upon his own movement within Europe, as highlighted earlier by Patti. There is a protective impulse underlying his desire to shield his own children from this experience in the future, which reveals how subtly his negotiations are patterned by race and the need to pre-empt, mitigate and protect against discrimination, incidences of which, such as the family's experience of racist verbal abuse from neighbours, and Patti's sense of a lack of equality in job opportunities, were also discussed during our interview. In terms of the benefits of migration-within-migration for Fijian families in Germany, however, dual citizenship places Manasa's children on an equal footing with their peers in terms of accessing further opportunities for social mobility that are exceptional even in terms of the resources available to state schoolchildren of equivalent age in the UK. Namely, their location on the European continent and proximity to an array of exciting ski locations. That said, paying attention to the subtler register of Manasa's aspirations here betrays a sense of the underlying social precarity he has experienced and its disciplinary effects in terms of conforming to cultural codes:

> P: Yeah. Like for the boys, like now we try to better things for them. Like when opportunities come up we try and make use of it. Like school trips or if they are invited by friends to go wherever. [. . .] They've changed so much and their friends um, most of them are English boys. And they go to their houses and vice versa.

> M: But then we always tell them, cos – before we always tell them
> [. . .] do this and say thank you, show respect back to them. And
> those things.
> [. . .]
> P: Yeah I think it's, it's good for them, especially for their education.
> Getting free education. Because that's our, our main thing – main
> aims, for them to have a better education.

Patti, Manasa and Jacquelyn all acknowledge the terms of their bargain with the military institution, whereby their children benefit now and in the future from the upheaval they experience. The inequities of this exchange in the short term, including administrative oversights but also racial discrimination and limited job opportunities, were present in all of their accounts. Jacquelyn has likewise been swift to ensure her two children can obtain dual citizenship, though her rationale is based on a longer-term investment. Similar to Manasa, Jacquelyn also wishes to protect her children from some of the pitfalls she has experienced when caught between different cycles of migration:

> Right, the citizenship, I just managed to get my boys naturalised last year. To become British citizens,[. . .] that's what I particularly wanted, mostly for them. I wouldn't say that I would want to take my boys back to Fiji, it's just a sense of education. Because when I came [to Germany] and applied for this job, I went into GLSU [and said], 'I've got a diploma in business management from Fiji' but [. . .] to apply for a post, it says [only] qualifications recognised [in] UK [will be accepted]. So I don't have anything to show for.

When it comes to applying for dual citizenship for Jacquelyn and her husband, the process is further complicated by a series of bureaucratic absurdities at various different levels, an example of which is the necessity to pass a 'Life in the UK' test, until recently only available in the UK. This was not only an obstacle in terms of needing to travel to the UK to take the test, but also in terms of the very conditions by which Fijian soldiers and their families who have been posted to Germany might qualify for British citizenship in the first place, as Jacquelyn explains:

> The 'Life in the UK' test used to be just in the UK, and to be able to sit the test you either have to be five years living in the UK and another prerequisite is you have to have a UK address to prove you've been living in the UK, which we don't have. So what happened was just

last month they said it's being hosted in [Germany] through Army education centre, and they're holding tests for dependants as well. The soldiers get to do a one-week course and do the test, but for dependants as well they do it now.

The obstacles that Jacquelyn and others encounter betray the slow process of legal and institutional change as the British Government and the Armed Forces struggle to respond to successive cohorts of Fijian personnel moving through recruitment rounds and deployments, and as they marry, have children, are promoted and in some cases begin to leave the Army.

What these everyday battles over visas, driving licences, work permits and qualifications, freedom of movement and citizenship also reveal is the intersection between geographic and social mobility, which I have shown is thrown into relief in new and particular ways by military forms of migration-within-migration. Many of these aspirations around citizenship connect the family, the nation and the British commonwealth in projections of transnational mobility, as evidenced by Jacquelyn's future plans:

> Our idea is for me and my husband is to go and settle in Australia. [. . .] Going over will probably be easier with a British passport than the Fiji one. And mostly the reason why we want to go down is to be near home – it's a little bit too far over this corner. And at least Australian qualifications. . . education-wise for the boys, can be recognised.

In her future plans – her bargain with the military institution – Jacquelyn seems to be aiming for a balance between moving on (to Australia), and return (to be closer to Fiji), looking towards the future, and also her past. This might be argued to be mirrored in the struggles of the British Army to modernise itself, caught between the historical conditions of colonialism that are foundational for its relations and attitudes towards F&C personnel, and a desire to transform itself into an outward-looking, globalist and multicultural organisation (Ware 2012). The participation of F&C personnel in the British Armed Forces is not a new phenomenon given the history of the British Empire, and the colonial continuities are clear – and increasingly contested – in contemporary discourses of national service (see, e.g., Basham 2016a and 2016b; Chisholm 2014b). But it is the quieter echoes I am interested in throughout this book: notions of self-improvement and social mobility that can be mapped onto military hierarchies of class as well as histories of race and empire in terms of its 'civilising mission'. Or, on the flip side, cultural assumptions that I heard referred to on numerous occasions regarding Fijian households and the perception of a higher incidence of domestic abuse; an element of 'culture' that it was thought had been imported from afar and needed to be corrected as F&C soldiers assimilated into British life.[10]

The experiences I have explored in this chapter, not only those of F&C personnel but of women married to servicemen more generally, include the kind of cultural and economic dynamics long critiqued in feminist and postcolonial scholarship, on heterosexual marriage and the division of labour in Western societies by scholars such as Carole Pateman (1988) in *The Sexual Contract* and Ann Oakley's (1974) *Housewife*, for example, or Ann McClintock's (1995) analysis of colonial economies of race and domesticity in *Imperial Leather*. The kind of historical continuities that I am interested in here coalesce around gender, heteronormativity and the sexual division of labour as well as colonial legacies of the enclave and the ways in which these are tied to white Britishness as embedded in hierarchies of class. In the final section of this chapter, I look further into the experiences of women married to servicemen living overseas in terms of privilege and mobility.

Privileged Migration and Its Discontents

And you know I've been to Canada, I've been to Kenya, I've been on tour. We've been to you know, crazy balls in Vienna. I've been down to Luxembourg, I've been all over Germany. I've drunk more champagne than I have water, I've met some amazing people, been to some incredible dinners. You know. And just seen some beautiful dresses and silverware.

Sophie, a young officer posted with the regiment and recently returned from Afghanistan, gives a thrilling account of her military career – it exudes glamour, beauty and a giddy but sophisticated youthfulness. Her account illustrates that military discourses of travel and adventure rely as much on social geographies of gender, class and rank, as they do upon landscapes and terrain. Scholars have identified some of the ways in which soldiers' identities are constructed discursively through the spaces of basic training (Woodward 1998) and, more recently, deployment in desert camouflage (Gonzalez 2010). These discourses rely on masculinised constructions of wildness and rurality or an orientalist adventurism. Yet military identities by no means exclude the production of a kind of glamour and sophistication as recalled by Sophie. My interviews with many women married to servicemen, particularly those married to officers such as Natasha below, revealed a repeated trope that relies on the construction of army life as cosmopolitan: if not glamorous per se, then at least productive of 'well-travelled experience, sophisticated style and *savoir faire*' (Vertovec 2010, 63).

> A: With the travel and everything do you view yourself as having this international outlook?
> N: Yes, we do. It's not a Singapore posting, it's not a . . . you know, glamorous . . . We've had lots of friends who've had much more glamorous postings and we've only ever done Germany and no one's raging to come out to see us because it sounds like a glamorous one! But we've done a lot of travelling which we wouldn't have done if we'd been in the UK I'm absolutely convinced of it, and yeah no we actively pursue the international . . .

Gender scholarship on 'global professional mobility' or 'privileged migration' (Coles and Fechter 2008, 1) has charted women's movements as they are determined by the careers of their husbands within networks of corporations, multilateral aid agencies, NGOs, international diplomacy and joint military forces, for example (see, within the same collection, Coles 2008; Gordon 2008; Hindman 2008; Jervis 2008; Walsh 2008). Coles and Fechter (2008, 4) have questioned the applicability of the term 'cosmopolitan' to describe the migratory experience of women such as those married to servicemen, 'because most of those involved retain much of their native culture abroad'. This brings such women's experiences closer in line with that of traditional 'sojourners' (Schiller et al. 1995, 48), expressed through the metaphor of a 'long vacation' (Kurotani 2007, 22). However, scholars of transnational migration argue that cosmopolitanism inheres not simply in the ontological conditions of travel and movement and the question of where people go or how long they stay. Rather, cosmopolitanism represents a set of dispositions and capacities (Amit 2007, 9), a particular 'orientation' (Vertovec 2010, 64). Cosmopolitanism in this sense might come close to the kind of outlook invoked by Natasha above, as she attempts to make the most of the opportunities afforded by living overseas. A further example might be the Anglo-German coffee morning.

Shaped by the garrison's long history in the German city, the Anglo-German coffee morning is a genteel form of cultural exchange between local German women associated with the garrison and women married to officers within it. The event was characterised by a combined sense of quaint curiosity and inherited obligation on the part of the women I accompanied there. We arrived at the home of the German woman whose turn it was to host the event and joined a group of about twenty other women. We complimented the host on the enormous Christmas tree twinkling at the centre of the house, and proceeded to mingle around a large table laid with patisseries, meats and cheeses. There was much admiration of the china tea service, some interest in my curious research project, and I received advice from one of the German women on where to purchase a second-hand bicycle. The Anglo-German coffee morning also came up in my interview with Pippa, who had not long arrived in the garrison and was just beginning to orientate herself within the social and cultural milieu. Although it was not clear whether she had attended the coffee morning herself, she was aware that such events were somehow exclusive, bound by internal divisions of (husbands') rank that were transferred seamlessly onto women whom she conceived of as 'senior wives': 'some of the more senior wives they do have these Anglo-German circles and I personally think they should open them out a bit more and publicise them a bit more.' Not only are such events determined by rank, but their exclusivity is also upheld through unspoken or informal means, such that one gains access to the coffee morning by invitation or association, rather than by public announcement like other events in the garrison.

As well as being the most overt, contrived mode of 'cultural exchange' between the British military and German civilian community that I encountered, the Anglo-German coffee morning is just as remarkable for the social structures it mirrors and reproduces *across* the Anglo-German (and military/civilian) divide. This represents what Vered Amit (2007) describes as the boundedness as well as the apparent fluidity of people's mobilities, in the sense that:

> travellers' voyages are critically implicated in the development of differentiated circuits of travel that encapsulate even as they facilitate movement. As a result, travellers moving through these specialised circuits are most likely to encounter other travellers like themselves. (Amit 2007, 11)

It is certainly possible to argue that the regimental community in Germany represents a particular circuit of travel, one that, as many of the encounters I explore in this book show, brings together people from a wide range of socio-economic backgrounds in the UK, who may not otherwise have socialised together at home (Amit 2007, 2). However, it is also important to recognise that this circuit of travel is by no means the only one in operation, and that people are also encapsulated by other 'overlapping categories of travel' (Amit 2007, 5). The categories of travel that encapsulate the Anglo-German coffee morning as a social circuit are not simply to do with nationality or military status, but a subtler equivalence that connects hierarchies of rank and social structures such as class, which must also be accounted for in terms of how cultural homogeneity works through race, here as whiteness. It is here that 'senior wives' find their well-matched, local equivalents in a group of women married to local business and civic elites. Moreover, it is a shared system of social conventions, a kind of cultural competence and savoir faire (the offering of a tastefully wrapped pot plant as a gift for the host, the correct use of the tea service) that oil the cogs of this machine.

What the Anglo-German coffee morning highlights is the role of culture as 'content or product' (Anthias 2001, 627) in women's attempts to make the most of their international lifestyles. The refined gentility of the coffee morning is a world away from the drab or dangerous machinery of military power as it grinds on elsewhere, in the garrison or indeed, in those parts of the world where women's husbands were at that time deployed. While the Anglo-German coffee morning was facilitated by continuities of class and social status, however, it was *consumed* in a way that emphasised otherness. The way the coffee morning was narrated to me beforehand as something I should 'experience' or 'see' for my project, our admiration of the food, our obvious curiosity, and some women's less reverent comments, after the event, about provincial German tastes in interior design, all contribute to the sense of how gender and class are produced by and produce social conventions that operate through alterity and recognition at the same time.

As Merje Kuus (2009, 550) has argued in relation to NATO internationalist discourse, 'militarism and cosmopolitanism appear to be incompatible at first: the former associates with nationalism and statism, while the latter eschews these notions.' If a military lifestyle can be aligned with a progressive, global perspective inflected with a sense of travel and adventure, however, then perhaps 'anyone can become a glamorous cosmopolite' by association (Kuus 2009, 558). Although the exclusivity of the Anglo-German coffee morning might appear to constrain cosmopolitanism to a class of British and German elites, many of the women I spoke to across the full spectrum of the community explained how their everyday practices were shaped in important ways by the experience of living in another country. Pippa recounts some of the tiny slippages and dislocations that prompted a mixture of escapism and frustration:

> P: There is always that little feeling that, I mean you're not always on holiday but there's a little bit of – it's quite cool that you're living in a different country [. . .] In other ways I find it quite frustrating – life isn't as convenient as the UK, you know you can't go to one supermarket, get everything – well, you could but, um, you know you can't get lamb! [laughs] Everywhere you go you can't get lamb except the NAAFI – little sort of foody things . . .
>
> A: So how much do you shop in the NAAFI and how much do you shop in . . .
>
> P: Um, I mainly shop in [a German supermarket] out of principle. Again, I just feel if you're in a country, you should throw yourself into it. I mean, that is a culture shock in itself the supermarket, and you know most of them don't have baskets [. . .] They don't have shopping bags, and still I forget to take them with me so I've got 4,000 in my cupboard because every time I go out I have to buy one! [laughs] So there's those little nuances which I half love and half hate because they're frustrating if you don't get your head round them. But the NAAFI, I think it's such a shame to limit yourself to limited and not particularly good-quality food and the NAAFI really is overpriced. I mean if there's some things you can't get anywhere else that you really want, you go to the NAAFI
>
> A: Like what for example?
>
> P: [laughs] Just like some brands, like Marmite – Tom likes Marmite – things like that. Umm . . . this is going to be embarrassing . . . Roast Beef Monster Munch! [laughs loud]

Scholarship on gender and migration has looked closely at material culture and its constitutive role in the production of identity and 'home'.[11] Scholars such as Ruba Salih (2003, 68) explore the role of material culture and 'the flow of objects' to accord subjects 'agency in the constitution of society and of their own identities' (Miller 1987 in Salih 2003, 68). Within this framework, homemaking is considered as a way of 'mediating a sense of belonging through the familiar' (Gordon 2008, 30). In relation to privileged migration, Heather

Hindman's (2008) study of women married to corporate executives relocated overseas illustrates how corporations provide monetary compensation packages designed as far as possible to maintain an 'equivalent' lifestyle for families living abroad. As Hindman (2008) argues, however, such economic incentives are nothing without the women's work which, through consumer choices and homemaking decisions, converts them into social capital: 'Thus if it is male labour that brings the couple abroad, it is the woman's job to erase that move' (Hindman 2008, 42). Despite the instrumentalisation of women's domestic labour in this way, the attitudes and practices that Pippa espouses might still qualify as 'actually existing' cosmopolitanism (Malcolmson in Robbins 1998, 2). This is not the kind of cosmopolitanism that functions as 'a luxuriously free-floating view from above' (Robbins 1998, 1), but one that inheres in everyday practices with an emphasis on pragmatism and tactics (Vertovec 2010 64). As Amit (2007, 12) argues in his consideration of the dual dynamic of escape and encapsulation that structures travellers' movements in privileged migration, military wives 'may not be seeking to ride cosmopolitan waves of international mobility, but in their efforts to win space for themselves in new places, their unavoidable and mundane encounters with "others" may well effect more or less subtle changes in perspective and organisation'.

Women such as Pippa may not, perhaps, be argued to transcend the gendered boundaries that confine her agency to domestic consumption and, ultimately, a choice of supermarkets. However, this apparently banal choice between national and international at least affords some escape from the overdetermined sovereign conditions of military mobilities represented by the NAAFI. Furthermore, if cosmopolitanism inheres not simply in the ontological conditions of travel and movement but also a set of orientations and capacities (Amit 2007, 9; Vertovec 2010, 64), could it be possible that women's active construction and performance of an international lifestyle serves as an imaginative landscape that substitutes the militarised terms of their mobility for ones that are far more 'civilised'? The example of the Anglo-German coffee morning and Pippa's practices of cultural consumption both demonstrate a set of micro-practices which, although often predetermined by the material and social structures of British Forces Germany, in some ways offer women the opportunity to transcend national borders, as well as the border between military and civilian, by seeking out their German equivalents, whether in the form of social conventions or consumer produce.

However, further examples of military wives' cosmopolitan imaginaries and, in many cases, their abrupt collision with reality indicate the degree to which the liberatory potential of such imaginaries fails to materialise as the transformative – and indeed transnational – effect it implies. As well as a potential site for both cultural consumption and familiarisation, shopping was frequently used by women as a measure of language proficiency, whereby multiple women equated their level of vocabulary as sufficient to be able to 'get by' in the supermarket, or not, in Stacey's case:

> I don't feel like I'm living in Germany until I hit the shops, and find a shop that no one speaks English, that's when it . . . you think, you know . . . But nine times out of ten you go in and you go 'guten Morgen', and whatever [you say] they can tell you're English just because [of] the way you dress, we stand out like sore thumbs. So they know and they end up talking English to you anyway. But it's not until really you hit a German shop that doesn't speak English then you think 'oh God' you know. But in general I like it, if I could move all of this back home it'd be better obviously, just because of being close to family and stuff like that but no, I like it.

Through an implicit mode of return, Stacey's narrative soon loops back to a desire for the familiar, or the incorporation of the foreign into the familiar at least (if Stacey could move all she liked about living in a provincial German city 'back home'). As I encountered these contradictions more frequently, such as when talking to Kirsty, who was married to a junior soldier and had not been in Germany long, I struggled to maintain the innocence of my questions, especially with regards to learning the language (and began to feel much less concerned about my own lack of efforts to do the same):

> K: [B]asically it's more of an experience while we're over here 'cause, well, [you] kind of get the chance to learn the language sort of [laughs].
> A: Yeah, have you done any of that?
> K: No! [laughs]
> A: Nor have I! [laughs]
> K: I think it's an experience more than anything else 'cause in the UK it's, I don't know, it's not as much of an experience, you can't really go out and indulge in the culture and stuff like that 'cause it's all English isn't it?

Kirsty's invocation of 'culture' as an 'experience' that she has in fact failed to pursue renders it something of an empty signifier and posits the cosmopolitanism that is constructed through it as a kind of wilful misrepresentation. This is in complete contradistinction to the form of culture that learning a language actually represents, involving a detailed, processual and long-lasting transformation on the part of the language learner and a long-term commitment rather than a one-off event. Moreover, where the German language might be viewed as an object of cultural acquisition and experience, it was most frequently cited as the biggest obstacle blocking women's access to German culture in any form, the 'language barrier'. The foreclosure of this transformatory aspect of living overseas is emphasised by Pippa, whose own efforts to learn the language had been thwarted multiple times when she signed up for free German lessons provided by the garrison, only for them to be cancelled due to lack of subscribers.

> P: But I don't know whether people just have a lot going on in their lives with their children and then they just get comfortable in their community and they don't generally show an interest in, you know, embracing German life and culture, um and whether that's, I think that does tend to be more on the soldiers' wives' side.
>
> A: Yeah – do you think it's to do with your outlook, how you've been brought up, your socio-economic means, your education things like that?
>
> P: Yeah, I do think, some of the wives come out here and they are really young, I mean I was twenty-nine, thirty, when I came out and some of them are just seventeen or eighteen and it's not what . . . you're not mature enough to say, 'Ooh, I'd like to embrace the culture,' or, say, go on a course. No, you just want to go out and get hammered, as in every country, that's as hybrid as it gets, going to Bar Negroni's and a few of the cocktail places, and I think maybe it's only when you become a bit older do you realise the benefits and the interests of being in a different country.

While Pippa distinguishes between different women's attitudes to consuming culture, these are distinctions she attributes to age, and, in so doing, she resists reproducing value judgements based on rank, class and socio-economic status. Her portrayal of some of the younger women married to junior soldiers is sympathetic to the degree to which, through age and inexperience as she perceives it, the consumption of culture (or rather, what she implies is a misguided version of culture constituting the overconsumption of cocktails in a bar that was broadly known as the go-to venue for British military wives in the city) represents women's limited choices but also, ultimately, the fulfilment of their desires at that particular moment.

But it is Pippa's invocation of the idea of hybridity (and, significantly, its failure) that is most interesting to me here, particularly for what hybridity implies about the liberatory potential of border-crossing as a process of transformation, where migrant experiences are argued to produce new, emergent subject positions that are neither here nor there, but which constitute a 'Third Space' (Bhabha 1994, 55). Through such interpretations, the 'liberatory turn' in migration studies (Pratt and Yeoh 2003, 159) has reformulated migrants as 'icons of hybridity' (Salih 2003, 5), a contested formulation that has nonetheless been used as a model for the cultural transformations posited as arising from migration and diaspora in a globalised age (Hutnyk 2010, 59). It is essential to note that the material and social context in which Pippa deploys the notion of hybridity differs considerably from the origins of the term in the work of scholars such as Stuart Hall (1988 in Anthias 2001, 625), Homi Bhabha (1994) and Paul Gilroy (1993). As I have shown in this chapter, people manage their mobilities more or less consciously by establishing cultural continuities along classed and ethnic lines, as both the German coffee morning, and many of Jacquelyn's, Patti's and Manasa's practices show. Like Kirsty's desire to learn the German language, Stacey's incorporation of the foreign into the familiar and Natasha's espousal of a 'cosmopolitan' lifestyle, people construct their own imaginaries of agency, choice and adaptation. This captures a sense of the more fluid social mobility that women *construct* of their highly bounded geographic location, for example. However, like Joanne's sense of 'moving on' and 'being held back', the limits of these transformations (as Pippa notes: 'That's as hybrid as it gets') betrays a complex set of contradictions where micro-opportunities for transgression and reinvention also reproduce their own encapsulation. The reliance of women's mobilities upon military hierarchies of class, whiteness and gender for example, and the military's structural and material reterritorialisation of British sovereignty and nationality overseas, can also have the effect of fixing women in place, for example through a military-sexual division of labour that confines their opportunities for empowerment to motherhood or the direct incorporation of their labour into the institution. In many ways, the failure of hybridity here underlines Anthias's (2001, 619) critique of 'the stories we tell ourselves that we are all becoming global, hybrid and diasporic'. Like 'globalist militarism' (Kuus 2009, 558), the hybridity and culture that women desire or imagine are 'constructions of social reality' (Young 1996 in Anthias 2001, 619). Furthermore, these are undergirded not only by privilege but, ironically, by the fixing-in-place of normative – and far from transgressive – gender roles and relations, culminating in grocery shopping and domestic practices as much as in leisure and culture (which is limited to a few cocktails in a bar frequented by other military wives). As Anthias (2001) argues and scholarship on privileged migration bears out (Fechter 2007), the 'alternative adaptation to that of translation (where new and more transgressive forms emerge)' is something of an 'enclavisation process, a living in a 'time warp', a mythologizing of tradition' (Anthias 2001, 628).

Conclusion

As this chapter shows, many of the conditions that shape the labour and identities of women married to servicemen are bound up in interlocking and multivalent forms of mobility. The mobilities of women married to servicemen in the British Army remain highly circumscribed and institutionally particular. They are difficult to compare, in any meaningful way, to recent frameworks for understanding gender and migration in transnational terms. What emerges instead is a set of cultural continuities that represent processes of encapsulation and enclavisation based on the creation of relations of equivalence, rather than new forms of diversity, hybridity and cosmopolitanism. A military model of migration remains in many ways rigidly confined to the reproduction of the nation state within a 'foreign' territory, the shoring up of boundaries, as opposed to cultural mixing and exchange.

It is unsurprising, therefore, that such mobilities produce the concomitant feeling of 'moving on' and 'being held back' as articulated by Joanne at the beginning of this chapter. It is true that this deep ambivalence limits the scope available for an assessment of women's role as agents of their own mobilities. Yet these limited conditions of possibility underline the need to pay attention to the local and internal patterning of military power within its international configurations. At least here, there are signs of more ambiguous, everyday spaces where military mobilities can be articulated in terms that are more animated, that embellish rigid structures with the looser threads of social ties and cultural consumption; imaginaries of travel and cosmopolitanism. In their micro-practices and wilful translation of the limited terms that constrict their options, women married to servicemen articulate routes that are informal and iterative and strive to 'grasp' whatever they can from limited resources.

Very few of the narratives I have explored in this chapter make possible the argument that women are merely accessories to military mobilities in any absolute, unquestioning way. The narratives and experiences I have documented are often ambivalent, often turn on an acknowledged compromise or draw on alternative frameworks to counter their co-optation into military prerogatives. Women frequently acknowledged the flaws in their imaginaries of travel or the difficulties in salvaging particular identities in relation to their paid or unpaid labour, and are knowingly undone by their own contradictions. In this sense, the push and pull of women's mobilities becomes a known feature of army life that can be harnessed to particular advantages or capitalised upon, and women learn strategically when to move with them and when to push against them. The material conditions of military mobilities are in this sense productive of a mobile subjecthood.

If it is appropriate to frame these micro-negotiations in conventional anthropological terms of the 'weapons of the weak' (Scott 1985), then what I have shown is military wives' fundamental 'struggle to control the concepts and symbols by which current experience is evaluated' (Scott 1985, 27). While this struggle might be 'singularly undramatic' (ibid.), it reveals how women keep moving and keep striving both with and against the flow of military mobilities. The foundation of these mobilities, however, needs acknowledging more broadly in terms of the diagnostics that might reveal the structures on which military power depends. It is a marital, not only a military, contract that connects these narratives and, moreover, can be argued to anchor military mobilities within a complex system of gender and (hetero)sexuality. Military mobilities, and women's navigation of them, are in flux only to the extent that they can be tethered, at the base, to a stable bedrock of marriage and the family. The many formations of gender, ethnicity and reproductive heterosexuality that circulate through marriage allow freedom of movement in some social fields, while in others they serve to fix women in place; a ballast against the unpredictable demands of military mobilities. Marriage, thus, is a stalwart of military power.

Notes

1. With respect to the history of the British Army, this includes the control of women and prostitution in relation to colonial forces in India, for example (Enloe 1989, 82; Gillem 2007, 10). In Katherine Moon's 1997 study, *Sex among*

Allies, the historical connection between military presence overseas and the control of men's and women's sexuality is reformulated across different national boundaries, no longer regulated by empire but played out through commercialisation and the transnational flow of labour and capital. Moon describes the licensing of prostitution via the America Town Corporation and the Korean Ministry of Health (Moon 1997, 18), arguing that the formalisation of prostitution into an 'R&R system' (Moon 1997, 28) represents nothing less than a fully incorporated, international mass entertainment industry with other R&R outposts in the Philippines, Thailand and elsewhere in Asia (Moon 1997, 34). As the US military rotates its personnel across a network of bases around the world, it facilitates a transnational process of inscription, for example where 'racist stereotypes of Asians within the American society have mixed with sexist stereotypes of Asian women to foster American participation in camptown prostitution in Asia' (Moon 1997, 33). More recently, Gillem (2007, 60) notes the liberal South Korean visa programme through which Russian and Thai entertainers have migrated to replace Korean women in their roles with respect to the US Army. This brings with it a new matrix for the inscription of national and racial identity around the military bases overseas, where 'an American soldier can find a Russian wife on Korean soil' (Gillem 2007, 64).

2. For example, scholarship on the basing policies and practices of national militaries in the UK and USA has revealed the reproduction of national belonging through cultures of travel, tourism and consumption (e.g. Demetriou 2012; Gonzalez 2013), showing at the same time how deeply the military's reproduction of national identity and belonging is bound up in cross-border hierarchies of gender, sexuality, class and race.

3. The pivotal role of women's reproductive labour as secured and maintained through the institution of marriage is implicit in much of the research on military family policy. The concept of 'greedy institutions' (Segal 1986, 9) has been used to argue that the family and the military exist in an inherent relationship of competition (Segal 1986, 32), while more recent scholarship has traced a growing resistance to the idea of 'total devotion' to either (Bourg and Segal 1999, 634). This is borne out in both the increasing number of women married to servicemen seeking to participate in the labour force and cultural trends that call for men to participate more actively in family roles (Bourg and Segal 1999, 634). Working in relation to the US Armed Forces, Bourg and Segal underline the significance of social norms for cementing the union between the military and the family, which they argue is secured by the extent to which a subject 'identifies with and is willing to work towards organisational goals and values' due to a 'sense of calling and duty' to both the military and one's family simultaneously and as mutually beneficent (Bourg and Segal 1999, 637). It is the elision of martial and marital values that underlines wives' 'affective commitment' (ibid.) to the military institution as an extension of their commitment to marriage. This 'affective commitment' might be argued to depend, as Enloe (2000) has argued, 'on whether a woman married to a soldier will invest her talents and aspirations – and her pride and satisfaction – in the militarized career of her husband' (ibid., 158).

4. In her work around a joint NATO base overseas, Sue Jervis (2008) observes that each separate military's boundaries of nation, service and rank must shift

in order to accommodate each other. It is the traditional gender order, she argues, including expectations surrounding both the voluntary and paid labour of women married to servicemen, that is first to be reinforced as part of each institution's 'unconscious defensive attempts to retain their distinctive identities' (Jervis 2008, 114).

5. See Julie Peteet (1994) on the role of Palestinian women elders as witnesses to violence and also Dowler (1998) on women's role in paramilitary activities in Northern Ireland.

6. The turn towards autonomy and 'lifestyle choice' in British Army family policy has been slow-moving. For example, when the drawdown of all British Army regiments based in Germany was announced while I was conducting fieldwork in 2012, there was much speculation among the community as to where in the UK they would be stationed. The most obvious choice from the perspective of many was that the regiment should return to the 'seat' of its historic regional affiliation, the place from which the regiment derives its name and cultural identity, the location of its permanent UK headquarters and regimental museum, and the area from which many of its soldiers were recruited. Many enlisted members of the regiment had extended family living in vicinity of this area, and some expressed hopes of being able to resettle among this broader network of support. In the end, however, the regiment was relocated to a UK barracks more than 260 miles – nearly five hours' drive – away from its regional 'home' in the UK, a journey that many pointed out was only slightly shorter than the drive back to the UK from Germany. At the time of writing, the regiment was earmarked for a further move after nearly ten years in the UK, where it was finally scheduled to return to a base close to its regional base.

7. The Quarterly Location Statistics (UK Ministry of Defence 2012) for the period of my fieldwork in Germany states that 'LEC employees are recruited overseas exclusively for employment in support of the UK Armed Forces deployed in a particular overseas theatre and on terms and conditions of service applicable only to that overseas theatre or Administration. This includes the dependants of UK military personnel [. . .] LECs are not civil servants.' In 2012 there were 4,670 LECs employed by BFG.

8. My approach in this book perhaps epitomises the feminist methodological and analytical pursuit that Patti Lather (2007) has called 'getting lost'.

9. This acronym has been changed.

10. What these assumptions overlook or gloss over is the question of domestic abuse within a wide range of British Army households and questions surrounding military-institutional causes and barriers to support (Gray 2016a, 2016b, 2017).

11. See, for example, Ayşe Şimşek Çağlar's (2002) discussion of the meanings invested in a coffee table and its positioning in Turkish migrants' homes in Germany and Turkey respectively.

Dining Out

I enjoyed the dinner party.

No, I wasn't working when I was at dinner, I said. Happily off the record: no noting of anecdotes, no participant observed. Instead, the freedom to be interested because interested. And they *had* been interested, in my research.

Yes, I said. A feminist study. The 'F' word, we laughed.

But then, returning from the evening into night,
to a barrack-room bed in the shadow of a sink-light,
the women I had met
passed through my head
like in novels.
Observed, narrated.

I replayed each detail one hundred times, checking if I had behaved well, listened as well as talked, if my choice of outfit and gift had been correct: a well-judged cowl-neck jumper, wine (nine euro fifty, price removed), the mention of a London exhibition, and the crafting of a casual nonchalance towards housework.

On that night, in the chink of light left over from the evening's chatter, vigorous nodding, and interjections into jokes (and having given sincere thanks for a really wonderful time),
on an unfamiliar pillow and contract-laundered sheets,
I felt a pull,
      like the dull thud of a bright balloon
                        on the string of its attachment.

The evening had unmoored me, exposed a set of aspirations on a list. I wanted to shift shape, fit in. Officer class: time, money, taste, success.

For others too, my presence had unsettled something; was, upon reflection, less comfortable than my attempts at assimilation had been able to achieve.

A few days later, the Welfare Officer asked to see me. There had been some concerns raised, he said. People weren't sure about my 'agenda'. Some of the officers' wives invited to the dinner party had declined to attend because I was going to be there. They just weren't sure. I nodded, but was mortified. The Welfare Officer said something intended to reassure me, about them all being university educated, married to officers of rank and, it was implied, invested in their husbands' promotional chances and sharply aware of the politics of socialising around the camp. We sent out another email about my research, offered another opportunity to opt out. No one emailed the office to do so, but I learned to intuit the signs.

So I moved, chameleon-like, through conversations. Sometimes I couldn't make myself blend in: the only non-wife at a dinner party of wives; the only non-mother on Mother's Day.

It was five euros for the Mother's Day lunch in the camp's canteen, including a free box of Quality Street and a voucher towards a scented candle from the regimental shop. All the fathers were still in Afghanistan. There were about three mothers per table, generally two children either side, then much sorting of food, counting of chicken nuggets, negotiating of cutlery, cajoling to eat carrots. I made my way through the room with my tray. I passed a larger table where many of the women married to officers were sitting, and though I knew many of them, I waved myself on, smiling: Hello . . . hello . . . hi. I sat with a woman I knew from coffee mornings and another whom I had never met. Much of my conversation was conducted with her five-year-old son.

Afterwards, there was a craft event in the family room and a bouncy castle set up outside. Noise levels were excruciating. At one point I got hit in the face by a ball from the ball pit, which stung more than I expected. Somebody's daughter got a bloody nose; there were tears.

But there was a good mix of people there that day – different ages, some new faces. I tried to mingle, moving from craft station to craft station, offering to refill paints, clean brushes, hoping to exude a proxy-official helper role through my association with the welfare office. I was looking for people to sign up to be interviewed. I had the uncomfortable, almost predatory sense of profiling potential participants, mapping the demographics of the room for balance, representativeness.

What of ethnography and being 'representative'? If ethnography is a curiously sticky process in terms of the attachments or identities we bring with us or can't shake off, then it is also contrived, full of artifice, in terms of the new attachments we must make, the new identities we must embody. It is through such artifice, rather than any neutral reflection of a pre-existing social field, that 'representativeness', such as it is, can be achieved.

I approached a woman working alone at a table on the edge of the room. Her children were on the bouncy castle; she was concentrating on her own design.

I didn't want it to be obviously about the fact that she was Fijian, but what else was I doing there if not navigating by the unreliable topography of race and class, sights and sounds, to select a sample of human subjects?

And yet, no one seemed to think twice about being approached, making an introduction, being friendly. Many times I encountered this in my reptilian dissembling: the ease of familiarity, the openness of people to new people being announced, asking all the polite questions, encouraging smiles. Always based on the assumption that I was another wife, perhaps a mother, newly arrived, settling in. I had to pick the right moment, and soon, to qualify my status: 'No, no, I'm here doing a research project.' They might reply with interest and ask what my research was about, to which I would say, 'Women married to servicemen living overseas.' A beat. The moment would hang in the air between us while they registered that I had effectively said, 'You.'

Shortly into my conversation with the woman at the table, she recalled the email about my project from the welfare office. Yes, yes, that's the one! My relief is palpable, I'm grinning madly. The woman was gracious and, I could tell, had perceived my discomfort, as well as what I was after. She agreed to be interviewed. The conversation cleared, but there was a lingering aftertaste; a self-consciousness that I couldn't shake, that was awkward for both of us.

These are the atmospherics of ethnography. They are sometimes unpleasant, but not always unhelpful. At the Mother's Day lunch, my self-consciousness fed on the unconscious bias that thickened the air in the room: the invisible process through which people had allocated themselves and others a place in the social order, at the back of the room or on the edges; round the large, laughing table in the middle or at a small table on their own. Our coordinates on the map are formed at intersections, according to axes of difference; our emplacement is relational, marked by our encounters with one another – you are like me, you are not like me; I am like you; I appear to be like you, but I am not really. Marked assumptions about class, race or age, combined with the lines drawn by nationality and ethnicity, all combine. Among all of this, sometimes I couldn't tell if gender was simply another set of social coordinates, or the whole social field.

Like the Ladies' Dinner Night in the officers' mess. Keenly anticipated, much discussed, widely acknowledged as a return to form after deployment, bringing together all the officers and their wives or invited guests for a celebratory dinner.

There had been some light-hearted discussion in the welfare office as to whether I needed a date, and some overtures had been made, unbidden, on my behalf.

In the end I was relieved to attend as a single guest. I was seated at the table with the Commanding Officer and the senior ranking personnel and their spouses. There was an even higher-ranking, external officer in attendance; he made a speech with jokes and proposed a toast to the ladies (we all sit down, they all stand up). The evening is fun, often funny; there is an interlude where the esteemed guest is challenged to knock the cork out of a champagne bottle in a daring way. The Colonel demonstrates, and all the other tables have a go. I ate and drank, relaxed a little. I was absorbed in conversation when the Mess Manager approached and bent down to my ear. 'Ma'am, the Colonel says please finish.' I look up: several around the table are looking gleefully in my direction. I blush, insist that my half-finished dinner is finished, draw my knife and fork together on my plate to prove it. Someone explains that they cannot clear any tables until the Colonel's table is finished, and they cannot clear the Colonel's table before everyone has finished, and I'm the only one left. Now the evening can proceed.

Earlier in the evening I had introduced myself to a woman whom I had never met. I asked her who she was with. She stumbled on an answer, it seemed awkward. Later, at our tables, someone referred to the beauty of the same woman in her red dress, to the approval of everyone listening. I was about to ask which officer she was the girlfriend of when someone added, just in time, that she was the Medical Officer, just returned from Afghanistan. I realised my error with dismay, though I didn't declare it out loud.

I had been duped, hoodwinked by the habitus of the Ladies' Night. With gender the frame for the whole evening (and so overdetermined, so fraught with dictates about dress codes, chivalry, beauty, standing up and sitting down, being served first or being served last, tricks with swords and jokes and toasts), I had been defeated by the bifurcated logic I sought to disrupt. Sitting there in mascara and high-heeled shoes, delighting in the floral bouquets and the champagne bravado, I had been caught up in the performance of Ladies' Night, where every 'lady' was an invited guest. I had reproduced the pitfall I had tried so hard to avoid: seeking to define women according to their attachment to their husbands. The social field of Ladies' Night was so overwrought, so totalising, that it had become impossible to imagine anything beyond it: a female officer.

This must be how power comes to settle into shapes and structures that, from the inside, seem unquestionable. It takes will, it takes *methods* (like critical ethnography?) to see beyond the prescriptiveness of gender as a social field.

But don't expect them to work all the time.

The Officers' Ball had been talked about for weeks. It was fancy dress, which seemed a popular move. Couples were coordinating their costumes, some people making their ideas public, others keeping them a secret. The theme was 'Roald Dahl'. Some costumes were direct character representations; some were more cryptic, forming a visual pun or clue. I had been invited to join the table of a joint-career couple, both of whom I had interviewed. The invitation was warm and generous, and I accepted, recognising a genuine kindness. But I was dreading it.

I went to town to shop for an outfit, having decided to go as 'Boy', after Roald Dahl's eponymous memoir. I thought myself witty and clever in this idea; I was pleased with it. It suited my interests and my subject matter; it undercut the expectation of glamour and catsuits. And it was a knowing and humorous adaptation of the jokes forged at my expense in the sergeants' mess, which centred around my short hair and occasional choice of green corduroy trousers (never mind that this is the officers' mess, and therefore an entirely different social circle).

I bought a pair of cheap knee-length shorts and a tie and borrowed a white shirt from the husband of the welfare office admin clerk. The shorts were ill-fitting, they settled somewhere around my hips and pinched such that there was a roll of fat above them. The shirt, tucked in, was a little more fitted than I would have liked. I wore long socks and sensible shoes, drew freckles over my nose and cheeks with eyeliner. I felt sick with nerves.

I take the short walk to the officers' mess at the appointed time. I meet some people I know well. One of their guests looks at my costume, puzzled. 'I'm Boy!' I say. She can't think: 'Is there a boy in one of the books?' she asks.

The ball was staffed by junior soldiers acting as waiting staff. Over half of them were problematically dressed as Oompa Loompas, the factory labourers with dwarfism as portrayed with colonial undertones in the 1971 film *Willy Wonka & the Chocolate Factory*. A woman asked if I was Matilda. I began to wonder at the wisdom of my costume choice.

Later in the evening, after dinner at the table of my hosts, I made attempts to socialise over by the dancefloor. The Welfare Officer and his wife were dressed as the Twits, the uncouth and combative married couple from the book of the same name. They were both wearing impressively grotty, long beards and sack clothing, complete with twigs and detritus and dried bits of breakfast cereal. You couldn't see their faces, only their eyes catching one another's, laughing as they danced wildly among the cliques of attractive young girlfriends dressed as sexy animals. I danced briefly, attaching to little clumps of people I knew. Someone spilled red wine down my borrowed shirt. There were two women I knew in the bathroom, and we said an awkward hello as I stood in my bra and ugly nylon shorts, desperately rinsing the shirt out.

Somewhere here, among the accumulating humiliation, there is a point where ethnography and its curious compulsion to *join in* merge perfectly with the ontological and affective demands of the British Army's call to live and be, and socialise, in particular ways. Participation becomes assimilation, tipping into complicity, raising the question of resistance. I thought it was a good idea to go to the fancy dress ball as 'Boy', but there was no one there to get the joke. I thought it was an act of resistance, defiance even, but standing in the bathroom scrubbing red wine out of a ruined shirt, it didn't feel that way.

I didn't want to go to the 'all-ranks do' either. It was held, excessively I thought, on the evening of the Families' Day barbecue, which itself followed the medals parade. I had returned to my room from the playing fields where the barbecue was held and sat on my bed, shattered. It had been a hot day. My face ached from smiling. I was a little sunburned. I didn't feel like drinking.

The all-ranks do was the only opportunity to attend an evening social event where everyone mixed together. But I'd had enough of curating my obligatory social life to ensure ethnographic balance.

I had been to dinner parties and dinner nights. To balls, barbecues and strange waiting parties on homecoming days. I had been to a parade back in the UK and the lunch that followed. I had been to a 'dining out' in the sergeants' mess where I lived, a dining out in another mess where I didn't. I had been to book clubs, pottery parties, a German coffee morning, standard coffee mornings, coffee mornings in different 'patches', a coffee morning at the home of the Commanding Officer. I had joined volunteers at the rehabilitation centre, I had joined in with cake stalls, banner-painting and fitness activities. I didn't feel like any more joining in.

But no. I had to go.

I went to try to see beyond the boundaries of each pieced-out, parcelled-up and highly regulated social setting and the access it provided to portions of the community. I went to see if an 'all-ranks do' was really possible. I was worried about not knowing anyone, but when I arrived I realised I knew lots of people. I met the families of those whom I knew from living in the sergeants' mess. I saw women I had interviewed, more relaxed now we weren't sitting across from one another with my iPhone recording every word. I spent time with colleagues from the welfare office. I was indebted to them. I went to show my face. I stayed longer than I planned.

CHAPTER 2

Ranking Difference and Distinction

Introduction

This chapter is about the stereotypes that attach to the figure of the British Army wife and the intersections of gender, ethnicity, class and national identity upon which they depend. In the last chapter, I explored the geographic mobility of women married to servicemen and highlighted the ambivalence of their bargains with the military institution. Here, I want to look further into the conversion of geographic mobility into social mobility, which I have shown is central to women's negotiation of their positionality and power in relation to the structures that determine many aspects of their day-to-day lives.

Many of the gender dynamics I explore in this chapter appear to be cast from the same mould that has defined British Army spousehood for centuries: as female in relation to soldiering as a form of labour that is expressly male (where women are emblematic of home and hearth worthy of protection [Elshtain 1995 (1987)]); or as heterosexual, monogamous and bound by the sexual contract of marriage (Pateman 1988) and, as such, distinguished from unruly and othered forms of sexual partnership or activity). While gender and (hetero)sexuality produce the clearest, most obvious delineation of military wifehood in the conditions I explore here, I show how container identities are also defined, subdivided and disciplined through the military-bureaucratic structure of rank. Paying attention to formations of rank as they are experienced and adapted by women married to servicemen reveals that rank itself cannot be detached from wider correlations with class and white privilege. This is significant because it helps us question the exceptionality of rank and the chain of command through which it is justified as a military technology of discipline and control. Rank as it emerges through the experiences of military wives is deeply embedded and intricately woven through multiple vectors of power and identity. By paying careful attention to the more complex interplay of internal modes of difference and distinction that operate within institutional hierarchies and divides, I want to question the fixity of rank as a structure of control, as well as the archetypes of class, ethnicity and gender that work through and serve to co-produce its disciplinary effects.

What the experiences of military wives reveal is a suite of military technologies that define and valorise gendered notions of propriety and obedience, promoting social mobility in particularly complex and ambivalent ways. This chapter offers some insights about how these disciplinary processes work and the messy dynamics on which they depend. I begin with a brief exploration of the markers of difference and distinction that women perceive as operating within the stereotype of 'the military wife', a group that is often managed or perceived as united by common experience. I then address the initial question of how technologies of rank are understood to extend to wives of personnel, and the gendered manifestation of rank in feminised and 'civilised' – or civilising – forms. Looking in further detail at the social patterning of rank beyond formal modes of discipline and command, I explore its spatialisation in and around the camp. Finally, I connect this social mobility back to the colonial continuities of military mobilities, questioning the implications for how we think about rank and class as embedded in white Britishness.

Stereotypes of Difference and Distinction

Scholars such as Margaret Harrell (2000, 2001) and Sue Jervis (2008, 2011) have explored the conditions and experiences that help to maintain gendered stereotypes such as the British Army officer's wife or, at the opposite end of the social hierarchy, assumptions about US junior enlisted soldiers' wives as 'big-haired trailer park babes with too many children' (Harrell 2000, 12). In *Invisible Women*, Harrell (2000, 106) faithfully reproduces three women's narratives based on life-history interviews to illustrate the ways in which 'they both support and challenge [. . .] class-based stereotypes' (ibid.). While I am likewise interested in documenting the narratives of women married to servicemen in the British context, I want to go further to critically deconstruct these stereotypes in order to understand how they gain, retain or lose their discursive power, both as they are socially constructed and subjectively renegotiated.

While Enloe (2000, 162) satirises a list of characteristics and attitudes to describe 'The Model Military Wife', she makes the important qualification that few women manage to fulfil such conditions, as well as conceding that some derive genuine satisfaction and material rewards from trying (Enloe 2000, 164). My aim in paying attention to how stereotypes work in women's narratives is likewise to explore how ideals of wifehood are co-opted and managed by women to make particular identifications. As such, my aim is not to measure the 'truth value' of stereotypes (Fechter 2010, 1282). Rather, I am interested in understanding their 'social or political functions' (ibid.) as modes of difference and distinction that are invoked by women and serve to reinforce, or renegotiate, the disciplinary effects of rank, for example, or the assumed unity of experience implied by any collective identity of 'military wives'.

Feminist scholarship has long emphasised the need to be concerned not only with connections that unify the experiences of women and help form collectives based on the experience of patriarchal oppression, but also with the operation of difference 'within and between the collectivities they belong to' (Yuval Davis 1997, 11). Enloe (1989) has likewise argued for the need to take the multiple positionalities of different women into account in any gendered assessment of military power, highlighting the 'mutually exclusive categories' (1989, 91) that maintain a militarized social order between '[p]rostitutes, girlfriends, wives, peace activists and women soldiers'. I want to engage briefly with some of the stereotypes and perceptions that produce broader notions and assumptions about the 'model military wife' (2000, 162) in a Western military context, before going on to explore different women's appropriation and rejection of what they imply. What women's negotiation of social stereotypes reveals is the complex operation of multiple modes of difference and distinction which are relational and emergent in women's encounters with each other and with the institution. It is these shifting boundaries and mobile forms of belonging that constitute wives' ambiguous and fluid position within a militarised social order where gender, class and ethnicity are overdetermined by rank.

My attention to modes of difference and distinction in this chapter is inspired by research on white British working-class femininities by Bev Skeggs (1997), in turn inspired by French anthropologist Pierre Bourdieu (1984) and his ideas about the exchange of social and cultural capital.[1] Skeggs's (1997) empirical study explores gendered constructions of selfhood among working-class white women in 1990s Britain. In addition to documenting the *content* of what constitutes class and gender for a specific group of women living in a particular place at a particular time, Skeggs's (1997) study sheds light on the ways in which stereotypes work less through the recognition of a particular value than women's 'constant refusal to be fixed or measured by [them]' (Skeggs 1997, 75). It is this focus on the 'relationship between positioning and identity' (Ibid., 74) that is a central inspiration for my analysis here.

For example, Elise, twenty-four, was on her first posting and described herself as 'a first-time wife – [that is,] I've only been married a year. My husband has only been home, let's say, three months since we've been married.' Elise and her husband knew each other at school but met again through Facebook in their early twenties, after he had joined the Army. Initially embarking upon a long-distance relationship, they married after she became pregnant with their first child and she moved to Germany shortly after. Elise was happy to expand upon her own typology of military wife stereotypes based on her observations of the women she had encountered in her time married to a soldier so far.

> This is my way of not just pinpointing something, because I . . . I don't want to put a tag on people. OK, so I'll just say there's three types. There's the strong-willeded [*sic*] ones, which I like to class myself as because for someone my age and has a baby and my husband's not been home, I've kind of kept it cool. You know. And I do things on my own, off my own back. Yeah. Then there's another type of army wives that aren't suited for the life. And that was someone I knew. And her husband wasn't away on tour but every time he was away she would break down and [. . .] she would just crumble [. . .].

Although during our interview Elise repeatedly insisted that as a young woman who had not been married long, she was 'new at this' or 'just learning', her stories of hardship – by no means unique or particularly extreme – made clear to me that of the women who were 'either made for it [. . .] or not', she considered herself to be in the former category. As in Skeggs's (1997) study of class and notions of respectability, the function of stereotypes in Elise's account of herself and others is less to do with their content than their use as a mode of positioning. What stereotypes of military wives provide for Elise is a clear framework for the assertion of her own strengths and capabilities with respect to the demands that the military institution makes of her labour, but also of her social and emotional resources: her capacity to feel and act in a particular way ('keeping it cool' versus 'crumbling'). What Elise's typology shows – less in terms of the content than in her *use* of it to define herself in relation to notional or specific others – is that women such as military wives 'are not just ciphers from which subject positions can be read-off; rather, they are active in producing the meaning of the positions they (refuse to, reluctantly or willingly) inhabit' (Skeggs 1997, 2).

The practices of *dis*identification that are part of this active and relational construction of the self were present in many women's views of the stereotypes attaching to the figure of the military wife. Maria, who might be argued to occupy a very different set of positionalities to Elise in terms of her socio-economic background, level of education, age, class and, in relation to the institution, her marriage to a senior-ranking officer, was aware of the preconceptions that might shape her own identity: 'There's not so much of the classic stay-at-home you know, cook for twenty-five people on a regular basis, throw lots of coffee mornings [. . .] I think that's probably a little bit outdated now, I think people want to do stuff for themselves.' Tracing the subtle shifts in women's narratives, or indeed the more explicit ways in which they invoke or interpret stereotypes and qualify their own views and identities in relation to them, indicates how flexible and fluid such tropes are when manipulated in circulation by their referents. Moreover, in the citation of stereotypes as an expression of extremes – of idealisations or demonisations of the figure of the military wife – women strive to assert for themselves a social personhood that is, by contrast, more authentic, more realistic. In other words, part of the function of stereotypes is the production of an identity that might be termed more liveable. Indeed, it might be argued that, for women married to servicemen, 'authenticity' is asserted through a trade in negative capital: it inheres in one's failure to reach prescribed ideals, the rejection or renegotiation of extremes. Real life, in short, is compromise.

As was clear from Elise's sense of her own strengths and abilities, one of the foremost stereotypes is a positive one based on resilience, strength and stoicism in the face of adversity. Like the pastiche of duty that emerges from her description of a wife busy with dinners and coffee mornings, Maria is (self-)conscious of the performance of coping that comes with the operational tour:

> I mean you've got interesting characters at the moment, you've got one trying to outdo their husband – sort of well 'Just 'cause he's away

doesn't mean I'm not going to get qualified in this, that and the other and dah dah dah dah dah' and, [I'm] like, 'Go for it, girl, but you know, all I'm trying to do is get through this' and you know? Everyone's got to take, they've got to just do what they want to do haven't they really?

By disidentifying with the excessive achievements and aspirations of others, and positioning herself in contradistinction to the extremes of behaviour around which stereotypes often crystallise, Maria is able to preserve the positive ideal of coping but assert a more moderate and modest approach for herself. It is interesting that Maria's conversion of the 'coping' stereotype into something more realistic or liveable relies on the expression of a kind of resignation, a willingness to compromise, that one senses is the real skill required: 'all I'm trying to do is get through this'. This is more than a simple act of disassociation, however – Elise and Maria cannot be argued to simply reject the ideals they cite – because each woman's liveable version of the stereotype remains dependent on the ideal it *appears* to reject. Hence Maria is able to convert her fallibility into a muted strength by contrasting her pragmatism to the overt and competitive performance of her friend. As Skeggs (1997) argues:

> The women of this study are aware of their place, of how they are socially positioned and of the attempts to represent them. This constantly informs their responses. They operate within a dialogic form of recognition: they recognise the recognitions of others. Recognitions do not occur without value judgements and the women are constantly aware of the judgements of real and imaginary others. Recognition of how one is positioned is central to the processes of subjective construction'. (Skeggs 1997, 3)

One might even argue that the conversions that stereotypes facilitate come full circle, flipping negative to positive and back again, not breaking but perpetuating the representation in question, and going some way to explain their stickiness as ready-made identities which, while being outmoded or idealised, persist as a kind of collective, constitutive other to women's everyday experience.

The primary mode of identification for Elise as a military wife is based similarly around notions of coping and resilience. When Elise expands her typology to include a third category, however, she reveals that women's identities are also regulated by ideas about sexuality that are far from secured by their containment within the framework of heterosexual marriage and an emphasis on domestic labour:

> And there's another stereotype – um how can I put this? So there's a homebody, then there's the crumbling type and then there's the–I-met-on-a-Saturday-night-and-just-married-her type [. . .] That when husband goes away they're out on the loose, on the wild side. The, 'Hey I know you from Saturday night, do you want to marry me?' and then [gasp] husband's away, so what do I do? And then, shit happens.

There is a subtle shift in the construction of the stereotype of the sexually unfaithful military wife here, which is defined primarily and externally in relation to the soldier who chooses her. Whereas the domestic stereotype of both the 'homebody' and the 'crumbling' military wife are defined in terms of women's own innate or learned abilities to cope with an army lifestyle, the sexual stereotype emerges as a universal trope: something out there among women that a soldier is unfortunate enough to be seduced by. Unacknowledged, however, is the fact that it is the military institution that produces the conditions of haste, absence and abstinence to test that marriage (Hogan and Seifert 2009).

The stereotypes that Elise enumerates are not surprising for their dependence upon received ideas of gendered domesticity ('homebody'), emotion ('crumbling') and sexual availability. Feminist scholarship has long explored the disciplinary effects of such established tropes across countless forms of social life and cultural representation, in literature (Millett 2016 [1977]), film and art (Mulvey 1975), for example, which has in turn revealed their reliance on race in complex ways (hooks 1996). Stereotypes around the category 'military wife' persist, supported in many ways by cultural representations (e.g. Cree 2020; Gray 2022). Although all the women featured here point out differences in people's interpretations of these stereotypes, what also emerged from many of my conversations was an expectation of sameness, even unity, among women married to servicemen. This is encapsulated by a refrain I often heard repeated among my interviewees, of being 'in the same boat' with other women experiencing the unique challenges of army life. Tellingly, however, the social, spatial and temporal meaning of this collective metaphor varied, such that it referred variously to the shared experience of being 'in' the Army, 'in' the regiment, 'in' Germany, or 'in' a period of deployment. Thus, being 'in the same boat' covers a multitude of experience that troubles the sameness it seeks to express. It could be argued that this provides a helpful multiplication of the terms through which women can find community and connection. But where this tension between sameness and difference, differentiation and homogenisation, emerges at its most complex is around the hierarchy of rank. Rank and its role as an institutionalised stand-in, proxy or signifier for multiple vectors of power shapes encounters between women married to servicemen in complex ways.

Elise's perception of the meaning of being 'in the same boat', for example, is reflected through her experience of meeting another woman when she first arrived:

> And I was like, 'Hi I'm new.' [And I came home] and I said to my husband, 'I met this really lovely lady.' And he was like, 'Oh what's her name?' 'Heather Lewis.' [And he said,] 'That's the SSM's [Squadron Sergeant Major's] wife!' You would never have thought that she was a high-ranked wife because she's so down to earth. Now I've met a[nother] sergeant's wife, and when I met her, she said my husband is Sergeant. And you know from that – well because my husband was only a trooper then – you're not going to get involved with me or want to talk to me anyways, do you know what I mean? [But] when I met Heather, she didn't say, 'My husband is the SSM.' You know? She didn't brag and that's what I liked. [. . .] But the funny thing is I was talking to her about the regiment and she was fully agreeing with me. I mean her life – like I say, I complain about my husband being away, [but] her husband's high ranked [. . .] so he's probably away more often than what my husband is. [But] she sees it probably as, we're all in the same boat so why be on a higher rank when you can just be friends with everybody?

What impresses Elise is the capacity of her new acquaintance to transcend rank – to ignore it – as a distinguishing factor between the two women and their experiences. The role of Squadron Sergeant Major (SSM) carries the rank of Warrant Officer Class 2, the second-highest rank achievable as a soldier, acting as senior advisor to an officer (holding the rank of Major) in charge of a subunit.[2] It is a visible and prominent role in relation to both professional and pastoral responsibilities for the junior soldiers in a subunit, and in reporting directly to established officers in the regiment. As a trooper's wife at the time, Elise's sense of being 'in the same boat' as a woman married to a soldier who is her husband's superior is attached to the experience of broader features of army life that Elise assumes are more important or impactful than rank, for example their shared location in Germany and the endurance of long periods of separation from their partners as well as family back home.

For another woman, Kirsty, who was thirty and also married to a junior soldier, the assumption of solidarity or community articulated through the metaphor of being 'in the same boat' was perhaps equally as surprising, but in a different way:

> A: So you went to a couple of coffee mornings? Was there any particular reason you didn't fancy going back?
>
> K: I didn't find them very welcoming. I don't know, over here you would think that because everybody's in the same boat they would all stick together and help each other out and be really welcoming when somebody new comes and stuff. But it's not – they've all got their little cliques and stuff and I don't know – it's like being back at school sometimes and it's not really that nice.
>
> A: So what was it like walking in? I mean I've been to a few of them [. . .] what was it like walking in there the first morning?
>
> K: Um, I was quite nervous actually because, um, one of the ladies did speak to [me] and she said she had a welcome present for me and she gave me a Yankee Candle, and I think it was the CO's wife or something, she didn't actually introduce herself so to this day I don't even know who she was, um . . .

In Kirsty's experience, her first social encounters with the community are shaped by conventions that are tightly bound up in rank, for example the custom of new wives joining the regiment receiving a visit and a small gift from the wife of one of the senior soldiers or officers. In this case, the gift was a particular brand of scented candle that represented something of a consumer trend while I was living on camp, with a range of scents stocked by the regimental shop and exchanged as gifts between members of the community. Many of the houses I visited featured one or more of these candles prominently on display. In her account Kirsty does not attach much significance to the goodwill gift, the gesture somewhat undermined by the impression that its giving was cursory and rushed, without a genuine social connection having been made on either side (hence Kirsty's vague recollection of 'one of the ladies', which betrays her perception of the CO's wife in terms of a kind of classed seniority, and the lack of introductions, giving the impression of social protocol met with bemusement rather than a sense of inclusion). Rank is arguably the overriding structure shaping this social encounter: it determines the expectations, behaviours and responses of both women, with the consequence that, paradoxically, the hierarchy of rank is reinforced at precisely the moment it is supposed to be transcended. Rank is inescapable in this performative encounter – the senior officer's wife presenting a welcome gift to a junior soldier's wife – because it has produced it. Kirsty's cynicism as a result is an indication of the degree to which the performances and protocols of rank are read as exactly that – as staged social interactions that require a learned, rather than felt, response.

The performativity (Butler 1990) of rank,[3] by which I mean the constitution of its meanings and effects through citational practices that are limited by the boundaries of the social field, is made clear in the conflicts that arose in other women's attitudes towards these same conventions. This was particularly resonant in respect to how formations of rank shaped their voluntary labour. Stereotypes about military wifehood include what Harrell (2001, 59) calls 'Traditional Officer Spouse Expectations', such as: 'Institutional Activities; Morale, Public Relations and Ceremonial Duties; Mentoring, Development and Role Preservation; Entertaining and Socialising; and Unit Readiness Support' (ibid.). In the context of her US study, such responsibilities were emphasised as strictly voluntary in army handbooks (ibid., 70), and yet could be taken into direct account in women's husbands' Officer Evaluation Reports (ibid.). This, argues Harrell, fuels a process by which labour that is officially 'voluntary' is transformed into what Harrell calls 'compelled duties' (ibid., 68). The tensions arising from this sense of obligation to the institution have been documented reflexively in research on the British military by Sue Jervis (2011), specifically the politics of flower arranging on a NATO base overseas (Jervis 2011, 2). In my own research, the particular place of flower arranging as a classed, gendered and ranked form of labour was exemplified by the case of Fiona, who had suspended her own full-time career in the UK after having children, and was engaged in multiple forms of voluntary labour while on a posting to Germany for two years. Married to a senior officer deployed with the regiment in a highly visible role in Afghanistan, Fiona conceded that 'although there shouldn't be a rank structure through wives there is, because it's all to various members of the regiments' wives to organise various things'. The job of organising the flowers for dinners and events in the officers' mess was described in conflicted terms not by Fiona herself, but in an interview with another woman, Victoria, who was also married to a higher-ranking officer in the regiment:

> Um. No there could, and I would hate – and I said to all the [. . .] wives, who – when they came, I said, 'Listen, you don't have to do anything. Don't feel obliged to do anything.' When [Fiona's husband] was made [a particular rank] I went straight to Fiona and said, 'Normally the [officer's] wife would do the flowers in the Mess because [that officer] is in charge of the Mess, so that's sort of your job. I don't want you to do it if you don't want to do it. I'm not making you do it. If you want to do it, brilliant. If not, I've been doing it, I'm very happy to keep doing it, if you want to come and help, fantastic. What do you want to do? It's up to you.'

Victoria was a prominent figure in the regiment in her own right, whom I heard referred to before I met and who was widely regarded as a stalwart member of the regimental community. As Victoria implies, the expectations regarding particular women's voluntary labour are formalised to the degree that they are often tied to the particular job role and rank into which a soldier or officer has been promoted. During my time with the regiment I saw Victoria carry out various voluntary duties that she appeared to embrace and invest with personal significance:

> Well [. . .] I like the Mess to look nice, and you know, I want it to look really pretty. For all the girls going in and you know, I'm proud of the fact, you know, that it's the regiment and proud that [my husband is part of] it.

This not only included the flower arranging that other women were unable or unwilling to commit to, but a set of other public duties that ranged from hosting welcome coffee mornings at her home, to occasions when she was positioned as the representative of her husband while he was deployed, for example standing ceremonially on a windswept parade ground judging fancy dress costumes and novelty skits for a 'family day' competition. Far from being confined to the wives of officers, the same kind of expectations are also managed (and again with some sense of conflict) by Jane, who was married to an NCO with a prominent role in the regiment. She was someone I had met early on in my fieldwork, who had been responsible for running cake stalls at various events I had attended and helped with:

J: [. . .] I've tried to be true to myself, I've done as much as I can, my family are my priority. So I won't mention any names but some of the other women before really took it so seriously and immersed themselves and did everything. There are a couple of things I haven't done that my predecessors did [laughs], which is go and deliver plants – welcome plants – to new people; go and knock on their doors. And I tried to do it initially for the first couple of months and I hated it, so I stopped doing it. So you know I think to myself: 'Is that really awful, should I have done that?' But I just didn't want to do it, I felt like I couldn't fit it in and you know, it wasn't me, so I thought sod it, I don't care! No – I've done as much as I can.

A: Does [your husband] accept that?

J: Yes he does, sometimes I say, 'Oh I don't want to go to coffee morning I get fed up with it', and he'll say, 'Just keep doing it, Jane, just keep showing your face, please, while I'm [in this job].' [. . .] There is rumour that depending on how your wife is and how she behaves depends on how further up the ladder you go. Whether or not there's any truth in that whatsoever I have no idea at all but that's the rumour.

A: Do you ever feel under pressure to bake a cake?! [laughs] Would you naturally . . .

J: No, I'm not naturally a cake baker, although I have got quite good at it recently! [laughs] It's out of duty that I do that, not out of love of cake baking!

A: I've noticed that you've baked cakes and you're always helping but . . .

J: But that's part of the expectation I think, of being [a senior soldier's] wife. I don't mind doing it I really don't, I'd rather actually be doing stuff than sitting around making idle chat sometimes.

What all the narratives I have explored so far reveal is the militarised – and militarising – influence of rank as an institutional technology and bureaucratic hierarchy, and its particular role as a conduit for social stereotypes and the compelled duties, performances and self-making processes that work through them. Rank in the British Army (and, more broadly, rank and its relationship to the production of contemporary Britishness in the Army through particular formations of gender, class and race) is almost entirely neglected as an area of sociological enquiry. Yet rank (like class in a British context) is one of the most stark technologies of discipline and control that marks the military institution out from other organisations. The data I explore throughout this book reveal just a hint of the myriad ways in which rank as a social structure is materialised, spatialised and performed in the everyday life of the military institution. Accordingly, rank emerges as a highly complex system of stratification which, at the same time as it is rarefied – and justified – as a condition of military exceptionality, is also enmeshed in much broader hierarchies of gender and class that connect it, for example, to the production of white Britishness and colonial histories of domination. I want to begin to map out some of these connections in the rest of this chapter, charting various formations of rank, gender, class and ethnicity as they shape the subjectivities of military wives.

In the last chapter I explored the military mobilities of women married to servicemen in migration with the institution, which included their conversion of geographic mobility into a kind of social mobility. In this chapter I continue to elaborate my analysis of military wives as mobile subjects, exploring not only their ambiguous position between military and civilian spheres, but also their appropriation – their strategic mobilisation – of other modes of difference and distinction that subdivide those categories. While rank is frequently materialised and understood in ways that appear linear and concrete, then, it operates through compound forms and subcategories and, like international mobility, creates overlapping circuits of encapsulation (Amit 2007, 12). It is true that women married to servicemen have been characterised as liminal figures on the edge of military belonging (Long 2022). Much of my analysis in this book upholds ideas about the contradictory and deeply ambiguous position in which women find themselves when both resisting *and* acquiescing to their own incorporation. Rather than their liminality, however, I insist on their mobility within the structures and frameworks that attempt to define them, through which the institution – and, in fact, many women among themselves – attempts to put unruly others back in their place. Thus I ask: what do the experiences of military wives as mobile subjects indicate about the fluidity of rank? Is the apparently fixed place one occupies in the military hierarchy in fact deeply relational and intensely variable, given what this research shows about the multiple meanings attached to rank at any one time and in any one place? In relation to women married to servicemen, the question then becomes: how is this shapeshifting, destabilising function of rank further compounded by one's ambiguous position on the very boundary of inside and outside? It is women's active negotiations of rank, their making and remaking of its meanings between different intersections of gender, class and race, for example, that I will elaborate further here.

Carrying Rank

In *Discipline and Punish* (1975), Michel Foucault uses the army barracks as a template for his theorisation of social control, involving *'enclosure'* (ibid., 141) to hold a population in place, then further degrees of more flexible and detailed *'partition'* (ibid., 143). According to Foucault (ibid., 145), the power of rank inheres in 'the place one occupies in a classification'. In this configuration, rank harnesses the power of internal, granular variation and leverages it against an external threat. My focus in this chapter is on the former set of internal divisions rather than the latter distinction between, say, the nation and its other in relation to the military base overseas and its 'host' nation. The wide-ranging *internal* schemata for difference and distinction that my analysis reveals appear to be at odds with an institution whose production of cultural homogeneity, disciplinary conformity and enforced community are at the centre of its operating model, where everyone is expected to be 'in the same boat'. Women married to servicemen might be argued to be in a particularly interesting location in relation to this central paradox of (externally facing) homogeneity and (internal) subdivision. What is revealed about the social structure of rank if considered from the perspective of a group of subjects whose positioning is argued to be beyond its reach, who are administratively constituted through the identity of a 'civilian' rather than a 'military' subject? What are military wives' experiences of rank from this externalised position? As a counterpart to the question of the 'incorporation' (Callan and Ardener 1984) of wives' productive labour that I explored in the previous chapter, I now want to explore the *extension* of rank to military wives as a disciplinary tool that works through surprising processes of adaptation and reappropriation. This reveals a more fluid, flexible aspect to rank that is adaptive – almost parasitic. The many compound forms that rank takes, as well as ensuring its ubiquity, are ironically key to women's reappropriation of rank and, arguably, the dilution of its effects.

When talking about rank in my interviews, it was very easy to become mired in the slippage between personal and professional power relations and some degree of regimental gossip. This is perhaps one reason why rank was frequently framed as a kind of regression by comparisons to being at school, as exemplified by Nick, a senior soldier who was part of the rear operations group:

A: Do people carry the rank of their husband?
N: Yeah yeah yeah they do, specially at a certain level.
A: And is that acquired or . . .

> N: I think it's what they've been used to, so maybe when she was a
> trooper's wife, she was treated like shit maybe, and then she's got
> to the point now where . . . [. . .] Well, I think, well – it's like when
> you get to high school again, it's like top year? You're being what
> you were treated like when you were at the bottom, you're the top
> of the class, you're the top of the tree, so it's your turn.

Nick's explanation here is evocatively close to Deniz Kandiyoti's
(1988) formulation of women's reproduction of what she calls
'classic patriarchy' (ibid., 279) in her cross-cultural study of women
in societies traditionally conceived of – including within feminist
scholarship – as disempowered and oppressed. Theorising women's
'bargain' (ibid., 236) with patriarchy, Kandiyoti reinterprets the
conditions of women's 'place' in relation to patriarchal structures
by emphasising their negotiation of passive forms of resistance as
well as modes of power inherent in their positionality between and
among women differentially positioned by its effects. Kandiyoti's
(1988) work occupies a significant place in research that complicates
simplistic appraisals of women's universal oppression. She argues:

> The cyclical nature of power in the household and their anticipation
> of inheriting the authority of senior women encourages a thorough
> internalization of this form of patriarchy by the women themselves.
> In classic patriarchy, subordination to men is offset by the control
> older women attain over younger women. (ibid. 279)

Taking selectively from Kandiyoti's (1988) observations about the
cyclical nature of power between different women as well as between
women and men is useful for thinking about the bargains made by
military wives in relation to the overarching – and, indeed, patriarchal – structures of the military institution. The cyclical nature of
power as it is passed through generations in Kandiyoti's (1998) classic analysis is a useful way of thinking about how women's power to
define their own *position* in relation to others constitutes a form of
resistance and assertion in itself, as well as, of course, a further form
of alterity and division.

The cyclicity of rank – as people move up the ladder, there are
always others coming in behind – is a form of mobility that is sometimes lost in the idea of a rigid and linear disciplinary hierarchy. At
once a set structure, a rigid hierarchy, rank is also animated by people's mobility through it – aspiring to a higher position, looking back
at how far one has come. Likewise, the places where the authority

of rank fails or is diverted by other means and for other purposes are important to exploring its adaptation and co-optation as a social tool. Erving Goffman's (1961) concept of the 'total institution' is frequently used to consider characteristics of military institutions (Belkin 2012; Hockey 1986; Jervis 2008; Scott 2011). Yet Goffman (1961) is clear that technologies of control are susceptible to failure: 'where enthusiasm is expected, there will be apathy; where loyalty, there will be disaffection; where attendance, absenteeism; where robustness, some kind of illness; where deeds are to be done, varieties of inactivity' (267). Acknowledging this fallibility, scholars have insisted on a more 'interactional and processual picture' (Hockey 1986, 9) of the British military institution. It is in this spirit that I want to assess some examples of rank at its most instrumental: as a mode of authority and discipline.

Arguably, it is the association between rank and discipline that underwrites functional explanations of its necessity (thus Pippa comments: 'I think the Army has to have the rank structure to work effectively. You know you can't have people . . . you know the authority has to be there'). Yet I was struck by the experience of Käthe, a German woman married to a senior soldier whom I had often heard dismiss some of the absurdities of army life with humour or cynicism. Her encounter with – and interpretation of – the formal chain of command complicates the division of military and civilian in ways that are surprising and complex:

A: So you feel that rank doesn't transfer to you and that . . .
K: No – rank, with me personally rank's got nothing to do . . . but I know that it has impacted on [my husband] in the past. I heckled the Colonel . . .
A: He told me!
K: In one of the briefings . . . yeah and [my husband] got pulled in the office and I went livid, he came back and I was like how dare they pull you! *I* did that and I just . . .
A: So what happened . . . it was in a briefing?
K: Yeah [the Colonel] did a briefing for the last Afghan tour, and he announced that instead of giving the guys two weeks off like planned, he would pull them away from us for another two weeks and put them on light duties and everything, so I went 'Wooooooo' like that really loud, and got lots of abuse and I was the only one and I looked round [to the other wives] and I was like, 'Why are you all quiet?! We spoke about this, you were all outraged by this decision!' Most of them were agreeing with me but none of them was stupid enough to say it out loud [laughs]. So then [my

> husband] got brought in – I don't know if it was the Colonel's
> office or the Welfare Officer's office but he got pulled up for that,
> and I was like, look you know, if a dog bites somebody in the
> street, you don't go slaughter that owner, you go to the dog.
> A: And so what was your husband's reaction to that?
> K: No, he laughed, he was just like, 'You have to do it, don't you?'
> He was laughing – I think he sees the point of how ridiculous that
> really was. [The Colonel] gave a speech to civilians so by all means
> expect a civilian reaction, you know?

It is Käthe's assertion of her civilian status that is interesting to me here, and the way in which she uses it to contest the proxy-discipline to which she is subject via her husband. The fact that there were mild disciplinary consequences to her actions is not the primary object of her irritation (although she points out how 'ridiculous' she perceives this to be). Rather, what generates Käthe's frustration is the fact that, in the military social order, she was replaced by her husband as the disciplined subject and thus erased (silenced, in a way) as the agent of the resistance she articulated during the meeting. Her metaphor of the dog and its owner is striking for the degree of subordination (between a husband and wife) that it implies, as well as the irony of its deployment as part of a story through which Käthe articulates her insubordination (and her husband's supportive response). Presumably, what was also denied Käthe when her husband took her place as the subject of military discipline was the opportunity to articulate her defence. In a further contradictory twist, Käthe's defence is based on the concept of civilian immunity to military discipline (the Colonel's obligation to 'expect a civilian reaction' when talking to civilians): the very immunity that has caused her husband to be disciplined in her stead.

Paying attention to the encounters between women married to servicemen and female service personnel also reveals that disciplinary power does not simply flow from one side of a military/civilian divide to the other, nor is it contained by the binary separation of public and domestic life. Laura, for example, a soldier with the regiment who had served for a long time and reached a distinguished rank, frequently dealt with military wives in her professional capacity working in regimental headquarters, but manages her disciplinary power by using her first name and trading on her identity as a mother:

> So a lot of the younger wives have never seen a sergeant [and] they
> think, 'Oh my God, my husband's platoon sergeant shouts at him',

and then I come to the counter and I say you know, 'Hiya, I'm Laura' –
if I introduce myself as Laura [. . .] or they bring the children in and
I speak to the children or I say I've got a little kid myself, they're a
bit more . . . But a lot of them, the younger ones [. . .] they probably
think, 'Oh God she's a female and a sergeant', and it's a bit sort of
daunting for those.

In her dealings with younger wives, Laura makes an active choice to
mobilise a 'civilian' identity – consciously informal, using her first
name, and connecting to her status as a mother – to counter military
hierarchies of rank. That said, it appears that the conversion is difficult
to achieve and that stereotypes forged through rank are particularly
hard to shake off, as Laura concedes that she might remain 'daunting'
to some wives despite her efforts to play down her rank and official
status. Even the narrative terms available to her for expressing these
differences in the first place – her use of age to distinguish 'younger
wives' – loops back to rank, age betraying the fact that these younger
wives are most likely married to junior soldiers who are in a subordinate position to sergeants such as Laura. Thus, in Laura's narrative,
age is really a metaphor, is willed into use as a euphemism even. As
at other times in her interview when she indicated her resistance to
dismissive or derogatory terms for junior soldiers such as 'squaddies', this is an ethical or political choice that avoids reproducing
rank and its implication of higher and lower status. The fact that the
implications of rank are clear, despite the substitution of its terms
for age here, betrays the difficulty of civilianising rank. While Laura
finds room to manoeuvre between 'military' and 'civilian' identities,
therefore, the example also exposes 'the lack of equivalence between
people and the problems with exchange' (Skeggs 2004, 17). This
example shows that, in an encounter where power relations are pre-
structured by rank, even the choice to underplay rather than assert
its significance is Laura's prerogative. It is Laura who sets the terms
for the exchange – as Skeggs (2004, 107) has argued, the possibility
for subversion or reappropriation remains with 'those who have the
symbolic power to make their judgement and definitions legitimate'.

Later in our interview, Laura narrates an alternative encounter
with another woman who 'spoke to me like shit basically, whose
husband is a rank above me'. In this case, Laura perceives a civilian spouse to be 'carrying' her husband's rank, which, because it is
higher than her own, reduces her power as it had functioned posi-
tively in her encounter with the wife of a more junior soldier. Her
response on this occasion is to reassert rather than renegotiate the

boundary between military and civilian, by foregrounding her disciplinary power as military personnel. Ironically, however, the resolution she seeks can be achieved only through the unofficial channel of the woman's husband:

> And he was like, 'Well, tell my wife that.' Well, actually [. . .] she's not military so if I went 'Hang on a minute, shut up and get out of my office' like I would a private solider or a corporal who spoke to me like that, I said your wife would be straight to the families' office. So I'm speaking to you as military-to-military that I don't appreciate [it]. So can you speak to your wife about how she speaks to people in my office?

In *Bring Me Men*, Aaron Belkin (2012, 41) formulates three aspects of military discipline in relation to military masculinities, including 'discipline-as-surveillance', 'discipline-as-punishment' and 'discipline-as-collapse' (Belkin 2012, 40). The last of these, he argues, hinges on uncertainty, confusion and contradiction to produce compliance and social control. 'Discipline-as-collapse' certainly resonates with the uncertainty, confusion and contradictions that emerge from women's multiple positionings in relation to rank. Looking beyond Belkin's (2012, 5) example of the conflation of masculine and unmasculine,[4] it is possible to see how categories of military and civilian also function in the same way. In women's experience of the discipline of rank above, and in the other formations I have explored so far, classifications around 'military' and 'civilian' status work together as a confusing double bind that secures the compliance of those, such as military spouses, who move between the two. The examples I have reviewed above demonstrate the subtle but nevertheless institutionally sanctioned ways in which rank shapes the multiple and contradictory positions available to women at different times, and in different combinations according to each encounter.

In all of the examples I have explored so far, rank is also somewhat elliptical – overtly present in conversations and stereotypes but oddly unsubstantiated, sometimes overwritten and elided, at other times itself a stand-in or a citation for other, subtler judgements or intimations. It is this more diffuse quality of rank that I want to pursue next – how it always works in mutual constitution with other vectors of power, some more visible than others. Although rank is so often hailed into being as absolute – when someone 'pulls rank' for example – and its authority is upheld in the chain of command as well as through cultural forms like dress and insignia, rank is never *just* rank. It is also deeply embedded in class, for example, in ways that are simultaneously reliant upon ideas about Britishness or British subjecthood, regional and ethnic identity, race as well as gender. To explore these compound forms further, and in order to move on from military wife stereotypes and keep some of their infantilising dynamics at bay in my analysis, I look closer at the material structures of rank as they shape its meanings in everyday life. I begin with the distinction – or connection – between rank as an institutional hierarchy of discipline and control, and class as a culturally specific social order (Bennett et al. 2008) that allocates value and sets the terms for exchange between women, and between women and the military institution. I begin with a brief exploration of the connections between rank and class in the formal structures of the military institution, before going on in the rest of the chapter to elucidate upon some of its local textures and social patterning through the spaces of the military base overseas.

Structures of Rank

Few scholars have pursued the imbrication of rank with gender, class and sexuality to the level of critical detail that Enloe (2000, 151) reveals in her examination of rape in the US military, where she argues that a 'class-dichotomized ideology of masculinities is woven into most military chains of command'. In another, historical, US context, Lutz writes of the subtle and selective dating practices that shaped romantic relationships around a rapidly expanding military base in a Southern state of the USA during World War II (2001, 57) pointing out that '[c]lass has always helped structure marriage choices in America, and so the signs of military rank – correlated but not identical with socioeconomic class – were important in decisions about how to deal with the new permeabilities war brought to town'. Yet class as a rarefied, pervasive and historically embedded social structure in British society (Bennett et al. 2008, Savage 2015) remains underexplored in understandings about rank in the UK military institution. In scholarship as well as in practice, the connection between rank and class in the social and cultural practices of the military institution is everywhere implicit but rarely acknowledged. It is as if class as a fundamental component of rank is so obvious, so deeply embedded in the social fabric, that it is everywhere unseen, unquestioned, hiding in plain sight. In short, rank camouflages class. Not only this, it is this particular relationship between rank and class – their mutual dependence but also the degree to which the dominance of class as a permitted hierarchy in military contexts is elided – and excused – by rank – that also serves to naturalise or conceal a whole other host of social hierarchies that are normalised as part of rank's organisational necessity. These include the patterns of gender and class that are produced through notions of femininity, for example, and colonial continuities with the racialised divisions of imperialism, as I will go on to explore later in this chapter.

Class and socio-economic status are deeply entwined with rank through the two-tier structure of the British Army and its bifurcated recruitment methods. Rank as a formal hierarchy is central to the organisation of the military institution whereby officers take command over 'other ranks'. Within this two-tier system – the officer class, and 'other ranks' below them in the chain of command – officers range from the rank of Second Lieutenant and Lieutenant, through the ranks of Captain and Major to Colonel, Brigadier and, eventually, General. 'Other ranks' is the term used to describe 'non-commissioned' soldiers, ranging from entry-level 'Privates' who might then work their way up to reach the level of Staff Sergeant or two further bands of 'non-commissioned officer' (NCO), Warrant Officer One and Warrant Officer Two, at the top. In many ways – and as I frequently heard asserted by personnel of all levels – the British Army represents an incredibly broad cross-section of class relations in British society, be this in terms of educational background, trade ('blue collar' or 'white collar') or other socio-economic measures. As a result, multiple formations and subcultures of class are accommodated and celebrated in British Army culture, including those that can be mapped onto the geographical identity of certain regiments associated with individual countries or particular regions within the UK. In the regiment I was with, many of the junior soldiers were recruited from white working-class communities local to the regiment's UK headquarters, whose presence was most familiar to them growing up through the public visibility of the regiment at local events, other activities such as fundraising at shopping centres, for example, or through connections to family members past and present. These junior soldiers enter at the lowest rank of Private, or the regimental equivalent thereof (troopers, gunners, sappers), often colloquially referred to as 'squaddies' (Hockey 1986).

An alternative route into a military career, and fundamental to the two-tier system engrained in the rank structure[5] is as a 'direct entry' officer via the prestigious Royal Military Academy at Sandhurst, where all officers in the British Army receive forty-four weeks of intensive, residential training.[6] Formal age and entry requirements are tied to further educational attainment at A levels rather than a university degree, but officer training is still closely connected to university-level education through a range of incentives and structures such as internships, scholarships and bursaries as well as the University Officer Training Corps (Woodward et al. 2017). While training at Sandhurst is 'infantry-based',[7] new officers apply to join a regiment or specialist unit of their choice. At the end of their training they receive a 'commission' as an officer and take up their first posting with a regiment or specialist unit at the entry-level officer rank of Second Lieutenant.

Rank may be a fixed administrative scale organising the chain of command in this way, but people's relationship to rank, and thus the ways in which it is understood, enacted and socially reproduced, is far from fixed or static. Rank, in fact, is characterised by mobility. People ascend (and, sometimes, descend); some progress quickly, others get stuck at certain points. Everyone, it seems, *aspires*. Social mobility, therefore, is woven into rank. It is in this sense that rank provides a measure of the opportunities that the Army offers, as Carol, whose own husband rose from the rank of a junior soldier to occupy one of the highest positions of responsibility available to an LE officer within the regiment, explains:

> In our regiment, we have two boys from [an area] which [. . .] if you looked at the socio-economic stats in the UK, must be in the top ten of the poorest areas in the UK. Those boys – I'm not saying what may have become of them if they'd have stayed in [their home towns], but what *has* become of them are two very hard-working, decent senior NCOs [non-commissioned officers]. Happily married, no nonsense, fantastic children. And already those children are more social – they become more socially mobile than where their father started off. And those children have far greater opportunity. And the only reason why is the British Army. It gives you that opportunity to make something of yourself. It really does.

While the Army is seen as the catalyst or cause of social mobility in Carol's framework, rank is not the sole measure of that mobility. The social mobility that Carol expounds reaches beyond questions of seniority in terms of rank, to inhere in the production of domestic stability (marriage, family) and employment (education, job security) for future generations. There are echoes here of the same bargain with the military institution that I examined in the narratives of Foreign and Commonwealth personnel in the previous chapter, except that here there is arguably more value attached to the achievements of the first generation ('hard-working, decent senior NCOs') in the present. Carol's account also underlines the socioeconomic range and undergirding class structure of the British Army and its discourses of self-improvement as an employer; an institution traditionally represented as taking the raw materials of boyhood in the form of junior recruits, and shaping them into upstanding, respectable men (Woodward 1998).

The aspirational drive that rank rewards reaches its apotheosis in one further, boundary-blurring category, the 'late entry' (LE) officer, distinct from 'direct entry' (DE) officers. For personnel joining the regiment as a Private, rank represents a ladder of sequential job roles through which a soldier acquires experience and responsibilities, working their way through promotions over a period of many years. If a soldier excels, they may be 'commissioned' as an LE officer, entering at the rank of Lieutenant, one rank above the most junior DE officers, who have commonly joined the Army straight from university via the Royal Military Academy Sandhurst. The LE officers I met during my fieldwork usually had more than fifteen years' service and were often around the age of forty. All of them were men. Many were married with children and lived in service family accommodation nearby. The vast majority of DE officers of their equivalent rank were young unmarried men in their early twenties (with the exception of one female member of the medical corps attached to the regiment for deployment to Afghanistan), straight out of university via Sandhurst and living in the officers' mess. While differences in age are a convenient marker for the distinction between an LE and a DE officer, the social relations produced around the border-crossing, transmigratory figure of the LE officer,[8] and what their position reflects about other ranks, are complex and hard to define, as Pippa explains:

> P: I think they all get on fairly well, the LEs and . . . Some direct entry officers' wives can be a bit snooty you know, I've heard a couple of 'Oh well, you don't mix with the late entry wives' but I think that's just . . .
>
> A: [. . .] Do you find yourself getting sucked into it or can you resist in any way?
>
> P: Yeah, well when I first arrived I got on quite well with a few of the late-entry wives but I don't really see them anymore and I'm not quite sure why [laughs] [. . .]

A: Maybe you [and women married to DE officers] have similar experiences?

P: Yeah yeah, you're from similar backgrounds you know, for example some of the LE people have teenage sons and daughters and they're in their forties whereas many major's wives are in their early thirties and have young kids.

More than any other figure in the hierarchy of rank, the LE officer represents 'progress' up the ladder and the potential for social transformation in ways that are explicitly understood in relation to class. One LE officer's description of the requirements for 'entering' the officers' mess, for example, was the acquisition of suitable attire. This, of course, includes the highly codified uniforms associated with particular roles and ranks, where a fastidious attention to detail renders the performativity of rank something like the performativity of gender (Butler 1990). Rank, in this sense, might be compared to a kind of drag performance that is so heightened, so overdetermined by the weight of institutionalised citations, that the 'reality' of rank is exposed as only ever parodic. Military uniforms are subject to careful material and cultural construction, involving domestic tasks such as ironing, sewing and polishing, and, when worn, are accessorised with an array of caps, badges, spurs and braids that are symbolic of multiple forms of status and allegiance. That is not to say, however, that the performativity of rank is not also playful and self-aware in its parodic and parroting forms. I often heard the esoteric or antiquarian features of military uniform – many of them, such as high-waisted tight trousers, leather-covered staffs or a special riding crop, evocative of high camp or sexual fetishes themselves (Crane-Seeber 2016) – openly and affectionately mocked while being used by officers. At the same time, these modes of dress extend beyond their symbolic function to shape embodiments of power, directing bodies to move and behave in particular ways: shoulders back, elbows in, heels together.

Military uniform, however, was not the only kind of dress undergirding the performativity of rank. For example, I was struck by an LE officer's advice to a senior NCO who was widely anticipated to be in line for a commission as an LE officer himself, that he would soon need to acquire a tweed jacket. The tweed jacket – traditionally the preserve of the British landed gentry and enduringly associated with classed leisure activities such as hunting – is not strictly a part of the army uniform. I initially assumed that this was a joke, but the LE officer laughingly confirmed that he had bought his own tweed jacket from a charity shop, and had advised his colleague to do the same. In such ways, the expression of rank depends on far more than the right uniform. Rather, it inheres in collectively sanctioned trends or traditions in civilian dress that are bound up in ideas about class and wealth, and which derive from a much broader set of cultural dispositions and learned modes of behaviour in response. Rank and its expression, adaptation and occasional subversion through material forms also becomes a pervasive signifier of consumption within the community, again as the trappings of rank find expression through aspirational stylisations of self. Along with the brand of scented candles exchanged as gifts among many women married to servicemen, for example, the regimental shop also stocked the same brand of boots favoured by the most senior officer's wife. These consumer trends and clichéd expressions of middle-to-upper-class family life find their way into wry humour and critique, which is directed both at the 'source' (those who are perceived to be the authentic or entitled bearers of certain sartorial or cultural conventions), as well as those whose imitations are perceived as derivative or self-aggrandising. Be it a scented candle, a Barbour jacket, a pair of Hunter wellington boots or the acquisition of a black Labrador puppy as a family pet, people's consumer choices are always-already 'ranked'; sharply observed and often ruthlessly called out, even at the same time as their normative function and symbolic currency is maintained through their use.

What this diversion into the sartorial and consumer choices of the regimental community indicates is that, while social class varies widely across the British Army, it is the compelled investment in class as an overall system of value that is foundational to rank as a disciplinary tool. Rank works to secure compliance not solely through the hierarchical arrangement of command whereby a person is always answerable to those who occupy the ranks above them. Rather, rank secures compliance as an overall system of values universally upheld by the whole community, in which everyone can see their investment manifest in the cultural trappings of class migration (Bennett et al. 2008) and the promise of upward social mobility. This social mobility is particularly keenly illustrated by the transmigratory figure of the LE officer. Visibilised in symbolic insignia and material culture, rank becomes a signifier of class and class a signifier of rank in ways that are overdetermined and strangely fixed – antiquarian, sometimes regressive – at the same time as people are constantly negotiating the fluidity and instability of their place in the system of values they ultimately uphold.

In the next part of this chapter I want to explore some of the gendered modes through which women married to servicemen are incorporated into these currencies of value around rank. Yet again, my analysis is invested in exploring the degree to which rank is a composite form of power, operating through gendered imbrications with class as well as heterosexuality, for example. Deceptively simple when construed as a structure for institutional career progression, rank emerges as slippery and elusive, both amorphous and all-encompassing, yet to some degree adaptable in practice. Considering the composite nature of rank helps to explain the confusion and elision that it produces. As a container term with particular explanatory appeal, rank allows highly complex and multiple structures of power to be naturalised as an institutionally sanctioned and functional necessity for maintaining order and discipline. Paying attention to the mobile positionalities of women married to servicemen troubles the exceptionality of rank, as well as any easy assumption about what exactly constitutes its hegemonic power. Next I want to look at how rank is made manifest through the social spaces of the camp overseas and, importantly, how it is moderated by people's inhabitation of those spaces and the meanings they make of them in the process.

The Spatialisation of Rank

On camp, rank structures the movements of service personnel and their families in formal and highly regulated ways. Although there are communal spaces that are open to all personnel and their families, facilities for personnel are all segregated according to rank, and civilians are permitted by invitation only. This is a spatial order that reaches its apotheosis in the form of the officers' mess and the sergeants' mess. The messes are by no means the defining space of the camp itself, with the parade ground in the centre flanked by the grander building of the regimental HQ with its clinking flag poles, then workshops, gymnasium and industrial-type units at the rear and housing blocks for junior soldiers. There are also multiple social spaces whose boundaries are defined according to alternative subdivisions – all-rank bars open for each squadron for example, a 'cookhouse' or canteen where soldiers below the rank of corporals eat and which I sometimes saw used as a communal space. Then the welfare office, the 'family room' where coffee mornings were held and two distinct 'PRIs' (regimental shops, one run by women married to servicemen and stocking gifts, cards, clothing, toys and other trinkets, the other run by the regiment and selling branded paraphernalia such as mugs and penknives, but also outdoor wear, camping equipment and mountain bikes). Of all the different zones and spaces on camp, the officers' and the sergeants' messes in particular are invested with meanings that are contrived and consciously reproduced, a process of mythologising that is overt and constantly reinforced in discourses and behaviours.

The officers' and the sergeants' mess were at two opposite ends of the camp. Each combines facilities such as bars, sitting rooms, formal and informal dining rooms, and annexed accommodation. Divisions are maintained through strict rules about who can enter which mess (each being closed to any rank that is not an officer or a sergeant, unless by special invitation). The material difference in the style and size of the accommodation is vast, such that it is not possible to describe all the intricacies of the distinctions here. They range from the type of food served and how (self-service at 6pm versus silver service at 8pm) to interior décor and facilities such as shared bathrooms in the sergeants' mess and individual rooms with ensuite bathrooms in the officers' mess. While the messes play a functional role in maintaining unit cohesion, organisational coherence and discipline within distinctions of rank, this spatial segregation also counts as an important element of people's assertion of social and professional mobility as they progress up the career ladder and are promoted to different ranks, gaining access to different social spaces as they go. Yet the functional and material hierarchy of spaces is constructed in surprising ways that are far from linear, with the highest-ranked spaces most valued, and the others held in less esteem. The particular value of each space is negotiated in relation to its constitutive other, as detailed by Steve, a senior soldier who explained his own investment in the social space of the sergeants' mess:

> S: Well, it's a gentleman's club, isn't it? [. . .] If you imagine, the sergeants' mess is the hardest gentleman's club to get into in the world. Why? 'Cause you have to do fifteen years in the army to join it, and you have to be selected. And only then can you join that club. So it's really prestigious.
>
> A: Yeah, sorry I hadn't thought of it like that at all.
>
> S: If I was going to join, you would have to be respected through [. . .] your fellow soldiers. You then have to have been to war at some stage, or a fight, or to have done your bit. And then you're going to be selected to go into there. And that is a really big thing, isn't it? If you look at it that way. Some people just think, 'Oh

> I get to eat not in the cookhouse in there.' But you know [. . .], if I
> wanted to join the Masons or something like that, I could just pay
> and join. [. . .] But could they join my club? No. Not at all. It is a
> gentleman's club.
> A: And is that an incentive to people?
> S: Well, that's what I said – the officers can't join our club, 'cause
> they're officers, they joined as an officer. I can join their club,
> 'cause I can become an officer and join that rank, and join that.
> But they can never do the same, so that's what makes that club
> very prestigious.

Explaining the function of the sergeants' mess, Steve is keen to
emphasise the acquired and, moreover, earned exclusivity of membership in this simultaneously classed and gendered space ('a gentle-
man's club'). In a conversation which centred around the question of
where I should live while on camp, Steve compares the two spaces in
explicit terms of class, bound up with ideas about not only economic
wealth and education but also masculinity and sexuality:

> M: I think that if you [live in the officers' mess], you'll get a real con-
> versation
> A: What do you mean by that?
> M: In the sergeants' mess, a lot of things are fabricated, aren't they?
> [both he and I laugh] Er, 'mine's bigger than yours' kind of thing?
> A: Do you think so? Have you noticed that?
> M: Course I have – 'I've done this' and you know, 'I've done 200
> press-ups today' when they only managed five. No, you *would* get
> a conversation over in the sergeants' mess, you'd get a childish
> conversation of some sort from the sergeants' mess, er, some seri-
> ous ones. You'll get a lot of moaning, which is like 90 per cent
> of everything. And [in the officers' mess] you'd get people being
> polite [. . .]
> A: But people are polite [in the sergeants' mess] . . .
> M: Yeah but it's a different type of polite over here. You know, once
> again it's the class and you know, you don't want to put people in
> this class but we are, you know, in the Army you are set in certain
> classes [. . .] To be an officer you've got to have a bit of education
> – er, a degree, you know – you've been to university, your father's
> probably got into a bit of money, you know, that's why you're in
> here or you know, Daddy used to be in the Army, an officer, that
> sort of life. Where [in the sergeants' mess] you've gone through the
> ranks, you know, instead of being brought up in a farm you know
> with three Labradors and a horse, 'I was bought up in a valley on
> a quad, robbing from the local supermarket' [. . .]

A: Do you think I'd have to change anything about my behaviour if I
   moved in [to the officers' mess]?
M: You'd have to buck up your ideas yeah [laughs].
A: Is it more formal?
M: Nah, do you know what I think you'll fit in [both he and I laugh].
   No – but in that way because you're educated, aren't you? [. . .]
A: So would you say it's education then, purely education?
M: No, I wouldn't say it's purely education – if you're after a . . .
   depending on what you're after as a conversation, you're going to
   get that [in the officers' mess]. Cos the conversation will vary, you
   know from if you want to . . . You couldn't have a good talk about
   politics [in the sergeants' mess], could you? 'Let's go to the bar and
   talk about politics', eh? No, no that would never happen.

So what does happen when civilians – women married to servicemen – enter the ranked, classed and gendered spaces of the Mess?
Francesca was a woman in her late thirties who had been living with
the regiment in the town and was one of those whom I often saw
on camp, at coffee mornings or popping into the welfare office. Her
husband was an established senior soldier in the regiment, and she
was considered to be an active and supportive member of the community. I interviewed her in the early summer as the regiment's soldiers were returning from Afghanistan, as plans for various periods
of leave, as well as official parades and regimental social events were
being made. She expresses the same collective sense of belonging to
the sergeants' mess as Steve perhaps, although in terms of a 'family'
rather than a 'club':

F: Like in the Mess it's kind of like we're a family 'cause we're all of
   the same band [. . .] Like, Dan's done [over twenty] years now so
   obviously we know practically everybody – we might not know
   some of the younger ones, but certainly everybody in the sergeants' mess. I look forward to the sergeants' [ball] . . . A lot of
   the wives get in a panic about it and get nervous about going and
   about what to wear but I really don't.
A: Are there any dress rules?
F: Yes. Um, it depends on if it's obviously cocktail – you're never
   allowed to wear anything above the knee in the sergeants' mess
   [. . .] cocktail is below the knee and if it's long dress then it's long
   dress. But um, this one is actually fancy dress, it's Hollywood
   theme, which I love – if it's fancy dress even better, it's just more
   fun, isn't it? I feel comfortable in the sergeants' mess, yeah, and I
   don't feel like I have to, you know . . .

A: What about going to things in the officers' mess?

F: I've never been in the officers' mess obviously, and I would [feel uncomfortable] then because obviously, it's not our mess, it's the officers' mess so it's different. But I have heard actually the officers' mess are more naughty than us apparently! [laughs]. Apparently we're the best-behaved mess, the sergeants' mess – so in a way, yeah you know, we 'have to behave' [because sergeants are subordinate to officers] but do we really because actually they seem worse than us? [laughs]

In Francesca's description it is possible to trace the ontological power of rank as it defines the limits of women's movements across the social space of the camp. In all Francesca's many years living around this particular camp, attending social events and coffee mornings in the family room or canteen, helping out on cake stalls for parades or medals days, attending all-rank events in the corporals' mess, doing spinning classes in the gym, navigating various admin processes with clerks in the HQ building, one space has remained off limits: the officers' mess. The collective adherence to the exclusivity of the messes (highlighted here by my own naive assumption that Francesca must have at least been to one event in the officers' mess at some point and have seen what it was like) establishes a stark border that makes certain spaces (and what goes on within them) accessible, visible and knowable to some and not others.

Much like Steve's assertion of the comparative value of the space of the sergeants' mess, Francesca's assertion of social and cultural capital is bound up in the value of the sergeants' mess in opposition to its formal status 'below' that of the officers' mess. In this sense, Francesca takes full ownership of her occupation of the space of the sergeants' mess. Her social capital (Skeggs 1997, 8) derives from the networks she has accumulated over the duration of her husband's service and her senior membership (compared with 'some of the younger ones') of a long-standing cohort. Her cultural capital (ibid.) might be said to inhere in her knowledge of dress codes and years of experience of attending many such events. Thus, within that particular bounded territory, Francesca feels comfortable, her experience an example of how 'Inscribed bodies literally embody entitlements' (Skeggs 2004, 17). They move in space 'as if they own it' (ibid.). It is perhaps this proprietorial sense – of rightful ownership of the place one has earned, or inherited, in a social order (wherever that may be) – that rank materialises through and across social space. In this sense, its effects might be argued to be paradoxically democratising.

Yet it is also clear from the rules of dress and comportment that attach to certain spaces at certain times that the spatialisation of rank is bound up in the production of femininities as well as masculinities. Joanne, for example, who was married to a senior LE officer, was particularly aware of the ideals of femininity that are perpetuated by rank and embedded in particularly freighted ideas about 'respectability' (Evans and Beach 2020). Joanne was not one of those looking forward to the ball that was due to be held for officers, in the officers' mess, around the same time as the one in the sergeants' mess:

> It'll be a load of rubbish 'cause they always are and that sounds really awful but they spend thousands on decorating the marquee and all the rest of it, then you'll have all your young officers flying their call girls across – they've got a Chinese one on this arm, a Latvian one on this arm, and I'll be sat here by midnight with a cup of tea. [. . .] I don't know if you heard but [at the last ball] there was a huge swimming pool in the garden in the officers' mess, and by midnight there was three of the officers' wives in there naked. It was all terribly hysterical and ha-ha, and things like that really annoy me. Like all the DE officers' wives all in there with no clothes on. And that really annoys me because if they'd have attended a corporals' mess and the corporals' wives had behaved like that, they would have been reprimanded, their husbands would have been on extra duties. But because it was them . . .

I had indeed heard this story before. It occupied roughly equal billing with a story about the 'all-wives' (that is, women married to servicemen of all ranks) Christmas party, which was held in the sergeants' mess for the first time shortly before I arrived, and which soldiers responsible indicated would not be permitted again. Both social events contain within them contesting and contested constructions of femininity, respectability and class, and both of them were mainly represented pejoratively when they emerged – often salaciously – in conversations and interviews. In relation to the Christmas party, stories were still circulating in late January regarding 'a twenty-five-woman punch-up outside the loo!', and the damage done to a set of eighteenth-century battle bugles that some of the guests had taken down from the walls and attempted to play. Class is as fundamental an aspect as gender in the interpretation and evaluation of rank as a form of discipline extending to wives here, something that was underlined by another woman, Magda. Like Francesca, Magda had experienced lots of social functions with the regiment, most recently in the sergeants' mess (in line with her husband's rank). However, her more cynical interpretation matches Joanne's in terms of the limited potential that such social events offer for meaningful social transformation:

> I don't know, I think I'm . . . sometimes when you walk into the Mess it sort of throws you into this fairy-tale mode, doesn't it? It's like really old fashioned and there's lots of silver, makes you feel quite 'ooh', but um, [. . .] I call it Council Carnival, because it's like all those people that stand at the bus stop and swear like troopers, dressed up in ball gowns and walk into the Mess, it's . . . That's tradition, that's how it's done but it's just a big fake act because that's not what it is. It's just a dressing-up event really.

Being cautious about the relationship between my research and the danger of interviews being side-tracked by regimental gossip, I did not follow up on the 'facts' of stories about social events in the messes, nor did I ask the people who were purportedly involved. It is the function, rather than the veracity, of the stories that interests me here. Namely, their capacity, through their circulation and retelling, as cautionary, even disciplinary tales. Of all of them, only the infamous case of the naked swimming was permissively reincorporated into regimental lore, legitimated in much the same way as the drunken antics of young officers (smashing up pianos, playing cricket in the corridors) were often tolerated as being indicative of derring-do and flare. The wives' naked swimming even gained a mention in a speech by a high-ranking army officer at another social event in the officers' mess, this time a formal 'ladies dinner night', alluded to as a sign of the notorious quality of the regiment's social life, to much playful cheer. Far from their husbands facing disciplinary action for the behaviour of their unruly wives, such acts go down as a mildly illicit 'in' joke, contributing to the regiment's collective identity and narratives of derring-do and 'dash'. Meanwhile, the standards and values by which different women's behaviour is formally and informally judged vary wildly in the messy and mutual imbrication of class, rank and the production of multiple femininities. In the next section of this chapter I look beyond the spaces of the camp to chart how some of these modes of difference and distinction are replicated in the domestic spaces beyond it, namely the housing estates around the camp, where the regiment's families live in service family accommodation.

Civilising Spaces?

Scholars have focused on the military control of space as a site where 'the connection between privileged geographical knowledges and the pursuit of power becomes most obvious' (Harvey 2001, 214; see also Gillem 2007). At the same time, the dynamism that is central to postmodern ideas of the social production of space demonstrate that 'military geographies' (Woodward 2004) are incredibly diffuse.[9] In Chapter 1, I explored some of the ways in which the local spaces around the camp where I stayed are reoriented according to centre–periphery relations, with regimental HQ at their core. I push my analysis further here to explore the social patterning of local spaces around the camp according to subdivisions of rank. The accommodation offered to married service personnel and their families constitute a large number of housing estates around the garrison town, where housing is allocated to families according to rank. These housing estates are colloquially called 'the patch'. There are housing estates where only officers live, with larger houses and gardens allocated the higher the rank. Likewise, there are estates where families of junior service personnel are housed, where accommodation in apartments is exchanged for houses of varying size and quality the higher a soldier moves up the career ladder.[10] This, as much as any other military-strategic technique, is a prime example of what, in a broader study of securitisation, Higate and Henry (2009, 63) have called a 'military-cartographic [. . .] impulse to distil dynamic social spaces into quantifiable, fixed territorial entities that provide for rationalised strategies of engagement'. To someone like Stacey, who worked for the regiment and encountered many different levels of personnel on a daily basis, the system appears arbitrary in the ways in which it categorises and flattens social relations, which in her case include friends married to officers from whom she is spatially segregated by the rank of her husband:

> A: So, what about moving – have you been in this house since you came here?
>
> S: Yes.
>
> A: Are you happy being on the patch? This is a 'patch', isn't it?
>
> S: It's alright. I still don't understand the reason why you have to divide yourself from the officers. I can understand maybe the colonels . . .
>
> A: So there aren't any officers on this bit here?

> S: Nah. And officers don't really come down this bit either [. . .] This
> is all soldiers, so WO1 [Warrant Officer 1] and below [. . .] Um,
> officers' patches are up by the stables where Heather and Amy live.

In her subtle register of self-regulation (having to 'divide yourself'
from others or the fact that 'officers don't really come down this bit
either'), Stacey's experience testifies to the panopticism (Foucault
1975, 209) of rank as a scheme of 'generalised surveillance' (ibid.),
where people are literally and visibly positioned in space, reinforcing
their place in this institutional social order. Paying attention to the
geographies of belonging that are produced by this spatial arrangement further highlights the productive power of rank as it shapes the
vectors of difference and distinction that women negotiate between
themselves. Rank as 'a type of power' (Foucault 1975, 215) in this
sense comprises 'a whole set of instruments, techniques, procedures,
levels of application, targets; it is a "physics" or an "anatomy" of
power, a technology' (ibid.).

Geographies of rank combine easily with stereotypes of class and
gender to render subjects knowable, as Joanne describes:

> You know anyway, you know by – certain [officers' wives] you can
> just tell, by the way they dress, speak, their children's names – you
> just can [. . .] It's generally the scruffier they are the higher up they
> are. But even if you couldn't tell and you got in a conversation with
> somebody, you'd know by where they lived, like it's well known that
> this patch is officers' houses.

In Joanne's assessment, rank is visibilised through its spacialisation,
a foundational element of its power that underwrites its expression
in other forms such as dress. As before, however, it is essential to
complicate the fixed assumptions and stereotypes that attach to
spaces of rank by studying how they are used and inhabited. The bus
stops that are located around the garrison's housing estates are one
such site. Several women mentioned the centrality of the bus stops
to their everyday routines, dropping their children off to be taken to
school in the mornings and picking them up again in the afternoons.
The buses that circulate around the garrison at this time take the
English-speaking children of military families to the MoD-run and
Ofsted-registered schools that are located around the garrison and
named after figures from the English literary canon. The boundaries of belonging demarcated by the bus stops are established in part

by the demographics of their use, in that they exclude a minority of married women such as Tessa, who does not have children:

> Um, it is quite weird 'cause all of my friends are – have got kids. There is a lot of kids, there's only one couple really that haven't got kids [. . .] So you do find that not having kids you kind of take a step back. And also if you have got kids when you first move out here, you're going to do the school run so you meet people on the school run. If you don't have kids, you don't get that opportunity.

For Jane, who lives in a different area of the town to many of the women in the regiment, the bus stop is a singular site for her encounters with the neighbours, especially when compared to her husband's network across the various camps in the garrison:

> No I don't know my neighbours, and obviously [my husband] has met a few of them round the different camps and stuff but in terms of here I only speak to my neighbours really when I go to the bus stop to pick up the children.

The bus stops constitute a socio-spatial network that is part of the circuitry of the garrison, although one that operates according to an alternative rhythm tuned to the clockwork mechanisms of family life. The feminisation of the bus stops as a maternal space camouflages the degree to which the belonging they facilitate is a product of the chain of command, which determines that only women married to servicemen of particular ranks live on particular streets. At regular times each day, the bus stops draw people out of their homes to gather at the end of the street in a space that is proximate, intimate even, as well as publicly visible. As such, the bus stop is host to the fluctuations of everyday intimacies between women, becoming a site that forces but also facilitates their compromise between public and private lives and performances, as Annie states:

> Well we call it the 'bus stop test'. In the morning we take [the children] down to the bus stop and most of the other wives on the street – well, not all of them but you do see most of them in the course of the day down there – and people have just got used to saying, 'I'm in a bad mood today' or, you know, the majority of the time it's just stick up and let her get on with it kind of thing but we know one another well enough now just to kind of say 'Yes, having a bad day!' or what have you.

While Annie's characterisation underlines the function of the bus stops as part of the community's self-disciplinary apparatus (the 'bus stop test'), they can also be argued to engender their own modes of transgression and resistance. Halfway between the private space of domestic life but public at the same time, the bus stops emerge as an informal space where social conventions – of polite conversation or the obligation to be cheerful – can be adapted to make allowances, where performances are public but do not have to be polished.

The bus stops around the garrison also emerge as a site for gendered and classed visibility, for sightings of different women and their own citational practices. It is this aspect that prompted Laura, a senior servicewoman with the regiment used to dealing with a range of personnel and their spouses, as an earlier example showed, to recommend the bus stops as a site of particular anthropological interest for my research:

> It's great when in a morning, 'cause half of them go out in their pyjamas and Ugg boots with a coat over the top [laughs] [. . .] Then you get the one with full make up on, can't go out the door without full make up on, it is interesting to see. . . even if you go by on your bike on a school morning, just come by on your bike and see what the bus stops are like, for people.

Laura's advice to observe the bus stops 'for people' underlines the public visibility of the liminal zone of the housing patches as a physical, embodied space through which particular militarised identities might be argued to crystallise. Cheryl, a woman who had not been living in Germany for long and was married to a junior soldier with young children, provides an alternative interpretation of the bus stops and complicates the stereotypes that Laura believes they confirm. For Cheryl, visible evidence to substantiate the stereotype of the 'glamorous military wife' has proved elusive:

> I think it's a myth because my brother-in-law's soon-to-be-ex-[military] wife, she was saying [. . .] she felt like she couldn't even leave her flat without putting make-up on and stuff like that. Me? I go down in my pyjamas to put my [child] on the [bus] – I don't care. You know. We call them the 'bus stop crew', all the mothers. You know we're in hoodies, pyjamas, trainers, knowing full right that as soon as we go back up we're just going to veg out, you know? And I was thinking, well I've not come across the glam army wife. I've only seen one or two but then I naturally assume that maybe they've got jobs.

While Cheryl's experience substantiates the basic descriptive content of Laura's observations, she offers an important qualification as to the value of the public and collective visibility they produce. Both Cheryl's and Laura's emphasis on visibility makes clear the significance of appearance as a primary mode through which women married to servicemen are 'categorised, known and placed' (Skeggs 2004, 100). Skeggs has argued that femininity is persistently 'read as a class-based property' (ibid.). Indeed, the bus stop scene denotes something of the changing dynamics around expressions of gendered 'respectability' in British social history (Evans and Beach 2020), particularly ideas around working-class femininities and physical excess, both in terms of 'excessive style' (Skeggs 2004, 99) and 'letting go' (Skeggs 2004, 102). While Cheryl places herself as belonging to a particular group or 'crew' and even fulfils some of the visible criteria Laura describes pejoratively, her narrative from within allows her to be author of her own social positioning. Like Laura, she is dismissive of the artificiality of the 'glam military wife'. Rather than seeking to exchange the excess of make-up and glamour for the 'restraint, repression, reasonableness, modesty and denial' (Skeggs 2004, 99) of legitimated middle-class femininity, however, Cheryl counters glamour with 'irresponsibility and lack of care of the self' (Skeggs 2004, 102). By refusing to trade 'up' in this way, Cheryl disavows the symbolic order – the whole legitimating framework – that values certain cultural dispositions and styles of dress over others. Instead, she appropriates the place she occupies – for now – within that order, making her own meanings out of the place she has been allocated on a part of the patch occupied by other families of junior-ranking soldiers. What Cheryl's 'bus stop crew' proposes is something about women's strategy of *staying put* within the bounds of gender and class, and appropriating their place within geographies of rank.

As I have explored throughout this chapter, rank takes shape in a range of composite forms that are complex and subtle in their effects. Yet the ranked modes of difference and distinction that I have explored throughout this chapter are far from subtle. Many of them work through processes of public visibility, are materialised in objects, produced through rarefied spaces, codified in signs, symbols and dress. Rank, in its visible audacity, appears something of a decoy – a high-camp, highly decorated distraction that permits other forms of power to operate through or behind it, unseen. One final example more than any other I have explored here demonstrates the totalising power of rank, this time in relation to race and the colonial continuities that connect rank and class to white Britishness yet serve to invisibilise them at the same time. What this final exploration underlines is that the totalising power of rank does not, paradoxically, inhere in its institutional ratification as an absolute, naturalised form of power and authority in its own right – a fixed and necessary structure of military discipline mandated by the exceptionality of the institution. Rather, the totalising power of rank lies in its capacity to conceal, camouflage and, sometimes, eclipse other forms of power through its apparent self-evidence, its ubiquitous visibility, its show. In other words, for all its elaborate expression, the totalising power of rank inheres not in its own innate art, but in the other forms of difference and distinction it allows to circulate, unseen.

Most subtle in rank, perhaps, is the interlocking system of value created through its imbrication with particular formations of gender, class and white Britishness via colonial continuities of power. The imperial legacies of British military power have been explored in historical studies, as they shaped the collectivities and motivations of subaltern soldiers from India in World War II, for example (Barkawi 2017), or as they continue to forge constructed ideas about 'martial races' (Ray 2013). Studies have also included officers' wives, in British India in the nineteenth century for example (McInnis 2017), or multiple forms of conjugal partnership that were subject to the racialised hierarchies of French colonialism in West Africa (Zimmerman 2020). Vron Ware's (2010, 2012) research stands as a singular critique of the ways in which the British Army's contemporary production of its own multiculturalism relies upon imperial continuities that reproduce Commonwealth subjects according to centre–periphery loyalties (Ware 2010, 324). In terms of the labour and identities of women married to servicemen, feminist postcolonial scholarship is useful for what it reveals of the historical significance of class categorisations as a vital part of the colonial dynamics of race, gender, sexuality and trade. This is clear in studies of the sexual division of labour in the British Empire (McClintock 1995), including the role of women colonists as middle-class adventurers and travel writers (Lewis 1996) or wives and governesses (Myers 2001) in supporting the national project. Studies of privileged migration, as I explored in the previous chapter, make the continuities with British colonial history of migration clear, such that military wives might be considered 'the successors – in the broadest sense – of colonials' (Coles and Walsh 2010; Fechter 2010; Fechter and Walsh 2010). The material conditions that undergird these continuities are evident in one soldier's account of his posting to Kenya. Rob, who was separated from his wife and living in Germany while his family remained in the UK, describes his former spouse's experience from his own perspective and with some hindsight regarding their marriage:

> R: In Nairobi or in Kenya, um, Mel had a visa to come into the country but she was unable to work. [. . .] So she's kind of, you know, I'd get up and go to work before first light, gone, and I'd come back when it was dark. Um, she was getting up, making sure the kids were done, on the bus, off to school. And then she waits until the kids come home. It would have been helped, I dare say, if we didn't have – 'cause we were fortunate enough to have a housemaid and a gardener, because out there everything gets dirty-dusty very quickly –
>
> A: And do you automatically get that allocated to you?
>
> R: Well, it was automatically allocated, kind of um, I'm not sure if it was part of the agreement with the Kenyan government that you've got to employ a certain number of . . . But it's kind of the way of life out there. And you tend to inherit the maid that was there before, sort of thing. So Mel was left with very little to do – a lot of time on her hands . . . [. . .] And I think in hindsight [it] would have worked better if I'd [. . .] gone married unaccompanied. Because Mel then would have been able to [. . .] have a career, a job, um because, you know, there's only so many. . . I mean the girls there, Mel isn't one of these who's into, you know, coffee mornings, going making cakes and things like that. Um, but there's only so many times you can go for a manicure, a pedicure, a facial, a massage, a spa day. Because, believe it or not, they get boring! And although the opportunity's there and the money's there to do it, you get bored of it.

The colonial legacies of British imperial power and its enduring Status of Forces Agreement with the Kenyan government are manifest in the material and social conventions that are handed down through successive waves of military wives. These conditions belie the historical continuities that make migration with the British Army, in this case, synonymous with white privilege. The conditions that Rob self-consciously describes (or rather hints at and almost disavows) betray perhaps a collective awareness that such practices are old fashioned, out of date – at odds with contemporary expectations of a kind of globalised, progressive modernity where gender parity is achieved and the military is a multicultural, forward-looking institution.

In terms of their reliance on a sexual division of labour, the conditions Rob describes are also ambivalent and traitorous in their effects. There is a sense in which the gendered division of labour upon which couples rely to naturalise their relations in migration (whereupon the husband leaves the house to go to work, and the wife is kept busy with domestic tasks) is here replaced by a racial division of labour. The anonymous Kenyan housemaid – understood as an accessory to Britain's Status of Forces Agreement with Kenya and an extension of the property that is passed on to successive occupants – becomes the housewife's imperial other (Spivak 1988). Because gender relations here are reconstituted through a postcolonial division of labour that shifts some of Mel's perceived domestic responsibilities onto another, 'privilege' creates a void that is filled with a brittle and feminised performance of leisure and luxury. Paradoxically, this brings Rob's understanding of his wife's experience in line with traditional migration research that argues that women in migration experience a loss of status and the entrenchment of traditional gender roles through increased isolation within the private sphere, although the means of this loss here include practices and identities of wealth and leisure rather than poverty and lack of resources. What is unchanged by privilege, however, are the patriarchal modes of femininity and the forms of labour and identities they support. Privilege has its discontents, therefore.

In many of my interviews with women married to servicemen, privilege emerged as an object of dissent and disavowal, or, like Magda's cynicism regarding the transformative power of the sergeants' mess, was dismissed as superficial – just for show. If the colonial continuities of the British Army produce privilege – however traitorous – through gender and race, then one further example of how these colonial continuities are self-consciously minimised or elided highlights the degree to which they are overridden and invisibilised by rank and its dominance as *the* military technology of entitlement and privilege. This was evident in the near-outrage articulated by Suzanne (who had been based in Germany for so many years with her LE officer husband, to the degree that it did not count, in her estimation, as a true overseas posting). Her estimation of postings that count as 'abroad' bear the markings of those conditions articulated by Rob during his time in Kenya:

> S: If you get a posting abroad, you get a cleaner, you get a cook, you get a . . . why?! Whoever you are . . .
> A: Whatever your rank?
> S: Yep. Well, I don't know about the lower but I've got friends who – the more bizarre the country, the more you get: you get an ironing lady . . . why?!

The object of Suzanne's consternation is not simply that families moving 'overseas' would automatically be allocated a local housemaid. Like Rob, the object of Suzanne's consternation is not the racial division of labour, but the sexual division of labour it disrupts: what is the point of having a local housekeeper when work such as cleaning, cooking and ironing are written into the sexual division of labour within military households? As Rob attests, disruption of this naturalised equilibrium left his wife 'with very little to do'. But, looking more carefully, it is also the fact that these resources are allocated 'whoever you are' that is problematic for Suzanne. This contravenes the system through which material resources such as larger houses and housekeepers are allocated to personnel according to their rank. Suzanne's reaction indicates that the privilege engendered through a posting overseas gains its meaning and value not as an act of travel to another country, but as a vicarious excursion in rank (and the material trappings associated therewith). This example is a final indication of the salience of rank in overshadowing other vectors of power – and the historical relations of domination beyond the military institution – that continue to inform military modes of difference and distinction. In Chapter 2 I explored some of the ways in which racial difference was wilfully unseen and ethnicity asserted instead through national identity and citizenship as ciphers. This is a mode of military multiculturalism that, as Ware (2012) has argued, does little to disrupt imperial legacies or contemporary inequities of race within the military institution. The very subtle connections I seek to draw tentatively into the light here, and which emerge this time in the tangential connections, ellipses and asides of people's speech, hint at the degree to which formations of rank connect intimately, and intricately, to contemporary white privilege and its origins in Britain's imperial past.

Connecting the question of women's social mobility – such as vicarious excursions in rank – back to their geographic mobility underlines again how women's navigation of opportunities for maximising their material or social resources derives not from travelling to a particular place and the opportunities that can arise from the creation of new, transnational social networks, for example, but rather remains resolutely rooted in military-imperial structures. This begs the question of how to *locate* military wives' mobility – how to understand their emplacement in terms of geography and space – if the cultural particularities (and racialised dynamics) of their location are so flattened, so invisibilised, as to appear almost incidental. Time and again, it is ranked measures of difference and distinction that powerfully override any other logic through which subjects might seek to understand their positionality within broader social relations.

Conclusion

Scholars of military history have argued that the professionalization of the armed forces, which includes the transformation of the 'bachelor Army' (Moelker and van der Kloet 2003, 204) into an army of family men (French 2005, 309), is commensurate with the decline of a 'system of surveillance that oversaw every detail of the waking and sleeping lives of its members' (French 2005, 332). Yet, as my examples throughout this chapter have shown, rank as a system of collective (self)regulation is both concrete and comprehensive in its presence, threaded as it is through space and social relations on and around the military camp overseas. The power of rank inheres in what Foucault calls the 'art of distributions' (Foucault 1975, 141). Rank does indeed emerge as a highly refined and artful practice that is intricate in its many forms, from the circulation of social stereotypes and the structures of the chain of command, to modes of dress, acquired tastes and processes of spatialisation both within and beyond the military camp. In such ways, the power of rank inheres in its capacity to classify bodies and construct identities according to their place 'in a network of relations' (Foucault 1975, 146). People are both geographically and socially – and constantly, it seems – *positioned* by rank in complex and multivalent ways. Key to any understanding of rank that accommodates the agency of those subjects who encounter its structures and stylisations on a daily basis is thinking about mobility. This undoubtedly includes mobility in a socio-economic sense: it is essential to recognise, as per Carol's perspective earlier in this chapter, that many find fulfilment, as well as material resources and financial security, in the pathway for self-improvement that the British Army promotes. But, in my critical analysis, I have sought to look beyond the material promise of rank in these terms, keen to avoid reproducing the value system that posits upward social mobility as a justification for its means. Rather, I look to the mobility of military wives and their various ways of both appropriating and, at other times, rejecting the totalising effects of rank, its essentialising tendencies, its dark arts. As per Annie's *dis*-identification with stereotypes of wifedom earlier in this chapter, the obligations that come with rank in the contemporary British Army can perhaps be reframed as a case of individual choice ('Everyone's got [. . .] to just do what they want to do, haven't they really?'). Yet many of the examples I have explored here underline the asymmetric power relations between women and the military institution, and a lack of equivalence between women positioned differently within it. Rank is a value system that works through many different currencies and modes of exchange. This helps to acknowledge, with Skeggs (2004, 48), the limits of women's mobilities, and to distinguish within and between military subjects 'who can move and who cannot, and what the mobile/fixed bodies require as resources to gain access to different spaces'.

Paying attention to the mutual imbrication of rank, gender and class illustrates the many ways in which their meanings and uses are renegotiated between women themselves. While these negotiations may not drastically alter the scripts and structures of ranked belonging on a broader level, their use-value inheres in the social mobilities they facilitate among women, and between particular women and the institution, on an everyday scale. Rank has come in and out of focus, more or less explicitly, throughout many of the narratives I have documented in this chapter. It is foregrounded then elided, appropriated and disavowed, then frequently upheld at a further point. My data show the many overt ways in which rank is formulated and expressed within British Army structures and culture, resulting in a false coherence that naturalises rank as an absolute and innate technology of military exceptionalism. Yet throughout the examples I explore here, rank becomes increasingly difficult to frame as an absolute entity in itself. I have shown that class and gender are often the salient citations through which the classifications of rank are performed and understood, and hinted at the less visible but equally intractable hierarchies of sexuality and race that accompany them. In this sense, rank operates through multiple 'formations' (Skeggs 1997) of power that are far from exceptional to – or contained by – the military institution and its rarefied managerial structures and esoteric cultural forms. At the furthest extreme of this logic, one might posit that rank has no 'real' basis as a singular form of power at all, emphasising through its performativity, its artfulness, the many broader (and equally constructed) citations through which its disciplinary power is achieved and understood. This lack of any 'real' basis for such an overdetermined, intensely produced, indeed, apparently 'exceptional' form of power, calls into question the nature of the 'civil/military divide' itself.

Notes

1. See also feminist adaptations in Adkins and Skeggs (2004), which argue for women's proactive and productive role in using and adapting modes of capital within processes of social stratification. Bourdieu's (1984) theory of capitals includes a person's cultural capital (Skeggs 1997, 8), which inheres in particular dispositions, forms of knowledge and their objectification, and social capital, relating to networks and relationships with other people or groups (ibid.). Such concepts offer the opportunity to explore how subjects interact (and transact) with each other and with institutional structures established by military hierarchies, as well as, crucially, how these forms of value are both formally and informally recognised and ratified (which Bourdieu [1984] characterises as symbolic capital – see Skeggs 1997, 10), but also how they seek to maximise their cultural and social capital based on broader schemes of value such as class and ethnicity. A theoretical framework for the analysis of rank in terms of multiple forms of capitals, along with ideas about military habitus (see MacDonald 2004 and King 2009), would be a fascinating undertaking, but my focus for the moment and in this chapter is on the empirical patterning of rank in people's lived experience.

2. https://apply.army.mod.uk/what-we-offer/army-life/ranks, accessed 26 May 2022.

3. I do seek to make a broad connection to Butler's (1990) ideas about the performativity of gender here, specifically the way in which rank might be viewed as a citational practice that draws from many different vectors of power and identity towards a similarly totalising effect. Likewise, it is easy to think of rank as performative in ways in which the performativity of gender has been simplified or misunderstood – as the mere putting-on of an act. While rank, like gender, undoubtedly lends itself to this kind of staging – through dress, for example – it is rank's dominance of the social field as a citational practice, its power to define and determine the language and forms of expression available to subjects at any one time in any one place, that I think characterises it as performative in a Butlerian sense. Thus, Butler's (1992) own qualification in regard to performativity is useful as a reminder here: 'The bad reading goes something like this: I can get up in the morning, look in my closet, and decide which gender I want to be today. I can take out a piece of clothing and change my gender, stylize it, and then that evening I can change it again and be something radically other, so that what you get is something like the commodification of gender, and the understanding of taking on a gender as a kind of consumerism. . . . [Treating] gender deliberately, as if it's an object out there, when my whole point was that the very formation of subjects, the very formation of persons, presupposes gender in a certain way — that gender is not to be chosen and that "performativity" is not radical choice and it's not voluntarism [. . .] Performativity has to do with repetition, very often with the repetition of oppressive and painful gender norms to force them to resignify. This is not freedom, but a question of how to work the trap that one is inevitably in.'

4. In this way I view my analysis as responding to Belkin's call to assess 'whether these observations come together in different ways at different sites' (Belkin 2012, 42).

5. https://www.nam.ac.uk/explore/british-army-ranks, accessed 28 April 2022.

6. https://apply.army.mod.uk/what-we-offer/regular-officer, accessed 28 April 2022.
7. https://www.army.mod.uk/who-we-are/our-schools-and-colleges/rma-sand-hurst/officer-training/, accessed 28 April 2021.
8. The idea of transmigration within and across military categories is usefully explored in an Israeli context around both ethnicity and the status of reserve soldiers by Lomsky-Feder and Rapoport (2003) and Lomsky-Feder et al. (2007), respectively.
9. Research that considers the socio-spatial construction of security in such ways troubles the tangibility of borders and the control of citizens across them to the extent that the very notion of 'security' can be viewed as 'having no independent reality outside of the social relations through which "it" is constituted and sustained' (Higate and Henry 2009, 100). Higate and Henry explore the UN's 'zoning' techniques in peacekeeping missions in Haiti. In addition to the restriction of people's physical mobility, the authors emphasise the curtailment of the everyday human relations that flow across and beyond that zone, for example through social networks and patterns of labour or consumption (ibid., 64). This flattening of 'social complexity and dynamism' (ibid.) into a two-dimensional 'red zone' (ibid.), they argue, homogenises and stigmatises every slum-dweller as a threat to security.
10. This represents one further layer of physical, geographical mobility on a micro-scale, where families can move house multiple times in a very small number of years due to the promotion of the serving member and the necessity that the family lives in the corresponding type and area of housing commensurate with the job, and so that the house they leave can be filled by the person who takes over their former job role.

'Female in Shower' and Other Signs

What is it to run a bath with the fluffy white bubbles of the previous person left behind in the tub? To swill round the sides, feel the slight residue of soap scum, splash the foam towards the plughole then fill it up again, with the steam of the previous person's presence remaining? To get undressed and get into the bath and lie where they lay, moments ago. To have entered a communal bathroom with its fluorescent hum, non-slip tiles and locking stalls, and glimpse a fleeting but intimate sense of the other person's self-care: the pink bottle of floral-scented bath foam, the signs of a body soothed and cleansed, before retreating back along the carpet tiles to a silent, single bed.

There is a charge here, something alive, something that connects bodies in sensory ways but is always deferred, never quite made flesh.

In the beginning, it was just me and one other soldier living on the corridor closest to the Mess. Most of the other NCOs lived in another building where the rooms had been refurbished. The rooms on this side were shabby and drab, but the advantages, people said, were the separate ladies' loos across the foyer and it was quieter here. That, I was told, was why the other soldier preferred it. Because it was quiet. His room was down the other end of the corridor to mine. There was a shower room towards the middle, with three shower stalls and a larger stall with a bath.

The first room I was given had no lock on the door, so I was quickly moved. My new room was at the end of the corridor near the fire exit, which led on to the open tarmac of a car park. The other soldier kept leaving it open. I closed it whenever I noticed – there was a secure keypad to get in via the foyer, why wouldn't he use that? But it kept being left open. Soon, and only through the process of walking and re-walking the corridors, forgetting the code (the date of an historic regimental battle victory), I realised that it was a convenient shortcut to come and go via the fire exit, and stopped closing it. I didn't think about security. I felt safe.

Initially, living in the Mess was communal only in the sense of these spectral signs of the comings and goings of a few others. The officers' mess was closed entirely. The sergeants' mess was running on a skeleton staff: the bar was shuttered off. I tried working in different spaces to get out of my room, at one of the imitation roll-top desks in the lounge area, crowded by regimental ornaments and miniature bronzes, or animal parts adapted for alternative use (an inkpot; a letter opener). It was the middle of winter and the lamps seemed inadequate to the task of lighting the dark wood, dark carpet and dark-red, faux-leather chairs. Once, someone built a fire in the hearth ready to be lit and left matches on the mantel piece.

If I was going to be late for dinner and had filled in my 'Pay as You Dine' chit correctly, there would be a single-serving portion plated up for me in a refrigerated cabinet. It would be there in the pale buzzing light at the very end of the dark room, past the long table, chair after chair after chair on dark-blue carpet, then the ping of the microwave oddly loud. If I left my laundry in the dryer too long, it would be taken out and neatly folded, whether by the kitchen staff (a German woman married to a soldier in the garrison), who might be in there washing tea towels and dishcloths, or by the solider, I never knew. When I went there once and realised I had dropped a scattering of dirty washing by the door, I was relieved to find that no one had been there for days.

I got used to my barrack room. I didn't nest in it, so much as arrange it to my purposes, swapping the armchair for a better one that I found in the room without a lock, moving it to the other side, also requesting a second lamp. I assumed that all the other soldiers living in the Mess tolerated the magnolia dinginess in similar ways. Yet on my very last night in the camp, I went over to say goodbye to the small group of senior soldiers I had joined at dinner on most of those winter nights, at 6pm every evening, the food kept hot on metal trays with tealights underneath keeping it warm. I was invited tentatively into one of their rooms where I was more surprised than I should have been to see scatter cushions and framed pictures, their own choice of matching bedspread. We sat – me on the sofa, another on the bed – while a couple of others stayed standing. The soldier offered me a glass of Robinsons Lemon Barley that he filled up from the sink in the corner with its mirror and shaver socket and overhead light. They said that I could have come by at any time, that they often wondered what the hell I did after dinner every night, that I could have come round and watched telly.

In the summer I had actually enjoyed a period living away from the camp. As the regiment returned from its tour in Afghanistan and members took Post-Operational Tour Leave (POTL), I was offered several opportunities to housesit for friends and acquaintances with pets. I started with two goldfish, then guinea pigs and finally a dog, before politely declining to look after a horse. These housesitting duties provided me with considerable insight into the dynamics of living within the community, such as grasping the orderly conventions of German recycling or realising the complete lack of privacy afforded by the layout and low fencing of the housing estates. These were trivial annoyances, but housesitting provided some important insights into the gendered dynamics that blur public and private space within the regimental community. On one particular day, I had helped a neighbour with her new-born baby, and on the way back from an evening event I was invited into the garden of another woman I knew for a late-night drink. I was feeling quite chipper, as my field diary attests:

> It has been a weekend of baking. While I took Sophie for a walk this afternoon, Sarah baked scones. We joked about the clichés while eating them. [. . .] I have been contemplating whether or not to take some tarts over to Meg and David's to say thanks for having me over for a drink last night. Maybe I will do that. I am conscious of the cliché, and of this all being my performance of domesticity but really it's just nice to be included in something that feels larger and brighter than one small khaki-painted room. [. . .] I have, I think, actually had a lovely weekend.

Such were the domestic practices of everyday life I adopted while housesitting, actively complicit in reproducing the gendered division of private and public space. There I was, with my market produce (white asparagus!), babysitting and jam tarts, building up my defences against five months of all-male dinners in the sergeants' mess, communal bathrooms and the institutional blankness of barrack-room walls.

But what about the pink-scented bubble bath, the scatter cushions, the Robinson's Lemon Barley? These are important blurrings that I can still only just make out, which I only ever glimpsed; intimacies that exist at the edges of this research and in many ways lie beyond what I can account for here. These stolen glimpses of something else going on, whether constituted by my inclusion in or exclusion from different aspects of community life, hint at the slippery, elliptical relationship between the public and private spheres and the different levels of intimacy and domesticity that surround, and in many ways are central to, regimental life.

By the early summer, all the regiment's soldiers and officers had returned from Afghanistan and the rooms along my corridor had been filled. This happened gradually, but I felt it as an intrusion. Only a few soldiers lived in their rooms, most using them only to change after PT (physical training), or on the nights when some of them seemed to stay over. The bar was open again.

One night, there was an event in the Mess which, it was explained to me, I could not attend because it was not a 'ladies' night' (though it was suggested I attend in male drag). During the night there were noises of drunken banter then snoring through thin walls, the smell of cigarette smoke from the fire escape.

This increased presence makes me nervy, self-conscious in what had come to feel like my own setting. I am resentful of what I come to think of as a heavy, macho, presence. One Saturday I am awoken by someone opening the door of my room and shutting it again quickly. I must have left it unlocked. The fire exit became exactly that: an escape route, a way to exit the building avoiding the main foyer, without being seen. I bump into someone as I'm returning from the gym in my running shorts. 'So you *have* got legs!' he exclaims.

Soon I am listening at the door before I leave, straining to detect the sounds of presence before scuttling out to the showers, which have become clogged with increased use, the soap scum slow-draining. Someone has taken a piss in one of the cubicles in the night and it begins to smell. These are remotely sensed, disembodied encounters, signs of living subjects. The smell of smoke, the hairs in the drain, the urine. They are different from the synergy of shared solitary presence when it was just me and one other soldier living on the corridor before. Anonymous and stripped of social context, they are base in their intimacy – generic, archetypal almost: too much.

Gradually, these multiple others become flesh, identify themselves. I am told the name of some of the new inhabitants, start to see them appear at breakfast. They acknowledge me in cursory ways. The dynamics at dinner time shift: I am quiet, eat quickly. The apparent confidence of some of the other soldiers I have got to know since I arrived seems to recede. Familiarity dissipates. Sometimes they seem resentful, quipping and rolling their eyes.

One morning, after I have checked the corridor is clear, I am in the shower, the stall locked, my towel on the hook. I hear voices in the corridor, listen closely. They get louder, closer, then I hear the other showers being turned on. I don't think they've locked the stalls.

The only voice I recognise belongs to a senior soldier whose wife I have interviewed.

I take my time, wait it out. They go on, laughing, talking, more and more animated. After a while I say thinly, 'Hello?' There is a sudden silence. They didn't realise I was in there, they say. I ask if it is OK for me to come out and they say 'Yes', and I say, 'OK I'm coming out', and they say 'OK' and I rush out so fast that my feet nearly slide off my flip-flops, making a rude squeaking noise. I round the corner at some speed and retreat to my room.

It feels like I have done something wrong. My first thought is: What will his wife think? Then I am more annoyed.

By lunchtime, I have composed myself. By then, I have converted it into a funny anecdote in the kitchen by the welfare office. By dinnertime, however, I have come full circle and am keeping it quiet. By evening in my room I am increasingly upset and I identify that feeling as shame. By morning I have decided to go and see the Welfare Officer. He nods sagely. The senior soldier has already been to see him. There should have been a protocol in place.

I am given an A4 sheet of paper with 'FEMALE IN SHOWER' printed in large letters on one side, and four bits of Blu Tack in each corner of the reverse. The Welfare Officer says sorry but the laminator has broken. I am to use this whenever I go into the shower. For my own protection, and the protection of others.

The sign becomes dog-eared and limp. I learn to find reassuring amusement in its shouty assertion of biological sex and the non-stickiness of Blu Tack on steamed-up tiles. Its damp folds mock me; my weakness, my sensitivity. When I interview a servicewoman she insists that sharing washrooms in Afghanistan, for example, is just a fact of contemporary British Army life. As well it should be. Months later, I see a photograph in a newspaper: a servicewoman emerges from a tent hung with the sign 'FEMALE IN SHOWER'.

My sign was the real deal. A bona fide military technology.

I should have been put in the officers' mess, explained a senior officer I had just met, though I had known his wife since the start of my fieldwork. In the officers' mess, he said, there were en-suite showers attached to each room. As the squadrons return, it's a bit like starting my fieldwork all over again. Introductions are made – explanations. I encounter regimental 'characters' I have heard stories about, or am introduced to the husbands of many of the women I have interviewed. With the officers' mess fully open again, there is some speculation as to whether or not I will be moved there for the last month of my stay. Barely a day goes by without someone asking me whether or not I will be moving. It is a topic of discussion when I am invited to dinner at the house of a couple who have become friends and meet a young officer, who mentioned my plight in his thank-you note:

> Dear Anna, I'm writing
> To thank you so very much
> For dinner last night.
> The food was excellent
> And the pudding to die for.
> It was lovely meeting Alex,
> Whom I think would prefer
> Life in the Officers' Mess.
> And also Henley.
> What a lovely
> Relaxed, hassle-free
> Dog he is.

People are keen to dispense advice, offer reasons why I should move to the officers' mess. Many of them construct it as a mythical place of sophistication or opulence, where one must dress for dinner, which is served at eight o'clock rather than six o'clock each night. The officers' mess takes on a chimeric quality as a place of superior facilities and better food; the height of military hospitality, something I really must see; a tourist attraction. Someone in the welfare office says I'll get better conversation there, more appropriate to my level of education. An officer warned that it would be much more fun but that I might wake up with a young subbie in my bed one morning. A senior soldier in the sergeants' mess remarks, 'I hope you've remembered your morning-after pills.'

Is this the sexual politics of rank? In the sergeants' mess, a young officer's charm and politeness were the object of negative cultural capital, often portrayed as duplicitous and sexually motivated by comparison with senior soldiers' age, experience and increased sense of responsibility, their respect for authority and status as 'family men' (even if divorced and single, as most of the men living in the sergeants' mess were). And what else was the regiment doing but carefully monitoring, and controlling, those sexual politics, through signs, social conventions and the division of social space?

Like my 'FEMALE IN SHOWER' sign, there are protocols in place for managing sexual politics on camp.

CHAPTER 3

Regimented Life

Introduction

In this chapter I explore the modes of belonging produced through the British Army regiment as a way to interrogate what military service *means* to people. Building upon the socio-spatial and discursive practices I have explored throughout this book, I want to go further, analysing the British Army's production of regimental belonging as a vehicle for people's affective investment in an institution that posits ideals of duty, service and sacrifice at its core. Looking at such ideals as they are personalised and adapted to produce new forms of belonging by women married to servicemen, I consider the disciplinary power of the regiment's will to cohesion, but also its potential for renegotiation through processes of 'civilianisation' as a form of resistance to militaristic values. Questioning how people make sense of different modes of regimental belonging – the meanings they make of the social and cultural attachments they feel, or are directed to feel – reveals a host of complex, affective ties bound up in familial, rather than military, relations. This offers a more nuanced understanding of notions such as 'duty' or 'service' as they circulate among, and attempt to bring together, the regimental community as a whole.

My concern with people's affective investment in regimental belonging and the ideas of duty and sacrifice that are promoted through it connects implicitly to war and combat as a central element of what the military institution is for. The exceptional status of the military among institutions has often been linked to the 'defence of the realm' and its mandate for the implementation of state-sanctioned violence. This, in conventional sociological terms, is part of what makes the military 'more than just a job' (Moskos and Wood 1989). The nature and meaning of soldiers' active service, and of the threat to which they were exposed, was very much a salient question during my fieldwork, conducted as it was during the regiment's deployment in a front-line role engaged in ongoing combat operations in Afghanistan. Beyond functional arguments for regimental cohesion framed around operational effectiveness, I connect the forms of belonging experienced by women married to servicemen – sensed and made sense of in so many ways – to the regiment's direct engagement in war-fighting activities.

As spectators round the edge of the parade ground, invited guests at ladies' dinner Nights and balls, or burdensome dependants queuing at the welfare office, military wives might, as ever, be characterised as liminal figures or vicarious consumers of regimental belonging. However, as my task in this book has been to explore the experiences of military wives as active and mobile subjects, geographically and socially, here I argue for their role as vital agents in the social and cultural reproduction of a regimental community. In line with the array of positionalities that women take up in relation to military power, the meanings they make of regimental belonging are multiple and sometimes contradictory – one moment in, one moment out, sometimes supportive, at other times disavowing or disavowed, both subverting and upholding its conventions. One of the places where this is most striking is in feminised or domesticated narratives of belonging that, while they are often constituted in close relation to the regiment, can be traitorous in their effects, reclaiming the meaning of soldiering as a form of labour. Here, the relationship I have explored throughout this book between the military and the family as twinned institutions reaches its apotheosis in the complex ideal of a hybrid martial and marital unit, the 'regimental family'. I begin by exploring the making of the British Army regiment as a container for collective identity and forms of personal and professional commitment on the part of soldiers, but also their wives.

The Making of the Regiment

In his history of the regimental system in the British Armed Forces, David French (2005, 77) argues that 'the willingness of officers and other ranks to invest the same emotional commitment in their regiment as they did in their family did not spring ready-made from the ground'. How the British Army produces and sustains social cohesion is the object of sociological debate (see, e.g., Basham 2009; King 2006 and 2007; Kirke 2009; Thornborrow and Brown 2009;

Ware 2012). Scholars have argued for the existence of a 'loyalty/ identity structure' (Kirke 2009, 747), based on the importance of close personal bonds between troops, as well as a 'functional structure' (ibid.), where cohesion is thought to be produced primarily through task-oriented training and activities, albeit with ritualistic significance (for a detailed debate, see King 2006 and 2007; Siebold 2007). A range of studies have provided evidence for the role of military families, and particularly wives, in supporting and sustaining unit cohesion within military institutions in the USA, for example, some of it justified on the basis of its own direct impact on policies designed to secure 'the commitment of male soldiers (and their wives) to the military institution' (Bourg and Segal 1999, 644; see also Bourg and Segal 1999; Cooke and Speirs 2005; Westhuis et al. 2006). The concept of 'greedy institutions' (Segal 1986, 9) has been used to argue that the family and the military exist in an inherent relationship of competition (Segal 1986, 32), a formulation that hints at military wives' position between the two, although this is rarely the main focus of such research. Recent studies argue that there is growing resistance to the idea of 'total devotion' to either institution (Bourg and Segal 1999, 634), as evidenced in the increasing number of women married to servicemen seeking to participate in the labour force and cultural trends that call for men to participate more actively in family roles (ibid.). The idea of a more balanced distribution of productive and reproductive labour is based on closer degrees of co-operation between military and family life (Bourg and Segal 1999, 648), an 'expansive model' (ibid., 637) of commitment that benefits both institutions at the same time. As well as the material remuneration that a military institution offers its personnel and their families, the union between the military and the family is thus secured by the extent to which a subject 'identifies with and is willing to work towards organisational goals and values' (Bourg and Segal 1999, 637) due to a 'sense of calling and duty' (ibid.) to both the military and one's family simultaneously, and as mutually beneficial (ibid.). It is this compound mixture of military and family values that prompts what Bourg and Segal call an 'affective commitment' (ibid.). Reformulated from the perspective of women married to servicemen, the 'affective commitment' required to bridge the gap between the military and the family might be argued to depend, as Enloe (2000, 158) has argued, 'on whether a woman married to a soldier will invest her talents and aspirations – and her pride and satisfaction – in the militarized career of her husband'. Thus women married to servicemen might be understood to be the principal agents of Bourg and Segal's 'expansion' model of resources (Bourg and Segal 1999, 648), whose labour is invested in smoothing the rupture of army life, and whose experiences of marital and martial duty blur the boundaries of what it is to be a wife and what it is to 'serve' in the military.

While this scholarship foregrounds the importance of social norms for military–family cohesion, less empirical work has been done to explore the precise terms through which women married to servicemen feel, make sense of, perform, embody and translate ideas about military belonging, duty and service on behalf of themselves and others. This goes further than an attempt to understand their motivations and obligations in regard to voluntary labour or the 'compelled duties' (Harrell 2001, 68) that extend to wives through certain soldiers' jobs, as I explored in the previous chapter. Women's investment in the cultural production of the regiment as a primary unit of belonging, encapsulating ideas about not only duty and service but also family ties, is a good place to start.

The regimental system takes up a culturally specific place in ideas about UK military belonging. Regimental belonging is a larger container for unit cohesion than subdivisions such as squadrons or platoons, and as such relies heavily upon cultural productions and symbolism to pull its broader community together. As the largest permanent organisational unit in the British Army,[1] regiments are expressly bound up in notions of home, roots and a kind of cultural heritage that is fiercely defended (sometimes literally, in terms of the historic influence of regimental belonging upon soldiers' willingness to go into battle[2]). Soldiers usually remain with the same regiment or corps throughout their career, such that, as stated on the National Army Museum website: 'To its soldiers, the regiment is therefore the all-important military family, providing accommodation, welfare, comradeship and a unique identity.'[3] Officers, too, retain a 'home' regiment while posted on two-year rotations or 'staff jobs' with other regiments and corps throughout their career. As I explored in the previous chapter through structures of rank, the regimental system is also freighted with legacies of class (Mansfield 2016), Christianity and monarchy rule, which are embedded in its command structure and cultural heritage (e.g. through each regiment's royal patronage). Thus, regiments are symbolic vessels of cultural patrimony in their own right, whose identity is constructed using products and performances that constitute a rich tapestry of belonging. The illustrious history and traditional nature of the regiment I was with was made repeatedly clear to me during my stay, for example. Steve, a senior soldier taking on the role of Mess Manager, explained:

> I know the history of [this regiment] like the back of my hand. You know, and when you go into that Mess and you look at the stuff that's in there – and there's so much history in there and – you can either walk past it and go 'Yeah it's just a painting', or you can actually look and think, look where we are and what we're with.

The material culture of the regiment pervades the social spaces of the camp, where the regimental crest and other insignia (such as its 'standard' or flag) can be found on anything from uniforms and cap badges to pens, keyrings, mugs, fleeces and ties. The sergeants' mess where I stayed was full of photographic portraits, honours boards, silverware and bronze figurines, all of them gifts that had been presented to the Mess by senior soldiers upon promotion to the officers' mess. In a very direct way, these material displays of regimental culture objectify soldiers' loyalty and service, as well as their personal achievements and progression through the ranks. Through such traditions senior soldiers quite literally leave their mark as part of the history they revere, and sustain the future efforts and aspirations of those they leave behind. As David French (2005) argues: 'The histories that regiments created for themselves may have smacked of antiquarianism, but the way in which they used them was anything but backward-looking' (French 2005, 83).

It is easy to trace a patriarchal line (and the securing of its future) through such traditions and rites of passage, a procession of forebears marked by silver statuettes and tankards, mounted knives and taxidermised animal parts. There is also the oral history of 'regimental legends', referring to the character and actions of former, mostly senior, personnel in a more colloquial manner, stories often focusing on their innovations in disciplining troops or playful contravention of military discipline themselves. In this sense, I often heard stories told about my own relative on camp – his progression through the ranks and occupation of key, high-profile roles within the regiment, as fatherly disciplinarian or good sport. He was pointed out to me in photographs, and people were generally full of admiration and respect. I was connected to him in such an active way, as a kind of representative of his significance to the regiment, that I myself felt the effects of his patronage as a kind of disciplinary force: to do well by him, to be polite and well brought up; not to bring his reputation into disrepute.

It is difficult to configure the growing number of servicewomen in this patrilineal production of regimental belonging. I did attend the 'dining out' of the most senior female soldier in the regiment while I was living in the Mess, who was taking voluntary redundancy. I observed an evening of practical jokes, drinking games and speeches that focused, it seemed, more on rhyming sexual innuendo than on her professional legacy as the highest-ranking female senior soldier that the regiment had seen in recent years. The homogenous demographics of the regiment concerned here, especially in regard to the low numbers of female service personnel, somewhat preclude any broader insights into the ways in which regimental traditions may be shifting with policies and practices designed to increase the gender diversity of members. Perhaps discouragingly, in relation to women married to servicemen, my analysis reveals a fundamental reliance on feminised and domesticated ideas of duty, protection and care connected to intimate and affective ideas about familial ties. But looking at the ways in which such discourses are strategically and selectively mobilised by women themselves in their assertions – and denials – of regimental identity reveals a more complex portrait of what wives seek to gain – and protect – from incorporation into regimental belonging. My argument here is not so much that regimental belonging for wives necessarily becomes deeply personal (though some women expressed that it was). Rather, my focus in this chapter is the degree to which the 'personal' is invoked as part of this professional – and deeply political – institution, through the model and mythology of the family. As in the quotation from the National Army Museum above, the family is itself a major and publicly performed mode of military belonging that goes far beyond its warm and fuzzy metaphorical function. As such, the family comes to function as a container term for many ambiguous and outlier relationships that may be harder to express or contain in overtly militarised terms, offering opportunities for women like those married to servicemen during an operational tour, to access and assert different modes of regimental identity for public recognition of their role and their relationships.

Jamie, for example, was someone I often encountered on the camp as she was employed by the regiment. As such, she was always willing and able to answer my questions about its cultural traditions and peculiarities, often with clear relish and in considerable detail:

J: Basically the short version of it is, at the Battle of Waterloo they were running out of food and supplies in the officers' mess. The officers had done the usual and binged and drunk everything in sight. So what they decided to do is, the officers and the sergeants messes would join together and share their rations. So that's where it . . . it dates back all the way to then and they still do it every year. But what happens is, the sergeants have to go and invite – all the officers wait in the Mess, and a couple of sergeants go up to the Mess and invite the officers down to the sergeants' mess, to come and join . . .

A: Oh! Sorry, so it's all of them together?

J: Yes, all together and they all go into the sergeants' mess because you can't go – you can't go into a mess higher than your own. That only happens with troopers.

A: [silence]

J: Oh, OK. Troopers can go into the corporals' mess if they've invited. I mean anyone can go into any mess if they're invited, but the rule is – that's why most events that are multi-rank, like all ranks, happen in the corporals' mess because troopers can go into the corporals' because it's not an official mess. But a corporal can't just go walk into the sergeants' mess or officers' mess, it don't work like that.

A: I never knew that, interesting, so yeah . . .

J: And then after they've eaten they play random games [. . .]

A: I've heard some stuff about it from the lads at dinner – rugby with a . . .

J: Cabbage . . .

A: Or something.

J: You know the mats in the gym? You know where you eat lunch and dinner?

A: Yes?

J: That gets padded out, it's deadly.

A: And then I guess the next morning everyone is, well . . .

J: Minging . . .

A: . . . Well, yep. And do you get to hear about it in the office?

J: Oh yes.

More than any other interview, my conversation with Jaimie, who was married to a middle-ranking soldier in the regiment, seemed to unfold in terms that were particularly instructive. Much of the interview took the form of an animated, engaging account of the regiment's quirks and traditions, each esoteric tradition or historical fact that Jaimie elaborated requiring a further layer of explanation. Jaimie demonstrated a comprehensive and affectionate knowledge of the regiment, which derived in part from her job. Throughout the interview she emphasised her privileged knowledge of and acceptance by the service personnel with whom she worked, to the degree that she perceived she had transcended her identity as a military wife: 'People generally relate to me more as Rupert's PA as such, rather than "Oh, Dylan's wife".' Jaimie was also clear about the emotional ties she had invested in the regiment, which were particularly acute at the time of our interview, just before the first group of personnel were due to return from Afghanistan.

> I work with [the senior officers] more than I see [my husband]. It's really weird 'cause I'm really excited for Sunday, for them all to come home, 'cause like, they're all my babies [. . .] if you think about it I spend more time with the boys in RHQ than I do actually with Dylan, so for me I've not just got a husband out there, I've got a whole regiment out there, 'cause I know everyone out there. Every single person down to the last trooper I know, even if I don't know them personally [. . .] it feels like I've got 400 husbands out there!

Although Jaimie might be argued to have transcended the limits of army spousehood through her employment with the regiment, her relationship with it remains couched in gendered terms of exchange. Jaimie's metaphors of mothering, nurture and marriage as a frame for expressing – and conflating – her personal and professional investments are striking. They open up the possibility of accounting for military forms of belonging in terms that go beyond masculinities and attendant formulations of homosociality (Belkin 2012, Hockey 1986), 'fratriarchy' (Higate 2012, 452) or 'mateship' (Woodward 2008, 377). Jaimie's mobilisation of ideas about wifehood, reproductive labour and nurture to articulate her position on both the inside and the outside of the military/civilian divide, indicate the importance of gender in conflicting ways. Jaimie's way of making sense of her role betrays many of the conditions through which women are marginalised as civilians in relation to military power in the first place (as 'beautiful souls' [Elshtain 1995, 3] or 'womenandchildren' [Enloe 1989, 1]). Yet it is also necessary to recognise that these gendered tropes are a crucial part of her capacity to renegotiate the meaning of her relationship to the military institution, both as her husband's, and her own, employer.

For another woman very differently positioned in relation to the regiment, the question of identity and belonging – and how to produce it, affectively, in terms of bonds within a squadron – is a project that confuses any notion of separate personal and professional duties. Annie was married to a senior officer who had taken up a staff job with the regiment in preparation for the deployment to Afghanistan, arriving in Germany six months before the deployment began ('Not long to [. . .] break into the regiment'). Her account illustrates a social field fraught with complexities and the pressure placed on them by the operational tour:

> [W]e're not [this regiment] by trade, [my husband] is [from another regiment], and I had a real struggle finding my own identity when we came [to Germany], funnily enough because I didn't feel part – it took a long time to feel part of the regiment [. . .]. So from the off, he said right we'll have the boys round, and then we'll have them round with their, we'll invite the wives as well, just have a chilli night or something at home. But interestingly the wives never came. [. . .] We had the boys round first and some of the junior ranks within [my husband's] squadron were like 'Oh, we've never been to an officer's house for drinks before', you know and 'Cheers that was really nice to come and . . .' [. . .] But um, one wife turned up other than me. And, bless her, she's someone that I wasn't surprised, with hindsight, I would have put money on it being her because she's very loyal to the, you know, she's very pro doing stuff for the regiment so she probably had a sense of duty, probably. [. . .] Anyway, it was more to flush the wives out so I knew who I was . . . We knew that the guys were going on tour and it was a safety net, I wanted to kind of meet these girls before they went. And I appreciated that quite a lot of them work during the day so I'm never going to meet them at coffee, and I tried to organise a night out in town because I thought, well, that's neutral and maybe they were scared to come to the house, which you can be, so I thought, well, we'll organise a night out in town. A few people came then but, again, basically the ones that I knew anyway. [. . .] You know I think there's a kind of unwritten – which doesn't necessarily make me in charge of those women but – I thought I don't want to have to turn up on someone's doorstep to do anything – and it be the first time I've met them. So from a purely um – just curiosity – I wanted them to know who I was and just to put a face to a name and, again, to sort of help [my husband] in a sense so that you know, he got the men on side you know. Here was someone coming in from another regiment, they might have been a bit 'Uh, well, he's not [from this regiment]'.

The regimental system provides both Annie and her husband – using the collective pronoun 'we' – with a sense of their institutional origins (their identity 'by trade'). Yet the professional obligation to break or blend into new regiments in time for particular postings or operational tours betrays the flexibility expected of men and women moving through the organisational structure, like officer ranks frequently do. This is a useful reminder that regimental belonging is acquired, not innate. What also emerges from Annie's efforts here is the functional argument that undergirds regimental belonging and enhances its disciplinary effects. Though Annie frames her efforts in terms of support for her partner's work, or 'just curiosity', the operational tour and the risks it entails are clear in her motivations. While she is reluctant to assert any formal authority 'over' the wives 'in' her husband's squadron, her many efforts to bring them together betray the sense of responsibility she feels, and her own personal anticipation of a moment where she may be expected to 'turn up on someone's doorstep' and offer support in the case of the death or injury of their husband. The conditions of exception that mark an operational tour shape the ways in which many of the power dynamics I have explored throughout this book are sensed and made sense of at particular times. I will return to the temporal specificity of these experiences later in this chapter. What Annie's sense of duty and responsibility shows in the meantime is that the imperative to 'belong' in certain ways, according to certain criteria, and at particular times, is constantly in flux.

Jaimie's experience, in contrast to Annie's, illustrates some of the ways in which women also exploit or refute particular conventions of authority and belonging in relation to the regiment. It is here that the experiences of women married to servicemen have the potential to trouble the categories through which military command is assumed to operate. Military wives' flexible position on the edges of regimental belonging confound and confuse the 'creation of insider and outsider categories' (Higate and Cameron 2006, 224) that is central to a regiment's disciplinary power, particularly in relation to the divide between military and civilian spheres. Jaimie's mobile positionality, for example, enables her to construct her own alternative relationship to the regiment, based expressly on her status as a civilian. This is a salient aspect of her professional competency working as she does in an outward-facing role dealing with the spouses of personnel. Here, Jaimie's status as a 'civvy' eases the tension and provides a 'friendly face'. At the same time, her civilian status also enables her to opt out of the regiment's hierarchical ethos:

> J: Like when [the Commanding Officer] first turned up it's like 'Yes, Colonel, no, Colonel', you know blah blah blah whatever. But

> now, it's like [he] comes in and [. . .] he'll say like, 'Can you make
> me a brew?' and I'll be like 'How many you had today?! Do you
> think I've got all the time in the world to stand here and make you
> brews?' And you know, you just have a joke and a laugh with them
> so instead of them being your boss, it's like . . .
> A: Well you just grow a nice working relationship, don't you?
> J: Yeah, but like some of the wives don't understand that, 'cause they're
> like [. . .] 'You can't talk to the Colonel like that.' I'm like – he's a
> *person*!
> A: But you're not in the Army as well, like . . .
> T: Exactly! It's like, he's a *person*, he's – yes he is the Colonel, yes he is
> kind of my boss, but . . . I'm not going to treat him any different to
> how I'm going to treat a normal friend or colleague.

Jaimie's manoeuvres bring her close to the experience of an 'out-sider within' (Hill Collins 2004. 103), crossing the boundaries into regimental HQ as a civilian with privileged access, to occupy a position that is deeply entwined with her role as a wife who also has a professional investment in the regiment as her place of work. As such, Jaimie might be argued to occupy a position that, although in many ways subordinate, enables her to perceive and articulate the absurdities of regimental hierarchy in a way that can speak truth to power, albeit only in small, everyday practices of rebellion: by at least joking with the Colonel about the cup of tea that it is her pseudo-domestic role to make, she turns it into an act of her own generosity, care and goodwill rather than an order or obligation. Yet, at the same time, Jaimie's status is also subject to the vicissitudes of multiple and intersecting boundary lines, as is shown when she explains her complicated relationship with the wives of senior offi-cers. Here, too, Jaimie must negotiate the terms of her subordination and carve out room to manoeuvre among others who expect her to uphold the formal conventions of rank:

> I work with so many different ranks from the troopers all the way
> up, to even the Brigadier when he comes in, you know so I know so
> many different wives, but some wives look at me as if to say, 'Oh,
> she's a corporal's wife talking to an officer – officer's wife' [. . .] And
> you'll get people like [senior officers' wives] who think that me, I
> work for them!'

Jaimie's ideas about her place within the regiment, but also what others misguidedly expect of her, perhaps betrays the flip side to

Annie's sense of responsibility and some sense of why her efforts to bring people together might have failed. As Annie herself conceded:

> Well, here there is [pause] . . . a very noticeable level of you know . . . you're [. . .] supposed to be 'part of the family', but . . . there is an '[XX] family', and within that family there is very noticeably a rank structure.

Both women's negotiations are forged through multiple aspects of their social personhood interacting with the structures and ideologies of regimental belonging. From the cultural capital (Skeggs 1997, 8) Jaimie accrues when sharing her knowledge with me about regimental history and rituals, to her affective investment in the regiment's soldiers through the metaphor of mothering, as well as her disavowal of the regiment's rank structure, Jaimie's positionality is constructed in a way that is incredibly fluid yet dense at the same time. Negotiating multiple divisions around military/civilian, rank and class here, undergirded by Jaimie's own identity as a cisgender, white, heterosexual woman and, thus, her alignment with the norms of the community, she nevertheless mobilises different aspects of her positionality to variously and strategically opt out of, or acquiesce to, the social relations that seek to push and pull her in different directions.

Looking at regimental belonging through the lens of military wives' experiences in this way proposes something more complex about how 'unit cohesion' works through ideas and assertions about gender. My findings show how institutional identities and affiliations are made and remade through informal cultural and social practices that coalesce around gender and sexuality in many surprising ways (Wool 2015b). What my analysis in this chapter reveals about the British Army regiment at the centre of this study is the degree to which it is culturally and socially reproduced through marriage and the family as a model and metaphor that encapsulates the normalising intensity of its disciplinary will to power.

Far from merely an organisational structure embellished with antiquarian symbolism, the British Army regiment comes with a will to cohesion that converts the public institution into a private concern, investing formal structures with intimacy and emotion, turning professional duties into ones that are conjugal. It is not surprising, therefore, that the regiment and the family converge in the hybrid category of the 'regimental family'. My analysis of the relationship between the military and the family here goes in a different direction from sociological understandings of greedy institutions (Segal 1986; Vuga and

Juvan 2013) to centralise instead the affective ties of the conjugal couple who are positioned between them. It is in the hybridisation of regimental and family belonging that social cohesion is forged, and the commitment of wives and their husbands is secured.

The Regimental Family

The material and symbolic role of the family both as a social unit and as a metaphor is threaded throughout the history of the British regimental system (see French 2005). Like family metaphors found in the biographies of military 'father-figures' (Jervis 2011, 31), the idea of the family regiment represents a mixture of discipline and benevolence. Family belonging thus becomes a central model for the kind of affective bonds, heritage, cultural lineage and generational commitment that the regiment uses to package and describe its own will to cohesion and community, and its role in soldiers' lives. Many times during my stay in Germany, I heard the regiment described as a 'family regiment'. Often, this idea expressed the small size of the regiment and its close-knit community, but it was also explained to me in various other terms. These included connections to British upper-class family lineage[4] on the one hand, or a more paternalistic tradition of raising wayward youths on the other; of sons following illustrious forebears to command the regiment as their grandfathers had done, or of the regiment rescuing multiple brothers in the same family from a deprived area of the UK. But the idea of the regiment being a 'family regiment' was also used as a way of declaring a progressive, liberal and forward-thinking approach to family welfare or the regiment's status as a family-friendly employer. Christopher, a middle-ranking DE officer, contended that family policies in the Army compared favourably to the conditions he had experienced while working in the private sector:

> On the flip side the Army – because it's [. . .] so family orientated, I think it's much more understanding when you have to leave to go look after your daughter or something [. . .] Or you know, just sitting in the office while you work and stuff [. . .] so you know all those negative things, the flip side is it's really family friendly and you can do that, you can bring your daughter in and people are understanding.

Family life was certainly a very palpable part of the regiment's day-to-day operations, and was highly visible in the spaces of the camp and as part of people's public lives and identities. Children and pets often played around the camp or in a family room equipped with a ball-pit and gaming consoles, for example. The welfare office organised regular events and activities for children (including baking sessions in the camp's kitchens and a trip to Disneyland Paris, although this was disappointingly undersubscribed). Especially after the return of the regiment from Afghanistan, wives popped in with babies in tow and fathers returned home for lunch or in time to read bedtime stories. During one lunch-hour, a high-ranking officer temporarily lost his young daughter in a game of hide-and-seek, whereupon most of the welfare office were ordered to join in the suddenly more serious search. In such ways, the conditions for the mutual incorporation and conflation of family and regimental life as encouraged in policy recommendations (Bourg and Segal 1999) might be argued to be ideal. Both men and women's family responsibilities, many of them complicated at different times by aspects of distance or separation, were permitted generous physical and discursive presence in regimental life. The family-friendliness of the regiment must be qualified, however. It is difficult to imagine a junior soldier losing his daughter during a game of hide-and-seek on camp, for example, or anyone but a senior officer being able to send a young lieutenant out with the order that he spend half an hour throwing pine cones across the parade ground for his dog to chase. Likewise, although many wives would concede that children were accommodated in many areas of regimental life, the giddy performance of fatherhood on camp is undergirded by motherhood at home. Multiple women cited their inability to go out in the evenings without checking first with their husbands for childcare, compared to the assumption that they were automatically available to babysit on occasions when their husbands were mandated to attend social functions in the Mess on a compulsory basis.

There is a distinction between the notion of the a 'family regiment' according to any of the policies or practices above, however, and the notion of the 'regimental family'. This latter formulation, appending the word 'family' to the regiment's acronym, as in 'The XX Family', is a wilful expansion of the regiment's terms of belonging. It is this proprietorial model of family life, the one where the family is the noun that is described – defined – by the adjective 'regimental' (like 'regimental mascot', 'regimental colours', 'regimental duties') that I am interested in exploring here. The regimental family, in this more proprietorial sense, emerges as a deliberate cultural production, an invocation to belong in a particular way.

One particular event towards the end of my fieldwork illustrates a lot about the ways in which the regimental family is produced and publicly performed, but is also structured by divisions and inequalities that result in tension and disappointment. On a scorching-hot day in early summer, the regiment held its 'medals day' parade, where soldiers marched round the parade ground in full regalia watched by an audience of wives, girlfriends, children and some visiting parents. Speeches were given and honours awarded while soldiers swayed with hangovers in the heat. After the parade, the welfare office had organised a 'families' day barbecue', which had been set up on the playing fields next to the camp. There was a large marquee with food stalls, a PA system for music, a children's entertainer, multiple bouncy castles, inter-squadron tugs-of-war and a free raffle with prizes including a brand-new vacuum cleaner. The regiment's new shop was also represented, having rearranged a choice selection of toys, scented candles and clothing under the sweltering canopy of a khaki tent. The event, it seemed, was supposed to have a distinctly 'off-duty' feel: there were crowds of families and their friends occupying picnic tables and groups of junior troopers standing at makeshift bars. Young officers, tired from the ladies' night dinner the previous evening, clumped together lethargically at the edge of the field, while women married to older officers sat on chairs with babies and dogs sleeping in the shade of the trees. Still further out, in a far corner, was a small group of Fijian families. In the welfare office the next day, some of us were discussing how it all went, as I noted in my field diary:

> [One of the staff] also suggests that perhaps they should have done one of those social mixer games where people hand out cards and have to match up with a pair to get to know each other. Mild weariness as [they] ask if I noticed that all the officers sat in a crowd right at the opposite end of the field to where the majority of the people were. When I said I had noticed, and that the Fijians were also all sitting apart, [someone] quickly said, 'Yes but that's just cultural difference.'

People's struggles to perform regimental belonging without slipping into the easy and familiar groupings of rank, class or ethnic belonging here betray the emotional labour (Hochschild 1983) that a regiment requires to reproduce itself. Given the performance of leisure that the families' day barbecue promoted, the staff's expectation that people should socialise together in a prescribed way, and in a way that benefits the organisational coherence of the regiment, is somewhat ironic. Such mixed messages show that the regiment's will to social cohesion can be confusing and contradictory. While the event was packaged as a sociable, relaxed affair, one of its functional objectives as explained to me the following day was for officers to mingle informally with 'their men' and get to know their families – a reconnection that was seen as particularly important in reuniting platoons and restoring equilibrium after soldiers' scattered retreat into Post-Operational Tour Leave. As platoon leaders, the young officers in particular were viewed to have failed in their professional responsibility to transcend divisions of rank and mingle with their soldiers' families (a responsibility which, ironically, comes with rank and associated ideas of classed etiquette and cultural competence). What staff at the welfare office had expected from the officers on families' day, was in fact the suspension of their own social groupings in favour of a continuation of their working relationships, though on more personal, familial terms – not, in the end, a transcendence of rank at all, but an upholding of it; a reproduction of the regiment's social structures and hierarchies, and the extraction of a kind of emotional labour by stealth. In many ways, the event failed in its functional objectives because the community *did* suspend formalities for the day, and with it the obligation to mix, retreating instead into comfortable groups to speak their own language, relax in their common backgrounds, and opt out of the effort to perform their professional duties. In the end, the only members of the community mingling were the children playing musical chairs. Even here, to the disillusionment of the welfare staff, there were complaints that the children's entertainer had failed to entertain *all* of the children *all* of the time.

These cracks on the surface of belonging reveal the regimental family in all its fragile constructedness and, moreover, the failure of its ideals. The regimental family, like many families, is comprised of tired, moody or recalcitrant members who just want to be left alone with their friends, like teenagers called down from their bedrooms to say hello to an aunt. Under the social stewardship of the officer class, the regimental family also emerges as a bourgeois production based on enforced fun and compelled duties, fraught with rules, social conventions and filial obligations: one moment 'join in'; the next, 'family hold back'. In this, the regimental family is fiercely aspirational, and it is this aspiration, the sheer force of its will to social cohesion felt, and thwarted, on occasions like the families' day barbecue, that reveals its failure to live up to projected ideas. The starkest division visible on the day, at least according to the dispersal of people across social space, remains the division between the families of Fijian personnel and the rest of the regiment. Yet this was wilfully flattened and naturalised under the banner of permissible cultural difference[5] in the post-rationalisation of the event by welfare staff. While overt, spatialised divisions of rank were suddenly considered inappropriate at the families' day barbecue, ethnicity and race are such visible and naturalised markers of intractable otherness excused by clichés of 'cultural difference' that the resulting divisions are unquestioningly accepted, waved away, wilfully unseen. Perhaps, indeed, it is because these differences are perceived as so self-evident, are so naturalised through cultural conceptions of racial and ethnic difference, that they invite a kind of pre-emptive surrender, a white flag of resignation, the division, across so many divisions, that people cannot fathom how to cross in any meaningful sense.

But perhaps these failures aren't so surprising. Because the institution of the family itself, of course, is also a cultural production, requires making and remaking from its genealogical roots, is a hierarchical, disciplinary structure subject to the fallibility, in practice, of collective identity and belonging. Any quick account of the ontological, day-to-day work of a family welfare officer within the regiment testifies to the degree to which family formations in the Armed Forces are, as in society more broadly, varied and multiple. There are step-families and multigenerational households, families split by divorce or distance, with some spouses choosing to stay in the UK (giving rise to administrative categories such as those soldiers who are classed as 'married unaccompanied', and live in the mess). There is, in the sense of this multiplicity, no singular, authoritative ontological reality of being a family 'in' the military, and it is important not to mistake the ideals and structures of the family as a model for anything resembling a uniform or universal experience. As in civilian life, also, our will to belong to one another in family formations – a possessive, sometimes oppressive bond – bends and often breaks under the pressure of human relationships. The hybrid form of the regimental family reflects this very reality, even as it aspires to alternative ideals.

The connections I have explored go beyond conceptualisations of the military and the family as 'greedy institutions' (Segal 1986; Vuga and Juvan 2013), not only because they demonstrate mutual imbrication as well as antagonism, as others have argued (Bourg and

Segal 1999), and not simply because I include the experiences of women married to servicemen (French et al. 2005). The gendered norms, discourses and feelings through which people's belonging is socially produced and performed illustrates the complexity of social relations as they blur the distinction between civil and military, public and private. The gender relations I have explored also counter and expand the terms for research on gender norms as delineated by the study of military masculinities. The practices I explore indicate a wealth of terrain for the exploration of gender and the military that foregrounds the family not as a supplementary or derivative sphere of influence, but as co-constitutive of military social relations and culture, as well as the identities of service personnel and spouses alike. I have explored the material and metaphoric connection between the family and the regiment here in ways that are arguably more realistic than ideals of both forms of belonging purport. Like the family as a unit of social organisation, the regiment is a production fraught with the pressures of proximity and belonging, the meting out of discipline and care, multiple vectors of power and inequality, and emotional labour forged by conflicting desires. In the next part of this book, I want to take these ideas about the role of the family and the regiment in people's lives and connect them to another 'imagined community' (Anderson 1991), that of the nation.

Genealogies of Regimental Belonging

As I have shown, hybrid discourses of family and regimental belonging emerge as an important sphere where social cohesion is strived for and the value of military service is negotiated. In the next part of this chapter, I want to look at what this means for the connection between military service, the state and citizenship as refracted through the cultural symbolism of regimental belonging and its link to national identity. The regiment with which I was based took seriously its national and regional affiliations within the UK and was heavily invested in the cultural work involved in sustaining them. Many regiments in the British Army boast histories that have tied them to particular regions of the UK for hundreds of years.[6] The genealogy of the regiment in question was deeply connected to a particular part of the UK with a distinct national and regional identity, from which the regiment historically drew many of its recruits. The localism of these networks was clear in the succession of brothers, twins, fathers and sons who followed one another into the regiment, and the fact that many of the regiment's soldiers hailed from roughly the same geographic region, producing a degree of cultural homogeneity. The regiment retained a large barracks and HQ in its home town, which was also the location of the regimental museum. This was the location to which the whole regiment 'returned' for its homecoming parade, as detailed in Chapter 2, and the place where soldiers were periodically sent to fundraise for the regiment, for example selling wristbands or remembrance poppies at stalls outside supermarkets or on the high street, which simultaneously reinforces the visibility of the Army as a local employer.

The cultural symbolism through which this conflation of regimental and national belonging is reinforced emerges in elements of the regiment's visual and material culture from flags and colours, through to the animal adopted as their mascot and the celebration of national holidays with special events. While these nationalistic elements draw careful boundaries around belonging in one sense, it is important to acknowledge that the materialisation of national identity in such ways, much like the material culture of the sergeants' mess, arguably makes it more accessible to those who have less of a direct claim to its specific constitutive power, but can appropriate and adapt its many forms to their own use. Jacquelyn, for example, a Fijian woman married to one of the regiment's handful of F&C personnel, explains her own translation of regimental belonging, which is refracted through a public performance of her own cultural identity as well as, but also as distinct from, the regiment's:

A: What is 'doing your bit'?

J: As in, if there's an event like the families' event they had last year, we try our best [. . .] We did a fundraising [event]. The Fijian families [from] the [regiment], we put in 30 euros each and we bought all the food, did the earth oven *lovo* thingy [and] gave [the food] out. We got about 400 euros; we gave it to SSAFA [Soldiers', Sailors', and Airmen's Families Association] as our contribution.

A: And is that also an important thing for you to do – is there lots of organising between the Fijian families?

J: I think we stick together [within] a regiment, yeah. As in for us it's a small regiment, we live our own individual family life, but if there's something that crops up that we need the whole crew to be part of, yeah the guys just spread the word and that's us.

A: Do you feel like a member of [the regiment], like regiment and traditions?

J: I would say I'm not very good at observing traditions. I know they do the St Patrick's Day or something, which I have no . . . I mean I know I've done research on the computer and read through a whole page of what St Patrick's mean and what not, but I think I don't really pay much attention with that. I do the bit that they require my help with or if there are events I try and show my appreciation as attending events, and um, popping into welfare now and again.

It is 'national culture' as a signifier that Jacquelyn adapts to offer her own identity in lieu of, or in an equivalent gesture, to the British history and traditions of the regiment. In Jacquelyn's account, the instrumentalisation of Fijian culture in respect of the regiment's demand for inclusivity and cultural representation is matched by her strategic deployment of it as a way to 'do her bit'. While Jacquelyn's Fijian cultural production satisfies the regiment's demand that its F&C personnel and their families are seen to 'belong' in a way that is consistent with the 'multiculturalisation' of the British Army (Ware 2012, 262), there is also a sense in which this somewhat superficial engagement frees Jacquelyn from anything more than a functional engagement by return. This is tellingly illustrated in her mistaking the regiment's national holiday for another nation's cultural celebration. Any ideological investment Jacquelyn might perform for the regiment is countered by her own matter-of-fact declaration of interest: 'I just know the people who I need to know – sort of need to know basis – welfare and the facilities they provide, whatever I need to use, that's about it.'

The functional approach implied by Jacquelyn's motivations is further complicated when other investments around ethnicity and national belonging are considered. These help to deconstruct the cultural homogeneity upon which cohesion among the (majority-white, British) community is assumed to be based. Towards the end of the operational tour, the welfare office began to arrange Sunday afternoon craft sessions for soldiers' spouses and their children. At these times, women came to the camp's family room to make 'welcome home' banners out of bed sheets supplied by the Quarter Master's stores. Of all the events for families that I observed during deployment, these sessions were the best attended, attracting women from different social groups whom I had not observed socialising together previously. Very soon in the creative endeavour, smaller groups of friends and acquaintances formed to produce separate banners and allocate tasks between themselves. Although ostensibly an activity for children, the event was attended by a couple of women who did not have children and some banners were worked on almost exclusively by wives. Following a debate about the colour of some lettering among one group, someone pointed out the lack of representation for soldiers of a particular nationality on the banner. As the regiment has its origins in one country within the UK, the banner was somewhat dominated by a very large national symbol pertaining to that country. Some women pointed out that their husbands weren't of that nationality, and that it wouldn't be right if their national symbol wasn't also represented. Separate national flags were considered before someone suggested that the Union Jack might do the job, although it was considered too difficult to paint and not sufficient to redress the representational bias. In the end, it was decided that the national flower of the missing nation would be added above the somewhat strikingly rendered symbol *and* national flower, of the dominant one.

The banner painting was a surprising occasion for tensions between national and ethnic belonging to emerge. After all, it had brought together a wide range of women based on their shared experience of the deployment, transcending usual divisions of class and rank, although the social groupings that formed within this soon reflected these differences. Only one F&C person attended this event and worked on a banner with her two children alone. As an example of wives' own materialisation of regimental culture, the banners are interesting for the alternative systems of meaning that they represent. Many of the other signs and symbols through which the value of duty and service was expressed pertained to the idea of soldiers not as citizens serving a nation state but as family men. These were expressed through sentiments such as 'daddy my hero' and 'welcome home daddies', further personalised by pink paper hearts and children's handprints. This personalisation of military service and its reformulation in the emotive terms of soldiers' role as fathers raises the possibility of an alternative interpretation of national and ethnic belonging. Contrary to the idea of national identity as an overarching framework that foregrounds the relationship of soldiers to the state and makes this discourse a foundation of regimental pride and duty, the banners portray a kind of family tree comprising ethnic origins, naturalised symbolism and the pre-military idea of where an individual soldier is 'from', such that might be represented (and is also feminised) by a national flower rather than a flag, for example. In this public expression of the meaning of military service created by wives, national identity emerges as something that precedes or predates the co-optation of a soldier's labour by the military institution and its prescriptions about serving the nation and regimental affiliation. No matter the national identity of the regiment as a whole, the women whose families came from different parts of the UK were insistent on having their diverse and particular origins represented. Here, nation and ethnicity come to stand for a kind of belonging that is expressly pre-military, through which people can be argued to renegotiate the terms of their investment in the regiment as something that is also bound up with personal, and not only institutional, histories. Like 'mateship' (Woodward 2008, 375), these familial modes of belonging illustrate 'just how contested and negotiated the idea of military service as citizenship is' (Woodward 2008, 379).

The example of the banner painting can also be argued to represent women's elision and evasion of the will to regimental belonging. If the regiment as a cultural production can often appear somewhat overdetermined, this is perhaps reflective of its false coherence as a collective. Arguably, such 'backstage' (Scott 1985, 287) moments as the banner painting, and the small cracks of dissent and ridicule that they reveal, reflect the vibrations of people's manoeuvres within the bounds of a total institution (Goffman 1961). In place of regimental belonging, the women creating their own cultural artefacts asserted the individuality of the soldier with a personal history of his own, their own privileged defence of and role in that history, as well the centrality of both the nuclear and the extended family to the meanings and motivations behind military service. This can be read as a strategy of self-affirmation (Woodward 2008, 377) by asserting the primacy of family ties over military forms of belonging and kinship. Such discourses reach the zenith of their institutional and political function in the work women do to translate the job of soldiering into terms that are liveable for families on a day-to-day basis. It is at this point that what might be described as practices of personalisation, which reframe the meaning of soldiering as a form of labour and reclaim it from the regiment, are paradoxically used to rationalise the deployment of its human resources in the production of state-sanctioned violence. In the rest of this chapter, I begin to explore these connections in more detail, between the affective bonds and social ties through which the regimental family is held (tenuously) together, and the conditions of exception that test them during an operational tour.

Absorbing Shock and Sustaining Awe

One of the primary tasks that military wives maintain during the tour is the necessity of translating the job of soldiering and the absence of fathers into a form that is palatable and comprehensible to children. Not only do such discourses draw on particular ideas about masculinity, fatherhood and soldiering, they are also helped (or hindered) by the ready socialisation of children according to gender norms, as Francesca elaborates:

> I think, speaking to my friend whose husband is away and has a boy the same age as Tessa, [. . .] he's into guns and stuff like that and he knows Dad carries a gun, where I say he's helping children to go to school, you know to protect them to go to school, to make everyone happy and get rid of the bad people because they can't go to school if the bad people are on the street.

As well as ideas about masculinity, femininity and violence as they are used to mark divisions between mothers, fathers, girls and boys, the narratives adapted and circulated by wives also depend on a range of well-worn, public discourses of contemporary, globalised warfare. This includes the image of soldiers as peacekeepers or the framework of humanitarian intervention as analysed by scholars such as Claire Duncanson (2009). Jacquelyn, for example, draws on ideas of international peacekeeping that derive from her Fijian background, through which she undertakes a selective translation of the meaning of her husband's 'national' service:

> They do ask questions about guns and what Daddy's doing. I felt from my point of view to explain to the boys what he's doing – I explain to them the other side is in the peacekeeping manner; that what Daddy's doing is more like peacekeeping, trying to keep the peace, rather than getting their head into [. . .] this whole war thing. [. . .] What I understand as growing up in Fiji is what the Fijian soldiers normally do when they go Lebanon, Sinai, it's always called the peacekeeping forces. So I thought that would be better explaining to them rather than thinking of them as a war as in 'a war'.

Jacquelyn's narrative permits an outward-looking, globalist humanitarian worldview that can be aligned with Kuus's (2009, 558) formulation of 'globalist militarism', as well as providing a counternarrative to the history and reputation of the British Army as a war-fighting machine. At the same time, her narrative serves to reassert the Fijian national identity of her family and disassociate her husband's labour from national service as constituted through British military identity (and, presumably, the colonial history that contributes to Fiji's commonwealth status and thus, ironically, the broader determinants of her husband's recruitment).

These examples reveal an active process of translation in women's discursive (re)construction of their husbands' identities as soldiers and fathers, which mediate between political and personal justifications for their implication in state violence. Given the fragility of the boundaries that women struggle to uphold, it is perhaps not surprising that there is a degree of narrative slippage between soldiering and paternal labour expressed in the trope that fathers are overseas protecting other children from harm. Most often, such statements were made by women with reference to the solider not by his name, nor as 'my husband', but as 'daddy', for example: 'She knew that her daddy was still out there looking after little children and keeping them safe.' When repeated in a conversation between adults, the mother's use of a child's phrasing works in the gap between the story told for children and the political reality that is left hanging in the air above it, a knowing disparity or dissonance that it is implicitly the mother's burden to bear. Such narratives are heavily loaded with ideas about duty, sacrifice and heroism that are integral to representations of the role of the Armed Forces in contemporary British society. Importantly, they also serve to incorporate the duty and sacrifice of the entire nuclear family. The father is deployed as the modern humanitarian actor, literally transferring his paternal labour to children who are less fortunate than his own. The deficit of care created by his absence from home is in turn absorbed by the mother. Children are also given a role in this narrative, in a formulation of soldiering that elevates the notion of self-sacrifice not only on the father's part, but also on the part of the child who is willing to give him up so that another child can benefit from his care. It is interesting, however, that the transferral of paternal labour is not seen to be at odds with images and ideas about the physical and technical prowess of the British soldier in contemporary combat operations, as Laura explains:

So you know, Daddy helps them go to school. That's how I've explained it, not that Daddy carries a gun. She's got pictures of him in uniform, where he hasn't got a gun. I know he's got a pistol to the side of him but she doesn't know that, but he's in his helmet and his glasses and his body armour.

As evidenced by the photograph of the hyper-technologised, well-equipped soldier (but with his gun hidden), families are proficient in creating the myth of awe without the shock.

The translations and conversions that women undertake are invested in making sense of the labour of soldiering, especially the violence and vulnerability this labour potentiates. These examples demonstrate the everyday struggle to reconcile the peculiar global and political status of the military institution and its state-sanctioned role in the production of violence, with soldiering – as well as parenthood – as a form of everyday labour. What these examples show is that the realm of the family is far from insulated against these geopolitical determinants of military power, the making of particular histories and the moral legacies they bear:

> Pete says people brag about things in the Mess. He said those things happen, but it's not a thing to big up in the Mess, you know, 'I'm such a hard person.' You know I . . . I quite agree on that. Because obviously [our daughter] as well, when she grows up, he said well actually she might think 'Dad's a murdering bastard' [laughs]. Yeah, you know – Afghan in years to come [. . .] the whole thing could change around, like us Brits and the Americans were really bad and we shouldn't have gone into Afghan, you know? And then if she sort of knows that, I think as she gets older . . . He said, 'Yeah, I was in Afghanistan but I don't want her to know those things.' He said: 'It's not for little girls' ears and not for my daughter to know that things happened over there that she might disagree with and not like me for in years to come.'

These narratives reveal the false innocence of the scripts surrounding soldiering, as well as the kind of discourses entailed in reconciling (or at least smoothing over) the confusing and contradictory relationship between the national family, the regimental family and the nuclear family. Women's narratives show how ideas and ideals about the family, and in particular its preservation and protection, have to be propped up and patched over again and again. People struggle to keep things clean and distinct but they often merge: soldiers are fathers, soldiers are fighters. Families attempt to secure some space, create some distance, prepare for the future, yet different forms of insecurity so frequently combine and collapse. As is clear from these same scripts, ideas about gender are recruited in the service of strengthening these fragile and failing boundaries – ideas about dads and little girls, about women's work, resilience and the burden of translation, all of it part of the work of normalisation.

The acknowledgement of the violence of soldiering in many of these narratives connects them to the broader sense in which Cowen and Gilbert (2008, 263), writing in the context of 9/11 in the USA, have argued that trauma as a national event 'is made interchangeable with familial grief'. Critical research on military power post-9/11 in countries such as the USA, Canada and the UK has illuminated the growing significance of the family as a *model and metaphor* for political relations' (Cowen and Gilbert 2008, 266; emphasis in original). As I have explored in this chapter, the family might be viewed as a twinned institution working alongside the military to replicate and reproduce the norms upon which both depend, from the micro to the macro scale. It is right to explore these dynamics in the explicit terms of the militarisation of the family, which illuminates the depths to which military power penetrates everyday life. And yet, like the pre-military meanings of national identity asserted by wives in their banner-painting, the family also emerges as a site of potential resistance. If military power is knowingly understood by families as spilling over, turning bad, turning-out-to-have-been-wrong, then the production of ideas about the stable, heteronormative nuclear family through some of the gendered tropes I have explored can also be viewed as a kind of pre-emptive defence. As a site for the deconstruction of military power, the nuclear family opens up the possibility that it can in part be defused, decommissioned. This might manifest itself in acts of discursive translation such as I have explored here, working always within the gaps between formal protocol, the official line, and the interpretative possibilities of representation. But the sphere of the nuclear family is also productive of a useful kind of pragmatism, a sense of everyday continuation, regeneration and reproduction that is driven by the labour of women married to servicemen in everyday life. This might be configured in negative terms as a retreat into the private sphere, a denial or depoliticisation, or even a societal ill – a kind of individualism that runs counter to the collective demands of the regiment and traditional ideas of duty and national service. Alternatively, the family becomes a resource for survival. It is to these more concentrated moments of threat, fear and relief that I turn in the final part of this chapter, looking at some particular examples of women's experiences throughout the duration of the operational tour as it unfolded during my fieldwork. Here I want to bring some of the socio-spatial analysis I have used throughout this book, to bear on the domestic sphere and the everyday spaces of 'home' that are so frequently posited as being preserved and protected from the threat of war while soldiers are 'away'.

Homecoming

In the analysis that follows, I explore the different registers of place and time that constitute an operational tour for military families, and the feelings that circulate through them. As such, the rest of this chapter is about the contrasting ways in which absence and presence, place and time, are felt. As articulated by the senior NCO Steve, who had seen numerous tours to Iraq and Afghanistan but had not been deployed this time round, many of these feelings about being away crystallise around the event of return:

> [I]f you're a soldier from the UK you'll fly back there and it's not just going to be your wife and kids, it's going to be your whole family that greet you. And that's really overwhelming and that's when you get the whole emotional side of life. Whereas here, you step off that plane, onto that bus, and you've got nothing waiting – you've got [someone] in a welfare office [. . .] with [monotone voice] 'Here's-a-burger, here's-a-beer, well-done-welcome-back-you-hero'. All well and good, but there's no emotion there, even for the married couples you know. When I come back from tour I would love my father to be there, to say 'Well done, you're a hero in my eyes', to make me feel a little bit . . . because my wife and children will always make me feel good when I'm down, or they will always respect anything I do, but I – and I love that – but I want it from somebody else, does that make sense? [When] you go back to UK [later], you can't break down to everybody, can you? 'Cause it's gone, that emotional bit has gone, it's like, 'Oh well, I'm glad you're back, last week.'

The regiment's troops returned gradually from Afghanistan towards the end of my fieldwork. Their return was staggered, each squadron arriving separately via a lengthy journey from forward operating bases to larger installations within Afghanistan, then to Cyprus for a period of 'normalisation' and from there on to Germany. Homecomings, when the soldiers finally arrived at the camp, were a curious mix of public spectacle and private emotion, of absence turning into presence, of relief shadowed by grief.

I attended several homecomings during my time in Germany and each one seemed to be an oddly condensed mixture of contradictory forces and feelings. Death and survival were both curiously present, and it was difficult not to think of the two servicemen who had been killed during the tour. My field diary records my impressions of the scene:

> A false start when the baggage lorry arrives and unpacks the camouflage rucksacks, helmets and flak jackets without the soldiers. A vague image of absence or death sneaks into my perception. Or something uncomfortable – the kit without the solider inside it. Hannah is showing me how her camera works as she asked me if I would mind taking some photos. I feel slightly odd about this as it filters my spectatorship of these intimate events through a looking machine that makes the voyeuristic feeling worse. I think that's how I feel – like I'm hanging round on the edge of other people's emotions, turning up to get a rush of sentimentality. It is very much spectating – the vast parade ground, standing at the edge on the grass, keeping a distance except today, when taking photos. [. . .] Every time I watch a homecoming it leaves me with some homesickness and an excess of direction-less emotion, a relief with no object I suppose.

In such a way, an imaginary of grief haunts homecomings, the constitutive other to the palpable sense of relief that was also present, feelings confirmed by the sentiments of some of the women I spoke to during the anxious wait for the coach to arrive, again from my field diary:

> Tricia commented that the last tour when she welcomed her husband back, she couldn't help thinking of another woman from the regiment who had lost her husband.

Eventually, tired men and women in desert camouflage greeted their loved ones (or not – many of the young soldiers and officers did not have family members present), who were waiting in new clothes holding up banners and homemade flags. Some women acknowledged that the public performance of homecomings was mainly for the benefit of the children, whose excitement did seem to provide a less anxious energy as they chased the coach and were lifted onto fathers' shoulders. Most families left as soon as they could, after kit had been registered and returned, with wives insisting that the real homecoming was arriving at their house, where many had also hung banners or prepared food and gifts. As Steven's perspective makes clear, homecomings represent the accumulation of many desires – not only the desire of husbands and wives to be together again but also a range of desires and expectations based on the recognition of a soldier's labour in very particular terms (war, heroism, the nation, fathers and sons). As is also indicated by Steven's account, home-comings are also viewed as a public site for emotion itself ('[When] you go back to UK [later], you can't break down to everybody, can you? 'Cause it's gone, that emotional bit has gone'). There is the expectation that emotions be forthcoming, expressed, unambiguous, fulfilled. Homecomings were so longed for, the focus of months of anticipation, weeks of counting down, that the moment of physical arrival almost collapsed under the weight of expectation: the banners illegible, the weather grey, everything suddenly parochial, couples bashful. It is these complex, spectral dynamics of anticipation and relief, hope, desire and disappointment, fear and love, that haunt the operational tour, and which I want to pursue further in the rest of my analysis.

A major part of my approach to understanding how military power is sensed and made sense of in this book has been to explore the socio-spatial dynamics of women's location in Germany. A fur-ther 'zone' that emerges from their experiences, however, has to do with the particular *time* when my fieldwork was conducted: the six-month operational tour when most women's husbands were away on active combat duty in Afghanistan. In the rest of this chapter, I use the spatio-temporalities of an operational tour to connect women's movements in local and national space to 'a-place-called-Afghanistan' and the fluctuations of global politics that are mediated through it. In such a way, I seek to build a picture of the *presence* of the war in Afghanistan as it is experienced by military wives living in Germany, in short, how a distant war *makes its presence felt*. This reveals women's 'affective labour' (Hardt 1999, 89) in the form of their heuristic responses to instability, separation, absence and vul-nerability, as well as revealing the 'collective subjectivities' (ibid.) that are formed in response. Looking beyond the effects of political violence as they are most viscerally attached to the bodies and minds of service personnel (Goodell and Hearn 2011; Wool 2013) or the hypervisibilised bodies of enemy 'others' (Amar 2011; Wilcox 2013), I describe a temporal continuum through which the 'theatre of war' becomes unsited and manifest in the everyday spaces of women's lives. I look closely at the textures and fluctuations of an operational tour from the perspective of women married to servicemen, looking at spaces and times of presence and absence, grief and relief, love and fear, public and private emotion, to explore the ways in which military power is sensed, including the everyday practices through which this more ethereal kind of presence is materialised, embodied and made liveable.

A-Place-Called-Afghanistan

The social construction of a-place-called-Afghanistan in Germany troubles the distance between the combat zone and the home to posit military wives as agents who work to smooth and absorb, if not resolve, the rupture and contradictions between them. One of the ways in which Afghanistan gains shape and form during a deployment is through world maps Blu-Tacked onto children's bedroom walls or display boards at school and nursery, a device that helped to 'locate' absent parents. In this way, soldiers' presence is pinned into position alongside last year's holiday destination or Granny and Grandpa's house in the UK. On such maps, a-place-called-Afghanistan is marked by its borders, terrain and capital city, even if this defies the limits of a small child's comprehension. Speaking of her toddler's nursery school, a servicewoman – whose own deployment preceded her husband's with only a few weeks together as a family in between – notes: 'And they had a map of the world, and she knew Mummy was there. And then a picture of Mummy on Afghanistan.' In this narrative trope, as before, the map is a device that functions at the meta-level of conversations between adults, where pathos is created between the innocence of a child and the knowing significance of Afghanistan for the adults, a gulf mirrored in the difference between the map's abstract topography – the shape and contours of a landlocked country in Central Asia – and the political geography that sustains a British military presence there and mandates the parents' absence. Indeed, if the trick of the map functions as a reassuringly abstract visualisation to a child, it functions as a knowing materialisation of the political significance attached to Afghanistan for adults. The power and pathos of the map as an expression of the presence of Afghanistan lies in its will to innocence, and inheres not so much in what it shows but what it hides.

The map on the child's bedroom wall is perhaps an appropriate manifestation of the complex and many-layered construction of a-place-called-Afghanistan in the regimental community. It betrays something of the process by which Afghanistan, remaining essentially distant and unknowable to women married to servicemen, becomes flattened into a two-dimensional site for narratives of war and its generic threats. 'Afghan' as the country was more often called, is always-already abbreviated as the object of international intervention and war, abstracted to a degree that renders Afghanistan itself curiously vague.[7] Correspondingly, its spaces are limited to a series of familiarised indigenous or military place names such as Helmand Province, Lashkar Gah or 'Bastion', or else are replaced by generic acronyms that are used with varying levels of comprehension, as is evident in Kirsty's misrecognition of an acronym when I use the term in its unabbreviated form: 'A: Was he on a Forward Operating Base or . . . / K: Um, no he was in a FOB or something, he basically lived in a tent.'

For women married to servicemen, the borders of Afghanistan are reconstituted according to the radius of a soldier's location (be this in an office on a base, in a tent or on patrol). Thus 'Afghanistan' might be described as a physical, embodied location only in so far as it is the destination of women's husbands, a paradoxical kind of disembodiment where the presence of Afghanistan in Germany is marked most sharply by a husband's absence.

Kirsty's experience indicates that the shapeshifting, ephemeral presence of Afghanistan in Germany eludes the Army's attempts at controlling its effects:

> K: They've done a briefing but [. . .] basically it was just these guys, some high rank, I don't know who they were, talking about um, how deployment's a very unsettling time for everybody and we have to be there for them and they have to be there for us. And I'm thinking 'Well, how can they [be there for us] when they're in a different country?' [. . .] and then they had this flick show basically, and they were showing us pictures of where they get washed every day and I'm like, what has this got to do with anything? I don't want to see their bathrooms and stuff like that, and rooms where they'll be staying and tents what have you, and. . .
>
> A: Why don't you want to see them?
>
> K: I just thought, what's the point? It's not something we really want to be thinking about when we're over here. We want to know like, how much danger they're going to be in and stuff, how much worry we are actually supposed to be worrying about, not where they get washed every day.

Kirsty's viewpoint illuminates the Army's attempts to demystify deployment by providing information and context regarding the tour, involving the construction – and normalisation – of Afghanistan through everyday spaces such as washrooms and tents. This emphasis on the personal and reproductive spaces of soldiers' everyday lives in Afghanistan is not insignificant, nor perhaps surprising, given the gendered division of private and public space I have explored in this book. While these spaces might not replicate home, they provide an alternative backdrop for more reassuring imaginaries of a soldier's location. The photographs of washrooms and living quarters function to let wives in on their husbands' home from home; they use a domestic scene to create a common ground between here and there. Kirsty is not persuaded by this gendered alignment of the reproductive side of soldiering with assumptions about the personal and domestic concerns of wives. The 'flick show' is to her an unnecessary distraction, would seem to conceal or elide the information she is really seeking: some quantifiable sense of danger, some indication of the exact nature of her husband's role in combat operations perhaps, and what this involves. Despite the regiment's well-intentioned attempts at familiarisation therefore, Kirsty maintains her own construction of Afghanistan, resisting its pacification. She does this by reasserting the distinction between public and private and reinstating the division between the combat zone and the home, in pointed contrast to narratives that attempt to reconstitute Afghanistan through the banality of the washroom.

And yet, just a few sentences later when Kirsty gives an example of one of the things she does know about her husband's time in Afghanistan, these everyday and banal forms of exchange *are* her primary way of locating and relating to his experience. Ironically, the washroom ends up being central to the one picture she is able to build of his location and, moreover, is also crucial for the practical role that she can play in that very scene through the materials at her disposal.

> I said if you do want to talk to [me] about it then you can. And he said, 'Oh right well, do you want to know?' And I said, 'If you want, if you don't want to speak about it then I'm not going to ask you and force you.' [. . .] And we've never really discussed it, I mean he has mentioned a few things 'cause um, he wanted a pair of onesies sent out, 'cause I wanted to get him something stupid 'cause he says all his mates are getting all these silly ones. So I got him a devil one, it was the only one I could find that wasn't just plain, yeah, basically, and he kept saying, 'Every morning when I go to the washroom and

stuff, all the Afghanis they think I'm the devil, the bathroom every morning just empties when I go there they think it's so evil, they're petrified of it . . .'

In the end, it is an apparently banal detail of her husband's everyday life in Afghanistan that provides Kirsty with her only deployment anecdote, the one scene that has been played out for her in which she can also locate her own presence. This scene takes place in the very space that minutes ago she was dismissing as irrelevant to her view of Afghanistan: the washroom. This is a space inflected with familiarity, of collective humour and practical jokes, constituting the only sphere of Kirsty's influence, when, by her choice of a fancy-dress outfit for her husband, she gains a role – albeit a remote one – in the performance it facilitates. That is not to say that this scene is completely void of the politics of the conflict in Afghanistan on a micro-scale, however. These are implicit in the shared facilities and routines of British Forces and Afghan Security Forces personnel, the joke that turns on the orientalist construction of a cultural other, and the noticeable undertone of antagonism.

In such ways, a-place-called-Afghanistan takes shape in Germany, constructed through social networks, media and institutional channels as well as material culture and discourse. In many ways, Afghanistan and Germany become twinned locations. Joint weather reports, news bulletins and messages to loved ones were broadcast constantly on British Forces Broadcasting Services (BFBS), for example. Desert bulletins and Afghan place names followed reports of European snow and sleet, a regular and pervasive reminder that is compounded by the women's location in Germany and not always appreciated. Amy, who was pregnant with her first child at the time of her husband's six-month deployment, complains:

> Yes I've definitely missed him more this time, and you're just constantly, just constant reminders, I mean even just getting into the car and listening to the bloody radio, that's what does my head in – the first two, three months when I was a bit you know, 'oooh', turning it on and they've got all these messages from Afghanistan and all this news from Afghanistan and you just can't escape it, unless you speak German.

Amy's description also draws attention to Afghanistan as a kind of presence that is constituted through time as well as space, for example a presence that is constant or one that is intermittent, and one that many women wish to forget. While the social construction of Afghanistan can be traced by exploring the ways in which its geographies are visualised, then, it is important to consider how the presence of Afghanistan manifests itself at different times during an operational tour, and through different temporal registers. This opens up further terrain for understanding how women married to servicemen might be understood to *inhabit* a-place-called-Afghanistan.

The Presence of Afghanistan

With respect to the study of military power, perhaps the most obvious way of accounting for time is that 'of which History (capital H) is made' (Massey 1994, 253). Understandings of military power tend to crystallise around the moments and places where battles are lost and won. The events of 11 September 2001 are the defining example in this context, marking what Tom Lundborg (2012, 1) describes as 'a border in time', an event that determines the present moment (in this case, a continuous chain of operations in Iraq and Afghanistan since 2003) and serves to separate it off from what came before (such as operations in Kosovo and Northern Ireland, for example). People's sense of this border in time was acknowledged in their narratives, where combat operations post-9/11 represented a sea change in the experience and perception of war, as Marianne recounts:

> M: [In relation to her husband's first tour in Bosnia] I think as well we just thought you know, it's just a NATO thing [. . .] I think with Iraq and with Afghanistan it's more of a fear of the unknown. And we hadn't lost anybody either until Iraq. The regiment hadn't lost anybody [. . .] '05 was the worst. '03 was the first one, what I call the war-y bit [laughs], which was horrendous. [. . .]
> A: Iraq was a real shock to the system?
> M: Massive shock.

The temporal register of the operational tour that was unfolding during my fieldwork can also be plotted according to the points when 'historical events' occurred.[8] The regiment had already suffered the loss of two soldiers in the first six weeks of the tour. During my fieldwork, two British soldiers were killed by members of the Afghan Security Force at a military base in Lashkar Gah, Helmand Province, where the regiment had some of its personnel. This incident, like all other security breaches, prompted the implementation of 'op minimise'. 'Op minimise' is a standard procedure by which all non-official communications between the theatre of war and the outside world are shut down. This means that, in the period immediately after an incident until op minimise is lifted, service personnel are not permitted to make any contact with friends or family.

From time to time in Germany, therefore, Afghanistan falls suddenly and unexpectedly silent. While 'op minimise' prompts a series of well-scripted procedures and protocols throughout the military organisational structure, for the community in Germany it manifests itself in a heightened state of awareness that is vague, frenzied and without object. In the silence and speculation that constitutes op minimize at home, the precondition for rationalising one's fear is that the system is designed to prevent leaks to the media before the military has been able to inform the families of the service personnel involved. Hannah, while recounting her experience of the day the British soldiers were killed, concedes:

> The brilliant thing about the system they run you know, as tragic as it is and as bad as you feel for those families, you know [that] if you're reading that news, [then] it's not your soldier, and that's the whole reason it exists, that's why they have op minimise out there so that there's no leaks.

The protocol followed by wives during op minimise involves monitoring the MOD website and crosschecking the information released by twenty-four-hour news media. In this case, it did appear that details of the event had been leaked to the press before they were released by the MOD. When Hannah saw news of the incident on the television, she checked the MOD website and there was no information available:

> And so I was sat here thinking, 'Oh my God, oh my God. Two soldiers have been shot in Lashkar Gah camp, where Edward works.' I was waiting for the car to come down the drive, I was beside myself. And I know – even though I knew in the back of my mind I was being silly and [. . .] the chances are it wasn't him statistically speaking [. . .] – I just knew they hadn't managed to get hold of the next of kin or whatever it was. So I was, oh I was in such a state. I called [the Welfare Officer] in the end actually. Just because – even though I knew that I sounded utterly stupid and neurotic, I was just going out of my mind, I had to speak to somebody. And I knew that he might know who it was, which he did. And I thought to myself, I don't want to be that person who calls and is like, 'Oh has anything happened to my

husband?' [. . .] But part of me did think, you know I haven't called up the welfare office for anything during this tour at all, I've never you know, phoned up in floods of tears or had a crisis or anything so I thought, 'No this is my crisis moment and I'm going to ring them.'

Through op minimise, an event is supposedly paused or frozen in time, its particulars held back so that its ramifications can be managed effectively and a soldier's next of kin informed. Yet this does not mean that the event does not *happen* in Germany. Rather, the event becomes manifest in the temporal form of waiting and is spatially reinscribed in unexpected places, such as the driveway of a suburban house where Hannah waits for the appearance of the families liaison officer, whom she imagines will tell her the news of her husband's death. Several women recounted this event during interviews, with others retelling those same women's responses second-hand (stories I had also heard through the welfare office). This illustrates the ripples and reverberations of an event three thousand miles away as it circulates through social networks in Germany. What it also reveals are the informal protocols for the collective regulation of information and emotion among women married to servicemen. Hannah's self-conscious awareness of 'proper' procedures or a 'proportionate' response to such incidents betrays the ideal qualities of stoicism and reserve required of wives during deployment. These ideals find their expression in hierarchies that fuse together women's intimate relationships with one another, on the one hand, and their relationship to institutional structures such as the welfare office, on the other. Recounting the same event, Heather asserts her responsibility and skill in managing the failure of another woman's emotional resources. She asserts the same rationalisations as Hannah, only her emotions are invested in defusing and converting the kinetic force of the incident as it ripples through the community. And yet, the cumulative effect of op minimise remains:

> And Hannah was in tatters. Susan was in tatters. [The Welfare Officer] dealt with Hannah, I dealt with Susan. And there was no one there for me, but I went to deal with two other wives. And my husband was, you know, as far away as anyone else. And I remember leaving Susan's and going up to [the park] and just started shaking. Just like [exhales]. But you know, I've just been – I'm thrown into making sure the other people are alright because I knew of course if it was [their husbands] you would know by now, you wouldn't hear it in the news. [. . .] And so they get all their tears and stuff and all their shaking, and I've taken that from them and stuck to that. And then I've got nowhere to go.

The continuation of an event in this way, its manifestation in a chain of places, times and emotions as passed from woman to woman, constitutes the everyday presence of Afghanistan in Germany. And it is a presence that is intricately shaped by the scripts of gender. Where the shock of death does occur, such as the occasion before my arrival when two servicemen from the regiment were killed while out on patrol, women spoke of a kind of transferral of effects from the theatre of war to the garrison in Germany. Ironically, it is in theatre, where the visceral events of war are experienced and witnessed directly, that the shock is more rapidly absorbed, as one young officer recalls of the death of his colleague:

> I think we hadn't really thought about him that much since he got killed. Um. Because we just couldn't, you know. [. . .] Obviously the, day he was killed was absolutely horrible and we – the way it works out there is, it's almost like an MSN sort of chat log and [. . .] they can track big incidents like that [. . .] And so his call sign came up as being, you know, vehicle hit, has hit an IED [. . .] We could basically see the incident evolving. But being absolutely helpless. And so that was pretty – you know, that was a very tough day. Then we had the repatriation, um, which again was, was pretty tough. There's a vigil service and then [. . .] at about four in the morning [. . .] we basically line up with the aircraft at the end, you know with the big sort of door at the back. And then it was the squadron officers sort of carried his coffin on and that was – yeah that was pretty, pretty tough as well. But then after that, that was like, right well we're only a month or so into this, we've just got to . . . [. . .] So I think really like, we quickly pushed all thoughts of that out of our mind.

But the continuation of this event can be charted through the unfolding of its effects 'back home', and the emotional labour of women married to servicemen. The officer's narrative is echoed in the recollections of his wife, Sophie, who attended the UK funeral of the deceased on her husband's behalf, taking over the process of ritualisation while those in theatre moved on to continue their deployment. Sophie frames this in terms of a direct transferral of grief and duty not only on behalf of her absent husband, but also in solidarity with other wives and girlfriends:

> And I just, I wanted to be there you know also for some of the other girlfriends who knew him a lot better than I did. And they were all there – I mean, we all sort of said we were there you know primarily because our partners couldn't be there.

This proposes an odd kind of reversal, whereby the event and its effects are spatially and temporally inverted: the soldier witnesses the violence of the event and experiences the death of his colleague in real time, albeit remotely through a technological interface. He experiences the physical proximity of the event, and his colleague's absence, as it unfolds in Afghanistan, yet its effects (at least those that are manifest in more public forms of grief and memorialisation) are suspended and continued instead by his wife on his behalf. In such ways, wives play a direct role in the continuation of public rituals, performing the duties of those 'left behind' in another sense, as mourners.

These dynamics of presence and absence, transferral and continuation from one place to another, throw into relief the struggle to maintain a division between the combat zone and the home, especially as people manage the intrusion of state violence into their everyday lives and relationships. Not surprisingly perhaps, the division between the combat zone and the home aligns with a gendered division of labour that posits soldiers as active, purposive, mobile subjects deployed on combat duties overseas, and their wives as responsive guardians of familiarity, stability and memory 'back home' (Massey 1994, 10). Despite this apparent divide, however, accounting for time and temporality reveals the dynamism and flow between 'here' and 'there' in such a way as to connect the micro-politics of everyday life (in multiple spaces) with the circulation of geopolitical power. This underlines the trickle-down of international political relations as they shape the everyday lives of women married to servicemen, as well as revealing the significance of their labour in regulating the effects. What this also illuminates is the connection between the linear time of military history-in-the-making and the cyclical, immanent time of subjects' everyday lives. The presence of a-place-called-Afghanistan is not only felt during the times when something happens, or in moments of violence and rupture. As Woodward (2004) has argued, violent force is merely the most obvious manifestation of military power, the apex of a pyramid that at its base includes the 'continual preparations which states make in order to be able to wage war' (Woodward 2004, 4). In the section that follows, I want to explore ideas about 'readiness' as a way to trace women's anticipation of, and continual preparations for, the risk of violence that soldiering entails.

Combat Readiness

Henri Lefebvre ([1961] 2008) posits the study of everyday life as central to a relational understanding of linear and cyclical time, a relationship that he uses the example of the military institution to express:

> The Army prepares itself for war; that is its aim and purpose. And yet moments of combat and opportunities to be heroic are thin on the ground. The Army has its everyday life: life in barracks and more precisely life among the troops. [. . .] This everyday life is not without its importance in relation to dreams of heroism and the fine moral ideal of the professional soldier. It is the springboard for sublime actions. Questions of rank, promotion and military honours are part of it. There is a saying that Army life is made up of a lot of boredom and a couple of dangerous moments (Lefebvre [1961] 2008, 41–2)

In her essay 'Politics and Space/Time', Doreen Massey (1994) advocates that everyday, routine time must be given greater consideration for a more comprehensive assessment of politics and power. Yet because this kind of time has so easily and frequently been 'coded female' (Massey 1994, 258), she argues, it has been excluded from politics and knowledge thereof. As I have illustrated here, paying attention to the same events as they unfold across time and space and are retold from different perspectives is a reminder that 'History' (Massey 1994, 253) and everyday time are not separate or sequential but simultaneous and mutually imbricated. The particular quality of routine time that Massey (1994, 260) is concerned with, however, is its cyclicity and immanence: time that is repetitious, the opposite to the kind of time where history and progress are punctuated according to a linear sequence of events. In the case of military power, this means bringing cyclical time into view alongside (and in order to disrupt) notions of military operations as temporally coherent or linear, as cause and effect, as well as spatially contained.

That is not to say that the routine rehearsals that play out in everyday life are not already a salient part of the military institution, however. Academic accounts of army life have occasionally included details of the everyday processes through which the Army reproduces itself, those daily routines and 'domestic' activities that function as part of the organisational hierarchy. In *Squaddies*, Hockey (1986, 50), considers action, domesticity and boredom as a 'disjuncture' in recruits' expectations of army life:

> There is, for example, a sudden immersion in activities of a domestic nature, all, as Bugler (1966: 5) has noted, involving a near-pathological concern for cleanliness, neatness and uniformity. These are activities which, set against an 'action-image', are seen as female in character. (Hockey 1986, 50)

As well as being feminised and devalued accordingly, routine time has also been connected to spatial incarceration and control. In a reworking of Goffman's (1961, 16) concept of the 'total institution', Susie Scott (2011, 93) considers 'temporal enclosure' and 'block living' in relation to prisons and the military camp, where routine runs counter to freedom and self-determination, combining spatial confinement with *the synchronised movements of disciplinary time* (Wahidin 2006 in Scott 2011, 93, emphasis in original). However, with the emergence of a reconstructed soldiering subjectivity that includes fatherhood and humanitarianism as well as the growing number of servicewomen, domesticity has also been appropriated by the Army as a token of its liberal modernisation. The phenomenon of the washroom 'flick show' that Kirsty critiques is indicative of a contemporary organisation that is invested in humanising its aims and methods, mobilising its everyday life (and the gendered ideas that come with it) to do so. This is echoed in many 'off-duty' images featured in the British media during the war in Afghanistan, for example,[9] which use domestic imagery – washing on the line in a Forward Operating Base, knick-knacks and television sets in a tent – to portray everyday life in a way with which broader society can identify and sympathise. In such images, the familiar tokens of everyday life are interesting for the contrast they present in relation to popular expectations of war: the novelty with which everyday objects are imbued when set against a desert backdrop, for example. One might argue that *real* 'real life' is still somewhere else. So what about the times when everyday life is not in any way exceptional or surprising, is not marked by contrast, but blends in perfectly with the background, meets our expectations, confirms our assumptions, such as washing hung on a line in a suburban back garden in Germany?

It is precisely these times and spaces that are rarely configured as part of everyday army life, perhaps because they go beyond what is considered banal (a valuable concept as understood by scholars such as Lorraine Dowler [2012] and Cindi Katz [2006] in formulations of military force) and are buried in the routine (banality, repeated?). There is a kind of implicit, hard-to-detect devaluation of the times and spaces of domestic labour here, which bears the hallmarks of gender. As Massey (1994) argues, even where understandings of the relationship between different kinds of time and different kinds of space vary considerably, the negative feminisation of one in relation to the other is strikingly consistent:

> Thus where time is dynamism, dislocation and History, and space
> is stasis, space is coded female and denigrated. But where space
> is chaos (which you would think was quite different from stasis;
> more indeed like dislocation), then time is Order . . . and space is
> still coded female, only in this context interpreted as threatening
> (Massey 1994, 258)

Massey's focus on the multiple dualisms that 'map onto each other and also map on to the constructed dichotomy between female and male' (Massey 1994, 258) can be usefully connected to Belkin's (2012, 58) configuration of gender and military discipline as involving the 'normative alignment' of 'substitutable binarisms'. Crucially, his argument focuses on the degree to which – while military discipline (and scholarship thereon) posits these oppositions as distinct and irreconcilable – they are experienced (and their power gains its disciplinary force) through conflation, confusion and 'the compelled embrace' (Belkin 2012, 5) of both.[10] Massey's and Belkin's analyses are useful for highlighting the spuriousness of binary thinking, which Belkin links to the smoothing-over of military power and its broader imperial contradictions, as well as to the centrality of heteronormativity in maintaining the 'illusions of normalcy' on which the military community relies (Serlin 2006 in Belkin 2012, 59). This is my critical rationale for paying attention to the everyday times and spaces in which processes of 'normalisation' – itself a military term denoting the period of adjustment that soldiers go through after an operational tour – are undertaken by military wives. My aim here is to counter the kind of binary thinking that designates the times and places of war while assuming that others represent states of peace; that privileges action and contrast but ignores what is continuous, repetitive or mundane; that separates productive labour from reproductive labour and foregrounds time as History rather than time as routine. Inspired by the feminist and queer analyses of scholars such as Massey (1994) and Belkin (2012) respectively, I want to show the interdependence of these states of being and realms of experience. One way to do this is to look at the interlocking temporal registers through which they are linked.

In her analysis of institutional timeframes, Scott (2011, 102) considers the interaction between the 'public calendars' and the 'private calendars' of seafarers. For seafarers, Scott notes, '[c]hildren symbolically represented [. . .] "lost time" that could never be recouped' (ibid.). While this implies an erasure or gap in time between the spaces of 'here' and 'there' as experienced by those, such as soldiers, who are 'away', the account of tour-time offered by some of the women I interviewed indicates that military wives work in the very tension between multiple wheels of collective and individual time, inhabiting this temporal gap between the public institution and the nuclear family, regulating the rhythms of the family being split between both 'home' and 'away'. Many of the measures that women use to smooth over these fluctuations are temporal themselves, as if using their own time to complement or sometimes counter military time, especially when the latter is beyond their control or unreliable. Women declare their own preferences and develop tactics for the management of time, as Heather explains: 'Leading up to deployment you just want them to go [. . .] My way of coping is that I almost push him away come the last couple of weeks [. . .] and then you get [. . .] sort of on a footing, and then I think it's OK.' An emphasis on establishing a routine, in order to balance work and childcare for example, also emerges as a valuable resource, to the degree that Angie finds some relief in the extended length of its duration:

> I find the deployment well, 'This is it, get onto it.' And the six-month time period [is a] one off and it's done with. I find it a little bit more frustrating with the training – going for three months, coming in, going for a week, coming in . . .

Military wives work both with and against the dictates of regimental logistics and its demand for synchronisation, converting the time of the tour into alternative forms. Like the map on a child's bedroom wall, counting down to a parent's return from Afghanistan was a popular technique. Some mothers translated the weeks into units such as the number of swimming lessons left until a father's return, or created 'a little chalk board of how many days'. Yet there remains a sense in which family time seems always to be working in tension with the unpredictability and possible failure of military time, as Amy, well aware of the myth of military efficiency, explains:

> I don't do the countdown for the kids, I don't believe in that because, if you do countdown and it comes to that day and his flight doesn't arrive or is delayed, well they're devastated. Jack knows he's due home in two weeks but they have no concept of time so two weeks could be a month. No but it's true. And I'll not even tell him the day he comes home, we'll literally just tip up. And I think that's just how I get on with things.

Women's micro-management of routine time smooths over the unwieldy mass movements of military logistics and the ripples of anticipation they produce at home, converting those movements into alternative forms or even hiding the passage of time so as to protect children from its disappointments. In such ways, women married to servicemen appropriate the kinetic force that, as much as operational systems or the events that interrupt them, propels the tour forward.

One further form of routine and repeated time that can be found in everyday army life inheres in the concept and condition of 'readiness'. Combat readiness is what Lutz calls 'war's shadow' (Lutz 2001, 7), which she connects to 'battle's other – the 'home front' (ibid.). Readiness entails the simulation, rehearsal and repetition of a series of calculated moves and practice mobilisations. The productive power of readiness is something that Lutz (2001, 87) attributes to its temporal quality of both presence and projection: 'because it involves peering into the void of the future and the blurry shapes of the present, it must also be mythic: It has to draw on culturally tutored imagination, fears and wishes.' The idea of readiness, its temporal quality and its role in the diffusion of military power, opens up a final aspect of the presence of Afghanistan and its significance for the women married to servicemen quoted in this chapter. This goes beyond the social construction of Afghanistan as a place, and the incorporation of events into routine and reproductive time as smoothed over by military wives. Rather, readiness, and the simultaneous conditions of present and future it contains, opens up a realm of experience that has less to do with the presence of particular places and events per se, than their *anticipation*. This presence of Afghanistan might be described as mythic, but the examples I have explored already in this chapter indicate a kind of presence that is keenly *sensed*. In the final section of this chapter, therefore, I want to pay attention to some of the ways in which Afghanistan *makes its presence felt*.

The Present Tense of Afghanistan

In this chapter so far, I have sought to animate 'Afghanistan' beyond its fixed status as the object of international intervention or the exclusive arena of soldiers' experiences. I have looked at the temporal contingency of an operational tour through the intrusion of violent events, at the same time as I have explored the continuities through which these are smoothed over in everyday life. The 'present tense' of Afghanistan brings these two analyses together to express the emotional register through which this contingency is felt, and the everyday processes through which it is managed. The present tense of Afghanistan is less about the times when events happen than their anticipation. It is about the imaginaries that rush in to fill the gaps of silence and unknowability that I have highlighted. However, it is also about the gestures, narratives and practices that women develop to enact these mythologies, to tether them to something here and now, to help materialise those multiple absences. Two very simple examples from men's and women's accounts of the communication links between 'theatre' and 'home' provide a starting point for what I mean. In the first, Bernadette and Malcolm describe their memories of the 2003 invasion of Iraq. As a soldier who had served in the regiment for over fifteen years, Malcolm had experienced many different deployments, from Northern Ireland and Bosnia to Iraq and Afghanistan. Married to Malcolm for the duration of his career, Bernadette had experienced each one in her own particular way. Of the invasion of Iraq, Bernadette recalls:

> B: I found out two months in as he was away that I was pregnant with [our son], and I couldn't tell him. I had to send it through the family officer to tell him you know, in the field.
> M: Yeah, [at the] troop briefing they were like 'We're going off here, we're going to take this place here, make sure there's no one in there. Adam, by the way your missus is pregnant.' I was like 'Can you just say that last one again I'll write that down, Sir – what?!' [laughs].
> B: I wouldn't have told him that way but I thought, well, if something happens . . .

The second example that illustrates my point about how war makes its presence felt is articulated by Elise, who had not long joined her husband in Germany and was relatively new to the community:

> OK, you're far away from your boyfriend, let's say. You can text him, ring him, can't you? You have conversations at night-time. But when your husband or boyfriend is in a war zone, and the Army control the phone calls, and you know if you miss . . . I missed so many phone calls, I was heartbroken. 'Cause that could be the last phone call [. . .] He could ring at three o'clock in the morning. You just never say, 'Oh can you ring back?' You just wake up and you talk to them.

There is a pre-emptive quality, a futurity implicit in Bernadette and Elise's experiences above. However, what I want to explore here is not so much the actual possibility to which women's pre-emption corresponds (for example, what those events are, the likelihood of them happening or whether or not they did happen, which in both narratives above is ultimately that their loved ones might be killed). Rather, my focus here is on the way in which the *anticipation* of those events manifests itself in alternative forms in the present, as women are going about their everyday lives. Thus, the presence of Afghanistan haunts their waking hours, and their sleep. What I want to express using this temporal register is women's daily inhabitation of a state of contingency – a kind of 'readiness' that involves an awareness of, preparation for, but in most cases the deferral of, the worst-case scenario. In other words, I want to question what it means to inhabit a state of 'what if . . .' and 'just in case'.

For example, I interviewed Kate, a friendly but reserved woman married to a mid-ranking soldier relatively early in my fieldwork, at a point when the regiment's return from Afghanistan was still a way off. Her husband was part of a platoon with a highly active front-line role in Afghanistan. Kate had experienced numerous deployments before and made clear that she was happily settled in the regimental community. Even so, her experience of this tour still took her by surprise sometimes:

> Every so many weeks I'll start feeling like, I'll get sad and I'll cry at the most ridiculous things. And I'll lie in bed at night and I can hear cars pulling up and I just – I don't know, I just think, 'Please don't, you know – please don't ring my doorbell.'

The motif of 'the knock on the door', implicit here in Kate's anticipation of the doorbell ringing in the middle of the night, emerged from many of my conversations with spouses and service personnel. The 'knock on the door' functions as a ready-made, collective euphemism for a soldier's death, referring to the visit his next of kin will receive from the family liaison officer whose job it is to break the news. Like Hannah keeping watch at her window during op minimise, for Kate 'the knock on the door' is manifest in material form here as the sound of a car (any car) driving up a quiet residential street at night. The present tense of Afghanistan is not simply about mythic projection, therefore; it is not simply the object of women's imagination.[11] Rather, the present tense of Afghanistan is felt in the very real spaces and times of everyday army life. Furthermore, it takes shape and form – is embodied, enacted and verbalised – through the kind of labour and identities that I have consistently shown throughout this book, are produced in the nexus of gender and the military.

Figuratively, 'the knock on the door' unsites death from the battlefield and places it at women's doorsteps, at the boundary of the public institution and the domestic sphere. Vered Vinitzky-Seroussi and Eyal Ben-Ari (2005) have considered military death in terms of the problem it presents for the military institution, which they underline is '*the* organization most strongly identified with the legitimate use of violence' (Vinitzky-Seroussi and Ben-Ari 2005, 651, emphasis in the original). The authors explore some of the cultural scripts that govern ideas about 'good' and 'bad' military deaths, determined by the kinds of operations that are their cause (humanitarian or peacekeeping missions, for example), and the kinds of soldiers killed (including their gender, age, marital and family status [Vinitzky-Seroussi and Ben-Ari 2005, 657]). As a cultural script that circulates internally within the military institution and pertains to those gendered subjects 'left behind' (Massey 1994, 10), 'the knock on the door' represents the domestication of a death whose cause is state-sanctioned violence, but whose effects are depoliticised as they cross the boundary and pass into the private, personal sphere.

The 'knock on the door' was most often an imagined event and not a concrete experience for most of the women I encountered, its invocation standing as a placeholder for the potentiality of a soldier's death. In this sense, its function is also a projection – a rehearsal. It is in this way that spaces such as the bus stop become sites of *feeling*, where the boundaries of different worlds – the private and public, the personal and political – collide but are also undone, as Kate recalled of the day when two of the regiment's soldiers were killed:

> And I was running late that day so my blinds were closed. So my neighbours walking past my house thought it was me. Because they hear [it happened to our regiment], they don't know who it is. But they know a couple of their friends are part of the regiment and they panic. So as I walk to the bus stop some of them were crying. Because they'd panicked, they didn't know if it was going to be [my husband], or going to be, you know, next door. Because it's always going to be someone you know.

Here, the dual dynamic of recognition and rehearsal with which women's storytelling is infused renders the present tense of Afghanistan cathartic almost. Like the twin dynamics of homecoming, it generates relief whose constitutive other is a proxy kind of grief. There is a sense in which women approach as close to the experience of grief as they can, with the death at its centre remaining collective, never individually their own. Kate continues:

> You can't sleep, you worry and you think . . . And d'you know this sounds really silly, I used to clean my house from top to bottom before I went to bed in case I got that knock at the door in the middle of the night. I didn't want the person giving me bad news to see how messy the house was. [. . .] Because if I'm going to have a stranger in my house telling my bad news I don't want them thinking I've lived in a mess. It was a ritual for me. I was – I would make sure – I would never go to bed without – because obviously if something happened as well I'd be shipped – I'd be flown wherever. And I thought the last thing I want is people, either friends of mine having to come in here and collect things for me, coming in to my messy house. It was just, it was something I felt – I didn't want strangers thinking that I was messy, that was all. The possibility of a stranger coming in here was quite, I thought, was going to be quite high. That someone was going to have to come in and collect belongings of mine to take wherever I was going to be.

In many ways, Kate's feelings and their translation into action through a kind of labour that is rarely configured as part of army everyday life, let alone war, represents the embodiment of many of the power relations I have explored throughout this book. It is in this sense that the present tense of Afghanistan also raises a difficult question at this final point: the question of women's capacity to resist the co-optation of their emotions, the internalisation of gendered identities and the incorporation of their labour in the interests of the gendered normalcy on which the military depends.

Conclusion

This chapter has illustrated some of the ways in which women married to servicemen work to sustain social cohesion within a regimental community. What these experiences also make clear, however, is women's central role in mediating the demands of the regiment as it blurs the divide between public and private lives, and the combat zone and the home. Again and again, women can be seen to meet the demands of the regiment halfway, frequently relying on their position as outsiders within, or on an ambiguous status between military and civilian spheres, to selectively co-opt and convert the discourses and identities upon which regimental belonging relies. In this sense, they assert the value of their labour and seek recognition of their place within a culture ostensibly maintained by hierarchies of command, soldiers' productive labour, national identity and state power. My analysis in this chapter reveals a broader framework for the reproduction of regimental belonging, however, and one that is equally dependent on the family as a mode through which both its functional and affective bonds are secured.

It is during the particular temporal and spatial zones of an operation tour when these bonds are most severely tested. By insisting on the 'presence' of Afghanistan as it is experienced through women's everyday lives and in places other than the theatre of war, I have sought to trouble wives' relegation to local rather than global, and personal rather than political space, or, rather, to counter the depoliticisation of reproductive time and the practices of domestic life (Massey 1994, 6). As such, my analysis underlines the need to pay attention to the many different *kinds* of time and the significance of multiple, concomitant temporalities in women's mediation of the presence of Afghanistan. The kind of time that I have explored in this chapter rarely features in accounts of military history and it goes beyond those times of rupture and discontinuity when events thousands of miles away in Afghanistan directly affect women married to servicemen. Equally as important, I have argued, are the times when nothing much happens, when normalcy is maintained. Paying attention to these quieter times, and the spaces through which they are experienced, reveals that they are far from empty, remote or insignificant. Indeed, these times and space are actively inhabited by women married to servicemen, their kinetic energy invested in maintaining the normalcy on which the military institution depends. Furthermore, as women's narratives and labour are invested in managing the spectres of state-sanctioned violence, the effects of military power become deeply sensed. Throughout this chapter I have sought to highlight the multiple times and spaces that constitute an operational tour and envelop military wives in their effects. If the spatio-temporalities of women married to servicemen count as part of an operational tour, however, then what does this imply about their complicity in military power and, ultimately, war?

Notes

1. https://www.nam.ac.uk/explore/regimental-system, last accessed 23 July 2022
2. Ibid.

3. Ibid.

4. The particular conversation that yielded this information also yielded a pertinent insight into the relationality of class and the rigidity of the regiment's classifying structures and social stratification. During an intellectually stimulating and animated debate with a young officer in the regiment, I noted what I believed to be the regiment's representativeness of a cross-section of society, from the working-class to upper-class origins of its members. It was quickly pointed out to me that the regiment currently included no 'upper'-class members, who derived, for example, from the British aristocracy. While this undoubtedly served to put me in my place as someone completely unacquainted with the higher echelons of elite society, it serves as an interesting illustration of the difficulty of stepping back from social hierarchies to view them from any other perspective than one's position within them.

5. This, Ware (2012) has argued, can so easily reproduce racism, despite being invested so earnestly in militarised ideals of multiculture.

6. https://www.nam.ac.uk/explore/regimental-system

7. Beyond the limits of my ethnographic data and this book, there are, of course, a whole host of historically and geographically specific articulations of Afghanistan as a social, political and cultural space that also work to constitute its multiple meanings (for a Western readership, that is, let alone the meanings of 'Afghanistan' from within). I acknowledge the risk of reproducing a reductive account of the borders of Afghanistan-the-place as it is reflected in my empirical examples, as my ethnographic data cannot support any kind of assumption about the material 'reality' of life in Afghanistan for service personnel or, even more remotely, the Afghan population. The kind of multi-sited ethnographic data that would illuminate the flow of space and time across both Afghanistan and Germany is therefore beyond the limits of this project, and the experiences of those men and women on tour in Afghanistan during my time with the regiment are to a degree consigned to the fixity of being far away in another place (and, of course, in the past).

8. I use 'historical event' to describe a security incident such as might be reported by the international or British media, for example. That is not to reduce or inflate (depersonalise or over-politicise) the meaning or significance of any one event. Rather, by 'historical event' I again invoke Lundborg's formulation of the process by which events *become* 'history', which he argues 'needs someone who can decide what a historical event actually refers to, where its borders are to be located, how these borders can be linked to the borders of other events, and how all these borders together constitute the basis of a narrative order that can take us from a specific point in the past to a moment that defines our present 'being' (Lundborg 2012, 2).

9. One startling example is a series of photographs by Alison Baskerville, published widely in the British press in 2012, featuring an image of women's underwear hanging on a washing line. The caption states: 'Trooping the colour: Brightly coloured women's underwear stands out against a dull background and more conventional items of military uniform.' The gendered terms of this engagement are clear (as heralded by the giddy headline: 'It's a girl's life in the Army! Portraits from the Afghan frontline show how female troops are winning hearts and minds in Afghanistan', http://www.dailymail.co.uk/news/article-2221475/Our-women-war-Portraits-Afghan-frontline-female-troops-winning-hearts-minds-Afghanistan.html, last accessed 17 March 2015

10. It is useful to expand this definition here: 'Parallel to the compelled disavowal of what is constructed as unmasculine, the military has also incited the unmasculine, and forced service members to inhabit it in order to be disciplined and conform to power. At the level of individual and institutional practice, military culture involves not just a flight from the unmasculine, but a simultaneous endurance and even embrace of it as well. Thus the creation of a masculine armed force depends on a surprising degree of engagement with the very sorts of unmasculine foils that masculinity seems by its very definition to be positioned against' (Belkin 2012, 24–5)

11. Although this spectral quality – sometimes literally taking the form of sounds in the middle of the night – might imply the need for a psychoanalytic approach (Gordon 1997), this is not my aim here. This is a distinction that is crucial to make in light of research that explores the impact of war through pathologies of post-traumatic stress disorder in military contexts (see, e.g., Mulligan et al. 2012).

Shock-the-Civilian Stories

The Welfare Assistant is complaining about a call he received from a wife who had run out of milk. She was in the German supermarket and wanted to know which bottle was full cream. He was in the middle of clearing up after a suicide, he said, so he could have done without it.

It is difficult to know how to listen, how to frame one's face, against a casual remark about a suicide.

Another time, it is being set up like a joke, with reference to a domestic scene, a girlfriend leaving, something about a tracksuit. Failure is the punchline, in that the soldier had lived. The theme is naive incompetence as pitched against the tools of military efficiency; he had used the wrong blade of the standard-issue British Army knife to try to cut his wrists. The narrative is accompanied by actions: the visceral sawing noises of a serrated blade, the flapping of exaggerated, half-dismembered hands. At the close of the story – as yet merely a story – the soldier is named. I had seen him a couple of times in the welfare office that week.

Like once, right, we're on detail to pick up this Ba'athist bloke bloated from the sun, fair bit of rigor set in. We were in a Snatch, meant for Northern Ireland not Iraq: the back door shut with a bit of rope. So I had the lads load him in, legs up, shoulders pinned down by two boys' boots. We're on our way but the driver brakes and somebody's foot comes down full force on the massive belly of the dead Iraqi and the dead Iraqi *farts*. We've got all the windows open but everyone's still puking like the time we pulled that floater out of a ditch, and the thing with corpses is, sometimes the air inside passes the vocal chords at perfect pitch and as we turned him round he made this sound like when we were clearing up after a suicide bomb, there was this bit of jaw and beard lying on the ground and the interpreter holds it up and asks the crowd, 'Does anybody know this man?'

The soldier is a skilled mimic, at least with off-the-shelf accents approximating a British listener's idea of Arabic. He acts out the fear of people running from cars when the door of the Snatch swung open to reveal the body inside; animates the panic after the suicide bomb, waving arms, a garbled invocation to Allah. Here is dissipated or decomposing flesh freighted with abject otherness, and not only by means of an ethnically distinct, racially marked, culturally reified enemy other. There is also the strange otherness of human bodies passed through violence into death: leakage, gases, inversions, limbs out of joint. Then a soldier's visceral response: sweat, vomiting.

What to do with all this bodily excess? All these dead, injured or scarred bodies, disposable life that cannot be disposed of, that returns and is problematically reproduced – then, here. These are war stories that must be understood – can only really be understood, *situated* – in the context of their telling. Because their objects – what (who) they tell of, the lives and deaths they contain – are by definition already absent, erased, silenced. War stories are citational, their content placeholders for glory, horror, pride, bravery, disgust. In the end, their objects obliterated, blown up, destroyed, they tell us only about us. It is a heady, confusing mix: sensational, sensate. It is laughter and shock at the same time, sympathy and disgust, moral outrage and scholarly fascination. Deep pauses, then tittering like schoolchildren, subversive yet predictable. We shake our heads in disbelief. It is a release, rich in subtext if you want it:

The soldier turns to me. I've seen him being all manly in the gym, he says, and I have. Flipping truck tyres, hitting sandbags, dragging thick rope. Hitting and dragging and flipping large objects like bodies he will never get rid of, the weight of which dogs his days.

Careful you don't spray it everywhere, the manliness, someone else says.

He is happy to talk about his PTSD and the Army's need to confront what will emerge for years to come from wars in Iraq and Afghanistan, he says. He calls them his shock-the-civilian stories. Good to tell at weddings. Good to tell in response to the salaciously posed questions of fellow guests, dared or whispered after a few drinks like a challenge almost: has he ever killed anyone? His war stories are a challenge by return, they assault our sensibilities, shut us up.

Shut the fuck up.

They land with a palpable ripple around the room. He pauses for them to take effect, takes another bite of lasagne, pours another cup of tea.

The narrative force of military power? Here is epistemic violence. Both in terms of the violent content of the war stories, but also in terms of their immediate effects: the regulation of power relations in a room, the fragmentation of the social order as the story ricochets around. And, more profoundly, the multiple erasures of subjecthood and humanity they enact, replacing real people – what was once a real person – with scraps of inert flesh, bits of racially profiled body parts. If the soldier's stories force the silence of the civilian listener (goaded into shock, made speechless, yet also captivated), they also announce a hierarchy of life: who counts, who doesn't.[1] They bring into the civility of the dining room a ravaged, uncivilised mess of victims and perpetrators, enemies and allies, blood and bone, piss and shit. It is a narrative pile-up, an assault.

Is there a sense in which these stories of vulnerability, violence, bodily emissions and decay are themselves a pre-emptive strike against the soldier's own abjection, an appropriation of the visceral exposure that posit him and his labour outside or beyond civilian codes of conduct? For his war stories, after all, construct an epistemic privilege, a power over life that is not only literal, in terms of the experiences they might recount as one who lived while others died or were killed, but which also derives from the privileged insight that violence affords into life's base susceptibility. Out of this potentially humanising insight, paradoxically, is created a zone of military exception, with the enemy expelled and the civilian as uncomprehending, ungrateful, other. The Dead Iraqi and other tales are a subversive act of reappropriation to mitigate against the risk that a soldier's productive labour will become devalued, outside of war, as an inconvenient, burdensome by-product of state power, a distasteful and awkward leftover; the fleshy, stinking remnants of state-sponsored violence, bodies and scars on bodies, exposed.

I had gone to the front lodge of the camp where a handful of junior soldiers were usually on guard duty. Mine was a trivial enquiry, but the soldier was in the middle of eating a Cornetto ice cream when I entered, and had quickly concealed it beneath the desk. My query required two hands to pick up some papers, fill in and rubber-stamp a form. Unable to put the melting ice cream down, there was a protracted pause of agonising indecision as the soldier glanced with increasing panic from the ice cream cone to the desk, to me and back again.

I related the story at dinner that evening, seeking to construct for myself some degree of status in relation to the trooper and what I saw as his comedic incompetence; or perhaps a knowing cynicism regarding the bathos of so-called military efficiency. One of the soldiers was stony-faced. Everyone else's gratifying laughter faded. The trooper had been in his platoon in Afghanistan, the serious solider said. A good lad. He had been injured in an IED attack. His internal organs were sliced through by shrapnel; he had one of the most impressive scars he'd ever seen. It ran diagonally from one side of his chest to his lower abdomen on the other.

If I was seeking to claim any social or cultural capital that I assumed might come from my place in the social order of the camp (as a guest, as a civilian, as someone the young trooper was obliged to assist, calling me 'Ma'am' as he did so), then that claim had been summarily rejected. Upheld, was the social and cultural capital of war and exposure to violence, against which civilian humour or critique was valueless, void.

War stories, then, are always political, always active.[2] They require reading and retelling in ways that acknowledge their narrative force as itself a form of military power and presence; an immediate, affective force in its own right. War stories are not straightforward vehicles for the construction of glory or heroism, or for making sense of senseless disintegration; nor are they necessarily a symptom of individual trauma or a performance of militarised identity based on the scripts of organisational discourse. War stories hover on the blurred edges of military and civilian codes; they dehumanise at the same time as they expose the common vulnerability of human flesh. They connect military and civilian bodies in ways that are a visceral leveller at the same time as they are infused with the privileged insights of exceptionalism.

If my own attempts at knowledge or critique were subordinate to military epistemologies on camp, subject to and silenced by the narrative force of war stories, then this begs one final question concerning the reproduction of such stories here. To reproduce soldier-storytelling within a critical frame is to engage in a spiralling, proliferating politics of representation and erasure. There is the question of complicity in epistemic violence[3] – the double erasure of the distant and othered victims of war violence (who is the dead Iraqi? A racialised subject made flesh only in terms of their destruction and decay), as well as the ethics of narrating the sensational extremes of military labour for scholarly fascination, as if for guests at a wedding. Finally, there is the question of redress; of what I am doing here if not spitefully countering my own subjection to the narrative force of a soldier's shock-the-civilian-stories, by writing about them later, seeking interpretative command of all the messy, fleshy bodies they represent, including the soldier's own.

'Can I put that in my book?' I asked the soldier. 'Please do,' he said.

And, reader, I laughed. No *killjoy*,[4] me. Awkwardly, shocked, my body at odds with what I was hearing, or what I knew; unsure; or shaking my head, but still I laughed. Or gamely, I laughed, at banter about my green corduroy trousers, Peter Pan haircut or stereotypes about 'lesbian' sandals. I laughed politely, to allay the collective embarrassment in the room when a senior officer joked that my heterosexuality was in doubt not because of my haircut but because I hadn't yet slept with a handsome subbie, indicating the young officer standing to his left in full equestrian riding attire, hat and crop, at the very same moment that his dog bounded into the room and nearly knocked me over by sniffing at my crotch. I laughed when his wife said that I wasn't being moved into the officers' mess because of the concern that someone would 'nail' me. At the end of a long, strange car journey to a NATO base where I was denied entry and had to be dropped off to have an ice cream, like a child, in the local town, I laughed at a joke made by one of the soldiers I liked most out of all the soldiers I had met, which spiralled out of control and ended with a punchline about my vagina. I laughed instead of crying, because if I hadn't laughed I would have thrown back my head and howled with homesickness and the sheer *weirdness* of the social situation I was in. The next day, I found out that the Welfare Officer had come to hear about the incident and that the soldier had been disciplined.

At other times, I laughed in admiration of the humour and wit of dry observations that skewered my expectations. I laughed at clever terminology that turned military exceptionalism and efficiency on its head. I laughed along with other people when they appeared to be 'taking' banter, usually in the form of a wry or harsh observation about their appearance, identity or experience. On another occasion I laughed, drunk, as I rode a tiny child's bicycle round the street outside with the wife of the Welfare Officer. When I was invited to the home of the Welfare Assistant for a barbecue and we sat round drinking sweet liqueur and joking about his nostalgic purchases on eBay, I laughed long and hard and it felt so good that the laughter is what

I remember above all about the evening, then gratitude. Deep, warm gratitude.

Those are the times I remember laughing. They all mean different things.

Notes

1. Whose life is grievable, whose isn't (Butler 2004).
2. Something like Tim O'Brien's formulation of shock and awe in 'How to tell a true war story' (1998).
3. I've explored some of these ideas around Spivak's (1988) ideas about epistemic violence in a fuller excavation of some of these fieldwork dynamics in a paper called 'Omissions and Admissions: Poetic writing, feminist ethnography and empathetic violence' (Hyde 2014).
4. See, again, Ahmed (2017).

Conclusion: The 'cotton wool effect'?

Early on in my time with the regiment, the Welfare Officer made a wry suggestion that my research should be titled 'Army wives: The cotton wool effect'. This humorous aside, the tensions it expresses and its encapsulation of the dynamics of my study at a number of levels (including the parody of academic style) resonated all the way through my fieldwork and beyond. The idea of the 'cotton wool effect' expresses military wives' 'dependant' status from the point of view of a welfare office working with limited training and resources, and perhaps something of a clash of management sensibilities,[1] to provide support services to over two hundred and fifty families during the particularly stressful time of a deployment. In short, it is a view forged in the experience of staff who are on twenty-four-hour call to handle issues 'ranging from "I've locked myself out of my house" to paedophilia [and] suicide . . .' The 'cotton wool effect' also evokes something of a self-perpetuating, cyclical interplay of care and dependency that is reminiscent of many of the experiences I have documented here, from the continuation of a 'British' way of life in Germany and the overbearing production of the regimental family, to the disciplinary power of rank and the domestication of war. The 'cotton wool effect' implies the pacification of women's needs with a somewhat infantilising comfort blanket of familiarity. As Pippa elucidates:

There's an absolute lethargy out here [. . .] you know the Army give you everything on a plate, they really do, they make it easy as possible for you, I mean you don't even need to think about phoning up the gas man or electricity and stuff, there's a step-by-step Guide to Life here. [. . .] So you know people are so used to having everything put on a plate for them that they won't go out and explore.

What ideas about military wives' dependency also imply in this sense is that the Army overcompensates and mollifies them so that they are in fact *dis*empowered (or, from the point of view of some perhaps, *over*-empowered) and come to depend upon or expect a level of support that is untenable and possibly even undeserved.

The Welfare Officer's idea for my title expresses the degree of weariness that comes with the job, and consequently perhaps a cynical view of women's status as the 'dependants' of military personnel. In many ways, the welfare office is the primary battlefield for women's material bargain with the military institution, the place where some of the conditions of British citizenship that the military maintains for its personnel overseas are administered, as well as, during deployment, support on a casual, ad hoc basis. Several times during the tour, I watched as the welfare office became the site of women's exasperated efforts to navigate the complex bureaucracy of arranging a house move or claiming benefits, which were thwarted by unreliable communications with a spouse in Afghanistan, wives' inability to access information directly, and the requirement for the husband's signature on one particular form or other. At these times, the welfare office was a site for women's assertion of their sense of entitlement to support, which was frequently articulated as their direct and rightful compensation for the degree to which the military institution determined so many aspects of their lives in the first place.

As the Welfare Officer intended it, and as these and other empirical examples show, the 'cotton wool effect' expresses a complex relationship of supply and demand (and the struggle to find a balance between them). What the idea of the 'cotton wool effect' also underlines, however, is that military wives' dependency – as an *effect* of the military institution – is not naturally occurring (say, in any biological or innate sense), but has been politically, socially and culturally manufactured. At the same time, the 'cotton wool effect' and its reliance on a common platitude (that of wrapping someone up in cotton wool) reflects the ease with which military wives' dependant status is normalised and simplified in a way that glosses over the complexity of the power relations involved. The challenge therefore, and one that I have undertaken in this book, lies in disentangling women's investment of their labour, identities and emotions from the proxy relationship to the military institution that their 'dependant' status implies. Paying attention to the ways in which women make sense of their relationship to the military institution – to their understandings of what they give and what they receive in return – helps to trouble the assumptions produced by the apparent dominance of the Army in women's lives, and of women's material dependency upon the Army by return. This is significant not only in pushing beyond scholarship in which the motivations and commitment of military wives are aligned with soldiers' organisational commitment or military effectiveness. It also has implications for the status of women married to servicemen as both the victims and the agents of military power, and broader still, how to think about women's agency within the bounds of highly normative social hierarchies.

In this book I have sought to unpack the assumption that military wives might be classified as militarised subjects in any unitary, absolute or straightforward way. Part of this task involves documenting the structural and discursive conditions that clearly shape the labour, identities and feelings of women married to servicemen. Thus in most cases my analysis begins with an aspect of women's lives that might be argued to be *made* by the military – the mandate for geographical mobility, questions of citizenship and service to the nation state, the social hierarchy of rank and its mutual imbrication with class, the will to social cohesion through the cultural production of the regiment, and the spatio-temporalities of the operational tour. Undoubtedly, the experiences I have documented reveal the myriad ways in which many women's lives are determined, to an often extreme and intractable degree, by the military institution. These are the limited conditions within which women married to servicemen operate. Yet, as my analysis has also shown, these conditions do not necessarily produce consistent, complete or stable effects. If, like the 'cotton wool effect', these effects can be revealed to rely upon demand as well as supply – on agency as well as dependency – then they are far more complex, contradictory and negotiable than they might at first appear. And if these effects, as they shape and are shaped by different women in different ways, are multiple and often divergent, then what in turn does this reveal about how military power operates? To begin this conclusion I review some of the effects of the conditions I have explored throughout this book. I will then go on to consider a framework for understanding the implications of these effects using ideas about militarisation, before coming back to the question of women's agency.

Military Mobilities

In Chapter 1 I began by exploring the conditions of geographical mobility mandated by the military institution. The aim was to chart some of the military-institutional forms of mobility that women negotiate on a daily basis, not only in terms of their own international migration, but also in terms of further, overlapping pathways of travel and movement undertaken across the spaces and boundaries of the military camp overseas. By exploring some of the ways in which women make sense of and manage these military mobilities, I sought to complicate the dynamic of 'following' that they imply. Instead, I emphasised the strategies and tactics used by women and men to convert these conditions and appropriate their effects. Many of these strategies are invested in asserting women's choices and, furthermore, in wresting these choices away from the military institution and couching them firmly in the context of the private sphere of the family. In this, however, women are deeply reliant upon traditional conceptions of the sexual division of labour within households and the gender roles inscribed therein. This gendered division of labour also helps to secure women's incorporation into the military institution as a casualised and localised reserve army of labour, constituting a hidden workforce within the garrison. In such ways and with gender as a key catalyst, women's productive and reproductive labour is instrumental to the day-to-day functioning of the military institution. While this positions women at the centre of overlapping circuits of mobility (holding everything together rather than peripheral figures trailing behind), it does little to unsettle the military conditions that are the causes of these effects.

One way in which women married to servicemen work within the constraints of their migrations with the military, however, is to convert their geographical mobility into social mobility. I explored the contemporary, globalised notions of travel and culture asserted by women, even as many of the conditions they described were evocative of expat and colonial continuities. Women's assertion of cosmopolitan identities, globalist attitudes and their attendant practices of cultural consumption complicate the degree to which the experience of living overseas is controlled and contained by the military's reinforcement of borders and boundaries of nation. However, looking at the gendered, classed and ethnic boundaries that many of these practices uphold illustrates the persistence of familiar structures of encapsulation, as well as the kind of social and material limitations that contribute to women's contradictory feelings of both 'moving on' and being 'held back'. Perhaps unsurprisingly, this chapter illustrated that many of the supposed liberatory effects of transnational migration are foreclosed by the cultural, political and material conditions under which women married to servicemen move overseas. As a model, however, the idea of transmigration offers some scope for understanding the adaptive, proactive and hybrid processes through which women refuse to be fixed by the boundaries of militarised belonging.

Ranking Difference and Distinction

In Chapter 2, moving on to tease out the complexities of social mobility as it is produced through and by the British Army, I explored the intersections of rank, class and other boundaries of difference and distinction on and around the military base overseas. The aim here was to unpick some of the homogenising assumptions and stereotypes that attach to the figure of the military wife and explore how women negotiate a sense of identity, selfhood and belonging relationally, between themselves. I documented a range of ways in which women articulate their social personhood and interpret, renegotiate and inhabit their place within a socio-spatial order. Rank was the primary structure I explored in this chapter, particularly in respect of its paradoxical function as both a foil and an enabling force for women's assertion of their own power and positionality. My analysis showed that women's identities are relational and fluid, and entail processes of disavowal, disassociation and resistance, as well as (often simultaneously) processes of recognition and assimilation in relation to rank.

I began by documenting some of the conditions through which rank might be argued to affect the spouses of service personnel. This includes the incorporation of women's voluntary labour as part of their spouse's job role, differential cycles of internal mobility between officers and soldiers, and the spatial distribution of the community in service family accommodation. Looking beyond these administrative or spatial conditions to their effects, however, testifies to the productive power of rank and its circulation through other vectors of power, resulting in a range of identities and assumptions that are co-constituted through gender and class. In such a way I showed how rank extends beyond its military-administrative function to regulate power relations between women married to servicemen and female service personnel, for example. Here I demonstrated that military wives occupy a highly ambiguous position between military and civilian spheres, subject to a range of power relations mutually constituted through rank, gender and class, at the same time as they are attributed – and assert – their civilian immunity to the formal discipline through which rank is upheld. In such a way, wives (and, indeed, service personnel) can be understood as working both with and against rank, selectively engaging formal and informal modes of difference and distinction in ways that transcend any neat division between military and civilian, and between rank and other composite vectors of power such as gender and class. Military wives' complex relationship to rank demonstrates that its effects are far more diffuse, but also far more negotiable than its formal technologies imply. Women are highly aware of rank and the conditions through which it shapes their everyday lives. Finally, then, my analysis focused on some of the ways in which women married to servicemen inhabit the places they are allocated in the stratified social order. By appropriating the gendered and classed performances and identities those places prescribe, women knowingly appropriate the effects of rank in a way that is tactical and selective. In this sense, women married to servicemen can be understood not only as subjects but also as agents of rank as a vector of power that they negotiate between and among themselves. Thus, rank cannot simply be understood as a linear social hierarchy that operates vertically according to the chain of command. Rather, rank produces disciplinary power in a way that is widely dispersed and highly fluid, to the degree that it is possible to question the exceptionality of rank as a mode of disciplinary power that seeks to normalise military control. Looking at how rank and class combine with ideas about race and the colonial continuities that still shape the British Army, however, is an example of how complex and overdetermined people's negotiations with rank are. The ironic consequence of rank's adaptability – its composite forms, its shapeshifting qualities and co-constitution through so many different forms of power in any one context – is its effectiveness as a technology of power that *puts people in their place.*

Regimented Life

In the final phase of my analysis – Chapter 3 – I looked at the politics of belonging produced by the regimental system, which I argued are deeply entwined with the ideals and structures of belonging inscribed through the heterosexual family. Exploring the cultural production of the regiment, I paid attention to women's participation in a range of activities that help to reinforce belonging, but also keep its demands at bay. These alternative materialisations of community and collectivity revealed some of the ways in which women married to servicemen take up a mobile and contradictory position on both the outside and the inside of regimental belonging, asserting the value of their – and their husbands' – labour in ways that sometimes exploit, sometimes subvert, its will to social cohesion.

I explored the knitting together of these ideals, narratives and desires of belonging through the compound form of the 'regimental family', a mythic formation promoting ideals of unity, duty and love at the same time as it manifests itself in a range of disciplinary effects. It is in this sense that the regimental family is also fraught with divisions, unequal power relations and, ultimately, failure. By tracing the gendered, classed and ethnic fault lines of these divisions, my analysis reveals the degree to which the regimental family is a cultural construction that requires propping up through the conscious performance of belonging, a performativity of which its subjects are highly aware. This family production, in both its ideals and its failure, reveals the depth and scope of heteronormativity as a social glue that binds the community together with extraordinary force.

Paying attention to regimental belonging also occasions some insight into women's relationship to the state as the author of military power, particularly with respect to national service as a mode through which military participation is understood. I illustrated some of the ways in which women fought to reframe ideas about national identity and citizenship in terms of family history and affective ties. Exploring notions of duty, service and sacrifice as they were tied directly, at the time of my fieldwork, to the regiment's combat operations in Afghanistan, I detailed women's translation of the meaning of soldiering as a form of exceptional labour connected to war and state-sanctioned violence. This fundamental exposure to the violence and human vulnerability of war in anticipated or imagined forms was the focus of my analysis of the spatio-temporalities of an operational tour. Here, I sought to rethink the relationship between the combat zone and the home and counter assumptions that posit soldiers as the agents of military power and their spouses as passive subjects waiting for their return. Instead, I emphasised the everyday practices through which women married to servicemen actively manage the flow of intimate human relations, the presence of absence and the continuation of violent events 'back home'. I began by paying attention to the social construction of Afghanistan as a place that takes shape as a kind of presence in the everyday spaces of women's lives in Germany. I revealed the simultaneity and continuation of the experience of war, as well as women's instrumental role in the pacification of its effects within the community. I argued that understandings of military power must be expanded to include those effects produced beyond the times and spaces where conventional scholarship has designated history is made and politics happens, or where military force is deployed. While women seek to keep the more spectral effects of military power at bay during a period of deployment, war is productive of a range of practices and scripts that are deeply gendered and which ultimately serve to reinforce and reincorporate the reproductive role of women in supporting the continuation and perpetuation of military power.

Considering Military Presence

My starting point for this research was to create a particular, spatially and temporally specific portrait of the military conditions that shape the experiences of women married to servicemen. As reviewed above, I have drawn on ideas about mobility and transmigration; about the performativity of belonging and identity, as well as multiple borders of 'self' and 'other'; about difference, distinction, discipline and control; and about the ways in which war and the threat of violence and human vulnerability make their presence felt. By looking at the mobile and flexible ways in which women co-produce the effects of military power, I have illustrated some of the ways in which their own manoeuvres help to reshape, divert, appropriate and resist the influence of the military institution upon their everyday lives. The picture this presents is varied, multiplex and often contradictory, demonstrating that wives' relationship to military power is far from uniform or fixed, despite the seemingly intractable material and structural forms it takes.

My aim throughout my analysis has been to look beyond the apparent self-evidence of military presence and those militarised structures of migration, rank, regiment and war that undoubtedly shape the lives of those I have sought to represent. Rachel Woodward argues that 'what military geography has to do is problematize the issue of presence and ask questions about the consequences of this seemingly obvious and taken-for-granted thing' (Woodward 2004, 154). I have sought to expand the terrain for questioning military presence in two ways. First, I have done so by paying attention to a range of alternative spaces designated as 'civilian' or 'domestic' zones beyond the army camp – the kind of spaces where military presence is less visible or overt. While they remain in many fundamental ways militarily managed, such spaces constitute the sites where military presence is camouflaged or converted into other forms, the boundaries of which are frequently blurred. Secondly, I have paid attention to the movements of women married to servicemen as they circulate through these spaces and the social interactions they facilitate and foreclose.

By paying attention to a set of alternative military geographies and, furthermore, exploring the ways in which these spaces are *inhabited* in everyday life, I have sought to demonstrate not only how military geographies order space, but also how that spatial order is socially reproduced through the interactions of people across it, such that its effects are more diverse than might be assumed. I have paid attention to the differential meanings of particular spaces at particular times, which includes paying attention to absence as well as presence, and continuity or routine as well as rupture and contingency. This shows how military geographies span great distances, but also how they are navigated according to the webs and connections of the most intimate human relations. Exploring the fluidity of everyday times and spaces in close detail, tracing the multiple mobilities of women married to servicemen, and the alternative, hybrid meanings they articulate, testifies to the degree to which 'military geographies are always shifting and changing' (Woodward 2004, 9). It is this understanding of military geographies as socially produced and in flux that 'brings with it possibilities for negotiation and challenge' (ibid.). The question of women's agency thus becomes central to what I set out to illuminate about the operation of military power in this book. In the next part of this discussion, I want to outline some terms for the more fluid conceptualisation this requires.

The Militarisation of Army Wives?

If militarisation is a way of configuring the productive nature of military power, how can it help us to understand the experiences of women married to servicemen? The relevance of militarisation to my analysis in this thesis lies in its expression of the processes rather than the presence of military power. Enloe (2000, 3) defines militarisation as 'a step-by-step process by which a person or a thing gradually comes to be controlled by the military *or* comes to depend for its well-being on militaristic ideals'. It is this processual, transformative quality that distinguishes militarisation from 'militarism', although the two are often paired together in a causal relationship as above. Lutz (2002, 725) has argued that, although the concept of militarism has evolved from the idea of a separate military ideology to describe instead 'the embeddedness of a militaristic mentality in civil society', it remains narrower in scope as a term because it 'suggests that warlike values have an independent ability to drive social change'. Thus another salient aspect of militarisation here is its expression of the military's mutual imbrication with other vectors of power in a way that is multiplex and hybrid. Accordingly, Lutz (2002, 723) argues that militarisation is 'a process of inscription' through which military power can be connected to the 'less visible deformation of human potentials into the hierarchies of race, class, gender and sexuality'. Lutz's emphasis on 'human potentials' (ibid.) also hints that militarisation might be used to express the less concrete *conditions of possibility* that determine subjects' relationship to military power in particular places at particular times. Scholarship that explicitly uses militarisation as a critical analytic (e.g. Bernazzoli and Flint 2009a and 2010, 158; Demetriou 2012, Dowler 2012, 491; Enloe 2000; Gonzalez 2010, 19; Higate and Henry 2011, 134; Kuus 2009, 547; Lutz 2002, 725) highlights the ways in which it 'is woven through the social fabric' (Kuus 2009, 548), thus accounting for the diffusion of military power beyond its more obvious forms.

Bernazzoli and Flint (2010) use the terminology of militarisation[2] for their study of garrison towns because, they argue, it refers 'specifically to interactions between the military and other arenas of U.S. society' (Bernazzoli and Flint 2010, 158). As the authors argue, more research is required to understand 'the ways in which processes of militarization are advanced or resisted in places without a military presence' (ibid., 165). With a garrison town as its setting and focusing on the experiences of women married to servicemen, this research does little, empirically at least, to decentralise the role of the military institution in understandings of militarisation. However, I do seek to contribute data and analysis to a sense of *how* that connection is understood. Rather than exploring the military institution as the apparent 'source' of militarisation in this book, my aim was to explore some of the more circuitous, contested and co-operative ways in which militarisation might be argued to function, the question being not where militarisation starts or where it ends, but how it circulates. In other words, I sought to trace the pathways of militarisation and pay greater attention to the processes and transformations that militarisation entails, and which give the term its analytical value.

Although the empirical terms of this project do little to problematise the centrality of the military institution to 'what counts' as militarisation, its analytics seek to illuminate the alternative forces that make of military power a presence that is more diffuse and far more difficult to disentangle from the social relations in which it is embedded.

In this book I have used the experiences of women married to servicemen to question a range of binarisms that, as feminist and queer studies have long established (Belkin 2012, Massey 1994), align with a range of gendered categories. This includes the binarism that posits the separation of military and civilian 'spheres'. However, it is this dichotomy that scholars have argued limits the usefulness of militarisation as an analytic, in that it denotes processes that 'take the 'civilian' and make it 'militarized' (Bernazzoli and Flint 2009b, 449). From the false binary between the military and civilian, they argue, flow a host of other unhelpful dichotomies, such as 'inside/outside; foreign/domestic; war/peace; violence/non-violence; state/society' (Bernazzoli and Flint 2009b, 449). This problem stands if militarisation is used to express military power in a way that is linear and unidirectional, extending outwards from the military institution to calcify everything in its path. My findings in this book, however, show that military wives traverse and trouble the conventional boundaries between military and civilian 'spheres' in multiple ways, occupying a mobile and ambiguous position that calls into question both their incorporation into the military institution and their civilian 'immunity' to its control. Writing of the blurred boundaries surrounding a US military base, Lutz (2001) calls for more attention to the mutual imbrication of military and civilian, and outlines a provocative and complex matrix for understanding how the experiences of subjects such as women married to servicemen are invisibilised by binary thinking:

> [C]ivilian has been a category rarely discussed explicitly in America [. . .] Throughout American history, black has been marked as race, white remaining invisible. Female has been a gender, male a kind of prototype human being, without gender. The identity of civilian is clearly the unmarked of the soldier–civilian pair. Despite the power of the military physically and economically, civilian is the majority, dominant category, and so is less recognisable as such. (Lutz 2001, 235)

Lutz's point illustrates the epistemological structures that have served to relegate the experiences of subjects such as military wives to the margins within critical research. But the connection with gender as posited by Lutz (ibid.) is more than allegorical. The kinds of experiences I document in this thesis have been largely ignored within scholarship that has made the study of gender and militarisation synonymous with the study of men and masculinities. A gendered analysis that is connected to women through marriage and the family, the domestic sphere and the sexual division of labour, however, reveals the feminised sexual relations on which those masculinities depend, and which research thereon takes for granted, leaves out, and thus helps to reproduce. In multiple ways, the experiences I have explored in this book represent the constitutive outside to military masculinities, a territory that lies beyond even the scope of research on the multiplicity, conflation or queering of those masculinities. In this sense perhaps, gender as an analytic does not help (see Stern and Zalewski 2009), even where it is used as a way to expand the definition of military masculinity and transcend the divisions of sex, such that women can be argued to perform it too (Belkin 2012, 3). There is no doubt that research on military masculinities has produced valid and productive analyses and I rely on them heavily in this book. The problem, I believe, is the epistemological effect of this scholarship and the dominance of masculinity as *the* normative framework for defining and understanding the relationship between gender and the military institution. Paradoxically, a focus on the discursive production of gender, through which masculinities have multiplied and spread, has reinforced this division. As a property of bodies that is socially produced, military masculinity has been related to the 'unmasculine' (Belkin 2012, 24) and feminisation as well as to 'civilian' constructions of masculinity (Higate 2003). But critical military research has done less to explore the imbrication of military and civilian categories with dichotomies of sex and gender through the military-sexual division of labour, for example, or the embeddedness of military structures within the institutions of heterosexual marriage and the family.

This only makes it more necessary to ask, still, where *are* the women (Enloe 1989, 7)? Gender, feminist and queer scholarship continues to build upon Cynthia Enloe's (1989) question in myriad, and increasingly nuanced, ways. It has been encouraging, since I began this research, to follow the many different directions that analytics around gender and military power have taken, including within research on masculinities – not only in terms of a diversification of settings away from dominant forces like the US and British militaries (e.g. in relation to Brazil [Silva 2017] and Japan [Dalton 2022]), but also through historical research of colonial contexts (Zimmerman

2020) as well as contemporary examples of militarised communities in countries such as the Democratic Republic of Congo (Baaz and Verweijen 2017), and in relation to constructions of fatherhood and the Lord's Resistance Army (Matarazzo and Baines 2021). Research in a US and British context has also shifted focus to questions of gendered embodiment and desire, breaking down taboos in scholarship that mirrored what was hiding in plain sight in military cultures (e.g. on women combatants and menstruation [Chua 2022] and the fetishization of soldiers' bodies in uniform [Crane-Seeber 2016]). Scholarship on British military wives and army communities in the UK has also focused on conceptualising women's experiences through the lens of their mobility and liminality as subjects (Long 2022), complicating the binarisms of gendered labour and the sexual contract. Such work must also push through increasingly difficult conditions of access (Rethinking Military Spouses: Critical Research Group 2021) to be able to gather the kind of finely observed, ethnographically informed narratives that counter the British military's increasing control over the representations that give the Armed Forces their meaning domestically. Further and more nuanced research on the lived experiences of a diverse range of civilian women (and men) in relation to military institutions is needed. The continuing conceptual complexity of a gendered, feminist, queer and intersectional lens of analysis may not offer straightforward answers, or a neat and tidy vision of human relations and the agency of subjects in relation to hierarchical structures. However, it does offer the opportunity for more granular, detailed and particular examples of the complexities of military force, war, state-sanctioned violence and the multiple femininities, and indeed masculinities, that are woven through them.

One further epistemological qualification is necessary when considering the productive power of militarisation. Stating that '[m]ilitarization does not always take on the guise of war' (Enloe 2000, 2), Enloe argues for a focus on what she calls its 'humdrum forms' (ibid., 3). It is in this sense that understandings of militarisation have facilitated what might be described as a 'cultural turn' in the study of military power. Enloe's insistence that cultural forms of militarisation be taken seriously turns on the reformulation of 'culture' as expressly political, not only in the sense that it is embedded in power relations, but also – and crucially – political in the sense of being strategically deployed (Gonzalez 2010). There is much in this book to testify to the processes through which military culture is made and reproduced, as well as resisted or reformulated. However, there is nevertheless a risk that the precision of militarisation as an analytical tool is lost in analyses that become bound up in what is doubtless a profusion of military productions and aesthetics, without paying attention to their effects or the ways in which those effects are achieved. Throughout this book I have shown the effects of military culture to be deeply ambiguous, contradictory, fluid and, indeed, fallible as they are mediated by the many different women whose experiences are homogenised under the category of 'military wives'. Enloe (2000, 3) is clear that a focus on culture does not mean that the influence of military power is either ubiquitous or inevitable, nor that militaristic values are natural or given in any particular (or all) societies. For, as she argues, militarisation 'doesn't shape everything all the time. If it did, it would be impossible to distinguish' (ibid.). It is in this sense that my attention to the temporal variability of military presence, as well as its operation through the social production of space, is important in qualifying those times when the productive power of militarisation is diverted or kept at bay by women married to servicemen.

Scholars have shown how militarisation can be a valuable analytic for demonstrating precisely 'how the everyday matters' (Enloe 2004; Thrift 2000 in Bernazzoli and Flint 2010, 160) in national and international politics, if it is explored in a way that is 'more contextual; society-specific, place-specific, and time-specific' (Bernazzoli and Flint 2009b, 450). As I have shown in my exploration of military presence and importantly, women's *inhabitation* of that presence, a more nuanced analysis of military power involves looking to the places and processes through which militarisation is resisted (Bernazzoli and Flint 2010, 160). Throughout this book I have tried to find ways and sites for keeping the agency of women married to servicemen in view, a challenge that Belkin (2012) formulates in *Bring Me Men*:

> I am mindful that any effort to identify a patterned social mechanism risks restricting or foreclosing the possibility of agency, a risk that is particularly acute given my emphasis on the troops' conformity. My task, as I see it, is to map the contours of a mechanism [. . .] so that future research might assess whether these observations come together in different ways at different sites. In this way, perhaps I can identify an important pattern while leaving room for agency and contingency in this as well as future narratives. (Belkin 2012, 42)

My analysis indicates that the agency of women married to servicemen is relational and exists in mutual imbrication with, rather than opposition to, constituent elements of coercion (Madhok et al. 2013, 3). In order to formulate what this implies for women's relationship to military power, I want to pick up again on a classic paradigm from within feminist research.

Bargaining with Militarisation

Taking issue with the use of the term 'patriarchy' as an easy signifier for any apparent instance of male oppression, Kandiyoti's (1988) argument in 'Bargaining with Patriarchy' was founded on the critique that the concept was both overused and under-theorised in feminist scholarship (ibid., 274). In a similar way, I have argued that, without further empirical exploration of how military power is renegotiated, co-opted or resisted by subjects on an everyday level, militarisation and its conceptual salience risk at best simplification, at worst misattribution, or, as with patriarchy, being 'treated at a level of abstraction that obfuscates rather than reveals' (ibid.). Alison Howell (2018) has made similar claims for the limits of the term 'militarisation': 'Like any concept it guides our attention in certain directions, but it also limits our scope' (Howell 2018, 119). She highlights the unidirectional, linear temporality implied by the term that I have also sought to complicate in this book. Where Howell argues for a broader, historical account of 'martial politics' (ibid.) to debunk the idea that '"militarization" is a new process by which the exception (war) encroaches on the norm (peace)' (Howell 2018, 118), I seek to qualify, rather than 'forget' (ibid.), the term here. This is where feminist scholarship that draws attention to the difficult and often traitorous co-constitution of agency, complicity and resistance (Madhok, Phillips and Wilson 2013) in relation to overarching structures and hierarchies such as patriarchy is so useful.

Through 'Bargaining with Patriarchy', Kandiyoti (1988) helped to establish the empirical study of women's everyday lives as a core tenet of gender research that sought to add nuance to the broader concepts of feminist scholarship and activism. Her central conceit of a 'bargain' draws attention to women's assessment of the potential losses and gains involved in their daily transactions within a given social order, emphasising their choices but also acknowledging the particular conditions within which those choices are made. Kandiyoti defines it thus:

> Like all terms coined to convey a complex concept, the term 'patriarchal bargain' represents a difficult compromise. It is intended to

indicate the existence of set rules and scripts regulating gender relations, to which both genders accommodate and acquiesce, yet which
may nonetheless be contested, redefined and renegotiated. Some suggested alternatives were the terms contract, deal, or scenario; however
none of these fully captured the fluidity and tension implied by bargain. (Kandiyoti 1988, 236)

It is in this sense that the idea of a bargain, including the qualifications above, was a central inspiration for this project, and has been
consistently helpful in my efforts to understand the agency of women
married to servicemen in relation to military power. In Kandiyoti's
(1988) broad analysis of power relations in a range of different settings, the terms of a bargain can be accepted or radically rejected
(281), resistance can be passive (283) and active (284), and women's
bargains are spatially and temporally specific (285). This is precisely
the kind of empirical variation that emerges from what I have shown
of women's multiple and contradictory approaches to rationalising,
resisting and acquiescing to military-institutional power.

The idea of a bargain with military power also helps to counter
the assumption that women married to servicemen unquestioningly
follow, support or invest in the military institution through a kind
of false consciousness (Kandiyoti 1988, 282), an assumption that is
countered by the knowledge and humour with which many women
narrated their experiences and opinions. Throughout this book I
have highlighted how women's narratives and strategies are shaped
by multiple positionalities but also by multiple layers of constraints.
It is in this sense that Kandiyoti (ibid., 285) argued that paying attention to women's bargaining approaches can help to 'dissolve some of
the artificial divisions apparent in theoretical discussions of the relationships among class, race and gender'. Perhaps most productively,
Kandiyoti's framework emphasises the specificity of the mechanisms
of social control at stake, the aim being to elucidate 'the place of a
particular strategy within the internal logic of a given system' (ibid.,
283). It is the tension between the limits of the given system, combined with women's mobile negotiations within them, that the idea
of a bargain expresses: 'Even though these individual power tactics
do little to alter the structurally unfavourable terms of the overall
patriarchal script, women become experts in maximising their own
life chances' (ibid., 280).

And yet, my analysis has shown that the effects of military
power negotiated by women, and the resources they draw upon
to do so, are not strictly limited to military structures per se. Many

of the conditions I have described in this book are 'made' by the military, but the *effects* of these conditions are produced through multiple pathways, come in composite and hybrid forms, and are shapeshifting and adaptive. This prompts the question of how exceptional and bounded military control as the 'given system' (Kandiyoti 1988, 283) at stake here really is. Most compellingly, many of the examples I have studied demonstrate the blurring of the divide between military and civilian 'spheres', where women are subject to and draw upon vectors of power that lie expressly beyond the internal logic of the military institution, indeed often rely explicitly on ideas about an external, civilian threat or immunity to military control. Time and again, the bargains women make depend on their ability to assert a position on the outside of the institution, or to assert an alternative interpretation of the meaning and purpose of their labour, identities and feelings. It is here that the heterosexual family and the gendered division of labour function as both a rationale and resource for women's bargains with the military institution. Indeed, one might ask in response, what role does patriarchy have in the upholding, and the undoing, of military power?

In a study of the Israeli Army, Edna Lomsky-Feder et al. (2008) use ideas about transmigration to posit reserve soldiers as hybrid military and civilian actors. To substantiate this conceptualisation, the authors cite conditions such as 'continuous mobilization, service, demobilisation, civilian life and mobilization yet again' (ibid., 599); a rejection of static ideas about linear movement or fixed duality (598); the potential for 'rupture, critique and resistance potentiated by permeable boundaries' (595), and finally the role of reserve soldiers, upon each 'return' to service, as conduits for the flow of ideas between military and civilian culture (599). The study assesses reserve soldiers' power and positionality in terms of social status, identity and finally, the operation of an implicit contract or bargain between the reservists and the Israeli Army (ibid., 605). In this book I have focused on the mobilities of women married to servicemen, exploring their own hybrid positionalities and transmigration across military and civilian 'systems' (ibid., 593). This has revealed that women married to servicemen *do* help to alter the scripts of military power. Empirically, in their day-to-day bargains with the military institution, women articulate a range of alternative positionalities and interpretations as to how military power works, sometimes 'civilianising' its effects, such that it is hard to tell where 'military' ends and 'civilian' begins. In such a way I have sought to demonstrate the fallibility of the line between the military and civilian, the falseness of a dichotomy that leaves military wives behind, apparently stranded between two opposing forces. What my analysis shows, however, is that this 'no-man's-land' is an expressly creative and regenerative space where new forms of power are forged. So, are military wives militarised? The answer appears to be so obviously in the question: 'military wives'. But perhaps, instead, the answer is in the point that the question misses, pertaining as it does to the fixed state of having been – past tense – militarised. We might insist, on rejecting this yes-or-no question, that the relationship of army wives to forms of military power is not a question of militarised or not militarised, military or civilian, home or away, war or peace. Rather, the very *quality* of militarisation that women married to servicemen represent and somewhat personify is its contingent nature as a process that is in flux, transformative, productive and emergent.

However, at this point it is necessary to return to the lessons that can be drawn from feminist paradigms for the study of agency, where, for example, Lila Abu-Lughod (1990) cautions against 'the romance of resistance' and the need to qualify the agency of those whom research such as this attempts, perhaps over-zealously, to 'liberate'. Instead, Abu-Lughod (1990) argues that empirical analysis must focus not only on the effects, but also the causes of inequality: 'We could continue to look for and consider nontrivial all sorts of resistance, but instead of taking these as signs of human freedom we will use them strategically to tell us more about forms of power and how people are caught up in them' (ibid., 42). The experiences of women married to servicemen are significant for 'the widening of our definition of the political' (ibid., 41) in a number of ways. Scholars have defined militarisation as 'the contradictory and tense social processes in which civil society organizes itself for the production of violence' (Geyer 1989, 79 in Lutz 2002, 723; Bernazzoli and Flint 2009b, 450). Thus the meaning of militarisation also turns on what it proposes about the production of violence in organised forms and the centrality of the state in military force. As I have shown throughout my analysis, everyday micro-politics can and must be carefully connected to understandings of nationhood, state-sanctioned violence, globalisation and war that are also in circulation through military power. This complicates women's relationship to military power as not simply a question of individual or everyday agency, but also one of complicity in the inequalities and violence reproduced by military power at its sharpest extreme.

'You can't help who you fall in love with'

By means of conclusion and in order to look beyond what I have been able to explore in this book, I want to raise one more possibility regarding the agency of women married to servicemen. Hiding in plain sight within my analysis here is a sense of one further analytic for 'widening our definition of the political' (Abu-Lughod 1990, 41) and problematising what we understand about militarisation. In many ways, it constitutes one of the defining places to look for the resources available to military wives for keeping the military at bay. Yet it lies even further beyond the scope of research on the military institution and is frequently forgotten in socio-structural analyses of the institution of marriage. Indeed, it lay beyond the limits of what it was possible to ask in my interviews, and thus it lies beyond what is 'discoverable' here. It is with a brief and deliberately inconclusive exploration of love, therefore, that I draw this book to a close.

Marianne, who had been through many deployments and relocations in over twenty years of living with the regiment, recalls the death of her husband's best friend, who had been killed during operations in which both he and her husband were involved during the Iraq war:

> So I had the knock on the door from the guardroom at five o'clock in the morning. And I knew – sounds horrible – I knew [my husband] wasn't dead because there was no welfare officer and no duty officer with them, so I just knew something had happened. And they'd only come to tell me that my husband would probably be ringing me, so they could prepare me for him ringing. It was particularly hard because he'd ring, and not speak. But sometimes he'd stay on the phone for five minutes and not speak, at all. [. . .] And then um, he was supposed to come home for R&R [rest and recuperation] and his R&R was cancelled deliberately. And their reasoning – and I agree with it – is that they're better staying with the men than they are coming home as soon as something like that happened. [. . .] And I agree with that, because I couldn't have said or known or done anything at that particular time. [. . .] I think you have to accept that there are certain things that I will never know. And it means that there is a huge part of the person that you love that you'll never understand fully, and I have to accept that, you know? I think that part of loving that person is accepting that you're not ever going to be let into everything. And it's not even that I think they're protecting you, I think they're protecting themselves.

In Marianne's theorisation of her experience, she acknowledges the epistemic gap that exists between her husband's intimate experience of human vulnerability and her own. During my time with the regiment I heard repeated many times the adage 'you can't help who you fall in love with', most often as a way to deflect or sometimes shut down my questions, at other times as a platitude to avoid a more private or personal explanation. Certainly, scholars have taken a critical approach to the kinds of caring labour that are secured through the obligations and ideals of love (MacLeish 2013; Wool 2015a), while others have drawn attention to the gendered inequalities that discourses of love and military service obscure (Gray 2022). I do not want to suggest, in some kind of final attempt to weaponise sentiment or romance against the intractability of military power, that love is some kind of free-floating or transcendental ideal that can somehow free people from the kind of structures and hierarchies which, as I have shown throughout this book, consistently and comprehensively weigh people down. Indeed, often the weight is such that bonds like love are broken or irrevocably damaged.

But if military power produces violence, rupture, distance and unknowability in the way that Marianne describes, then love – not love for one's country, or for one's regiment, but love for one's spouse, in this case – must also be included in our understanding of how it is made liveable for those who serve its ceaseless demands. I can only offer a brief acknowledgement of the role of love in how military power is sensed and made sense of here, thanks to Marianne's willingness, more than anyone else I interviewed, to explore what love meant for her relationship with her husband and, implicitly, the military institution. Love, for Marianne, emerges as a significant social and emotional resource on which she draws not so much to resolve but to acquiesce to the irreconcilable tensions that army life produces, and to manage unknowability at multiple levels. Love, in Marianne's conceptualisation, is the creative, kinetic force through which she transforms multiple distances into proximity.

The central lens through which I have analysed women's experiences in this book is gender, undergirded in no small way by heteronormativity. Throughout I have revealed the imbrication of military power and gender in many different forms and, in co-constitution with other vectors of power, as productive of many different effects. This reveals women's negotiation of a host of material conditions, social structures and discourses, through which they assert their own identities and experiences in relation to the hierarchies of the military institution and each other. What has eluded the empirical and analytical reach of this project, however, is a sense of the more intimate human relations that are complicated by military power, and which complicate in turn any attempt to understand the depths to which it penetrates. Many women with whom I spoke rejected the simplistic assumptions about their experiences that are perpetuated through clichés such as being 'married to the military'. Yet the more personal meanings attached to love and marriage were not something I could always intrude upon to counter platitudes about duty or resilience. There is scope here for a great deal more research on military intimacies, on the interplay of gender and affect, sexuality, belonging and desire. It feels appropriate to my task in this book – the task of trying to lay bare the contradictions that are part of the everyday operation of military power – to finish with Marianne's conceptualisation of an epistemic gap between her and her husband, therefore. It feels appropriate, in acknowledgement of the partiality of any picture one might try to provide, to end with what remains unknowable; like Marianne's sense of her husband's experience, of what remains unresolved between their difference perspectives on army life. At the very least, out of such uncertainty, we can say that military power – like all the technologies of power we navigate – is far from monolithic, far from absolute.

Notes

1. According to my interview with a member of welfare personnel, the shift from military discipline to 'dealing with civilians' requires a personal transformation on the part of the soldier responsible, as well as a professional transformation for which further training is required: 'Dealing with stuff that you just should never ever deal with, which the professionals should be dealing with.'
2. Another term the authors suggest as part of a debate on the language of military power is 'securitisation' (Bernazzoli and Flint 2009b and also debates in Stavrianakis and Selby 2013).

Abu-Lughod, L. 1990. 'The Romance of Resistance: Tracing Transformations of Power through Bedouin Women'. *American Ethnologist*, 17, 41–55.

Abu-Lughod, L. 1991. 'Writing against Culture'. In R. Fox (ed.), *Recapturing Anthropology: Working in the Present*. Santa Fe: School of American Research Press, pp. 137–62.

Adkins, L. and Skeggs, B. 2004. *Feminism after Bourdieu*. Oxford: Blackwell / Sociological Review.

Ahmed, S. 2004. *The Cultural Politics of Emotion*. Edinburgh: Edinburgh University Press.

Ahmed, S. 2017. *Living a Feminist Life*. Durham, NC: Duke University Press.

Ahmed, S. 2019. *What's the Use? On the Uses of Us*. Durham, NC: Duke University Press

Akibayashi, K. and Takazato, S. 2009. 'Okinawa: Women's Struggle for Demilitarization'. In C. Lutz (ed.), *The Bases of Empire: The Global Struggle against U.S. Military Posts*. London: Pluto Press, 243–69.

Al-Ali, N. S. 2002. 'Loss of Status or New opportunities? Gender Relations and Transnational Ties among Bosnian Refugees'. In N. S. Al Ali and K. Koser (eds), *New Approaches to Migration? Transnational Communities and the Transformation of Home*. London and New York: Routledge, 83–102.

Alcoff, L. 1991. 'The Problem of Speaking for Others', *Cultural Critique*, 20, 5–32.

Amar, P. 2011. 'Turning the Gendered Politics of the Security State Inside Out?' *International Feminist Journal of Politics*, 13, 299–328.

Amit, V. 2007. 'Structures and Dispositions of Travel and Movement'. In V. Amit (ed.), *Going First Class? New Approaches to Privileged Travel and Movement*. New York: Berghahn Books, 1–14.

Anderson, B. 1991. *Imagined Communities: Reflections on the Origin and Spread of Nationalism* London: Verso.

Anthias, F. 2001. 'New Hybridities, Old Concepts: The Limits of "Culture"', *Ethnic and Racial Studies*, 24, 619–41.

Ardener, S. and Callan, H. 1984. *The Incorporated Wife*. London, Croom Helm in association with the Centre for Cross-Cultural Research on Women.

Atwood, K. 2013. 'Families' Emotion Work in Transnational Settings: The Case of Military Families', *New Global Studies*, 7, 1–22.

Baaz, M. E. and Verweijen, J. 2017. 'The Agency of Liminality: Army Wives In the Democratic Republic of the Congo and the Tactical Reversal of Militarization', *Critical Military Studies*, 3(3), 267–86

Basham, V. 2009. 'Effecting Discrimination: Operational Effectiveness and Harassment in the British Armed Forces', *Armed Forces and Society*, 35, 728–44.

Basham, V 2016a. *War, Identity and the Liberal State: Everyday Experiences of the Geopolitical in the Armed Forces*. London: Routledge

Basham, V. M. 2016b. Gender, Race, Militarism and Remembrance: The Everyday Geopolitics of the Poppy', *Gender, Place and Culture: A Journal of Feminist Geography*, 23(6), 883–96.

Basham, V. and Catignani, S. 2018. ;'War is Where the Hearth is: Gendered Labor and the Everyday Reproduction of the Geopolitical in the Army Reserves', *International Feminist Journal of Politics*, 20(2), 153–71.

Barkawi, T. 2017. *Soldiers of Empire: Indian and British Armies in World War II*. Cambridge: Cambridge University Press

Bastick, M. and Duncanson, C. 2018. 'Agents of Change? Gender Advisors in NATO Militaries', *International Peacekeeping*, 25(4), 554–77.

Bennett, T., Savage, M., Silva, E. B., Warde, A., Gayo-Cal, M. and Wright, D. 2008. *Culture, Class, Distinction*, 1st edn. London: Routledge.

Bernazzoli, R. M. and Flint, C. 2009a. 'Power, Place, and Militarism: Toward a Comparative Geographic Analysis of Militarization', *Geography Compass*, 3, 393–411.

Bernazzoli, R. M. and Flint, C. 2009b. 'From Militarization to Securitization: Finding a Concept that Works', *Political Geography*, 28, 449–50.

Bernazzoli, R. M. and Flint, C. 2010. 'Embodying the Garrison State? Everyday Geographies of Militarization in American Society', *Political Geography*, 29, 157–66.

Bhabha H. K. 1994. *The Location of Culture*. London: Routledge.

Booth, B. 2003. 'Contextual Effects of Military Presence on Women's Earnings', *Armed Forces and Society*, 30, 25–52.

Bourdieu, P. 1984. *Distinction: A Social Critique of the Judgement of Taste*. London: Routledge and Kegan Paul.

Bourg C. and Segal, M. W. 1999. 'The Impact of Family Supportive Practices on Organisational Commitment to the Army', *Armed Forces and Society*, 25, 633–52.

Belkin, A. 2008. 'Spam Filter: Gay Rights and the Normalization of Male–Male Rape in the U.S. Military', *Radical History Review*, 100, 180–5.

Belkin, A. 2012. *Bring Me Men: Military Masculinity and the Benign Facade of American Empire, 1898–2001*. London: Hurst.

Bell, D. B., Schumm, W. R., Knott, B. and Ender, M. 1999. 'The Desert Fax: A Research Note on Calling Home from Somalia', *Armed Forces and Society*, 25, 509–21.

Brah, A. 1996. *Cartographies of Diaspora: Contesting Identities*. London: Routledge.

Bulmer, S. 2013. 'Patriarchal Confusion?', *International Feminist Journal of Politics*, 15, 137–56.

Butler, J. 1990. *Gender Trouble: Feminism and the Subversion of Identity*. New York and London: Routledge.

Butler, J. and Kotz, L. 1992. 'The Body You Want: An Interview with Judith Butler', *Artforum*, November, 82–9.

Butler, J. 2004. *Precarious Life: The Powers of Mourning and Violence*. London: Verso.

Caglar, A. S. 2002. 'A Table in Two Hands'. In D. Kandiyoti and A. Saktanber (eds), *Fragments of Culture: The Everyday of Modern Turkey*. London and New York: I. B. Tauris, 294–307.

Castaneda, L. W. and Harrell, M. C. 2008. 'Military Spouse Employment: A Grounded Theory Approach to Experiences and Perceptions', *Armed Forces and Society* 34, 389–412

Chalfin, B., 2008. 'Sovereigns and Citizens in Close Encounter: Airport Anthropology and Customs Regimes In Neoliberal Ghana', *American Ethnologist*, 35(4), 519–38.

Chisholm, A. 2014a. 'The Silenced and Indispensable: Gurkhas in Private Military Security Companies', *International Feminist Journal of Politics*, 16, 26–47.

Chisholm, A. 2014b. ' Marketing the Gurkha Security Package: Colonial Histories and Neoliberal Economies of Private Security', *Security Dialogue*, 45(4), 349–72.

Chisholm, A. 2016. 'The Culture of Whiteness in Private Security'. In C. Kinsey and J. Bernestein, (eds), *Routledge Research Companion in Security Outsourcing*. London: Routledge, 257–69.

Chinkin, C. and Kaldor, M. 2013. 'Gender and New Wars', *Journal of International Affairs*, 67(1), 167–87.

Chisholm, A. and Eichler, M. 2018. 'The Private within the Private: Accounting for the Household in Global Privatisation of Security', *International Feminist Journal of Politics*, 20(4), 563–82.

Chrystal, P. 2018. *British Army of the Rhine: The BAOR, 1945–1993 (Cold War 1945–1991)*. Barnsley: Pen and Sword Military

Chua, J. L. 2022. 'Bloody War: Menstruation, Soldiering, and the "Gender-Integrated" United States Military', *Critical Military Studies*, 8(2), 139–58.

Clifford, J. and Marcus, G. E. 1986. *Writing Culture: The Poetics and Politics of Ethnography*. Berkeley: University of California Press.

Cockburn, C. 2012. *Antimilitarism: Political and Gender Dynamics of Peace Movements*. New York: Palgrave Macmillan.

Coles, A. and Walsh, K. 2010. 'From "Trucial State" to "Postcolonial" City? The Imaginative Geographies of British Expatriates in Dubai', *Journal of Ethnic and Migration Studies*, 36, 1317–33.

Coles, A. and Fechter, A.-M. 2008. *Gender and Family among Transnational Professionals*. New York and London: Routledge.

Coles, A. 2008. 'Making Multiple Migrations: The Life of British Diplomatic Families Overseas'. In A. Coles and A.-M. Fechter (eds), *Gender and Family among Transnational Professionals*. New York and London: Routledge, 125–48.

Cooke, T. J. and Speirs, K. 2005. 'Migration and Employment among the Civilian Spouses of Military Personnel', *Social Science Quarterly*, 86, 343–55.

Cooley, A. 2008. *Base Politics: Democratic Change and the U.S. Military Overseas*. Ithaca, NY: Cornell University Press.

Cooley, A. and Marten, K. 2006. 'Base Motives: The Political Economy of Okinawa's Antimilitarism'. *Armed Forces and Society*, 32, 566–83.

Cowen, D. and Gilbert, E. 2008. 'Citizenship in the "Homeland": Families at War'. In D. Cowen and E. Gilbert (eds), *War, Citizenship, Territory*. New York and Oxford: Routledge, 261–80.

Crane-Seeber, J. P. (2016). 'Sexy warriors: The Politics and Pleasures of Submission to the State', *Critical Military Studies*, 2(1–2), 41–55.

Cree, A. 2020. '"People want to see tears": Military Heroes and the "Constant Penelope" of the UK's Military Wives Choir', *Gender, Place and Culture: A Journal of Feminist Geography*, 27(2), 218–38.

Dalton, E. (2022) 'Women as Helpmates: The Japan Self-Defense Forces and Gender', *Critical Military Studies*, 8(1), 39–57.

Davies, C. A. 1999. *Reflexive Ethnography: A Guide to Researching Selves and Others*. New York, Routledge.

Demetriou, O. 2012. 'The Militarization of Opulence', *International Feminist Journal of Politics*, 14, 56–77.

Der Derian, J. 2001. *Virtuous War: Mapping the Military-Industrial-Media-Entertainment Network*. Boulder: Westview Press.

Dowler, L. 2012. 'Gender, Militarization and Sovereignty', *Geography Compass*, 6, 490–9.

Dowler, L. 1998. '"And They Think I'm Just a Nice Old Lady": Women and War in Belfast, Northern Ireland', *Gender, Place and Culture: A Journal of Feminist Geography*, 5(2), 159–76.

Duncanson, C. 2009. 'Forces for Good? Narratives of Military Masculinity in Peacekeeping Operations', *International Feminist Journal of Politics*, 11, 63–80.

Duncanson, C. and Woodward, R. (2016). 'Regendering the military: Theorizing women's military participation', *Security Dialogue*, 47(1), 3–21. doi: 10.1177/0967010615614137.

Elshtain, J. B. 1995. *Women and War; with a new epilogue*. Chicago: University of Chicago Press.

Enloe, C. H. 1989. *Bananas, Beaches and Bases: Making Feminist Sense of International Politics*. London: Pandora.

Enloe, C. H. 2000. *Maneuvers: The International Politics of Militarizing Women's Lives*. Berkeley: University of California Press.

Enloe, C. H. 2007. *Globalization and Militarism: Feminists Make the Link*. Lanham: Rowman and Littlefield.

Enloe, C. H. 2010. *Nimo's War, Emma's War: Making Feminist Sense of the Iraq War*. Berkeley: University of California Press.

Enloe, C. H. 2013. *Seriously! Investigating Crashes and Crises as if Women Mattered*. Berkeley: University of California Press.

Eran-Jona, M. 2011. 'Married to the Military: Military-Family Relations in the Israel Defense Forces', *Armed Forces and Society*, 37, 19–41.

Erez, E. and Bach, S. 2003. 'Immigration, Domestic Violence, and the Military: The Case of "Military Brides"', *Violence against Women*, 9, 1093–117.

Evans, M. and Beach, K. 2020. *Making Respectable Women: Changing Moralities, Changing Times* Cham: Springer International Publishing AG.

Fechter, A.-M. 2010. 'Gender, Empire, Global Capitalism: Colonial and Corporate Expatriate Wives', *Journal of Ethnic and Migration Studies*, 36, 1279–97.

Fechter, A.-M. and Walsh, K. 2010. 'Examining "Expatriate" Continuities: Postcolonial Approaches to Mobile Professionals', *Journal of Ethnic and Migration Studies*, 36, 1197–210.

Fechter, A.-M. 2007. 'Living in a Bubble: Expatriates' Transnational Spaces'. In V. Amit (ed.), *Going First Class? New Approaches to Privileged Travel and Movement*. New York: Berghahn Books, 33–52.

Federici, S. 2012. *Revolution at Point Zero: Housework, Reproduction, and Feminist Struggle*. Oakland and Brooklyn: PM Press.

Finkel, D. 2009. *The Good Soldiers*. London: Atlantic Books.

Foucault, M. 1975. *Discipline and Punish*. London: Penguin.

Franz, B. 2003. 'Bosnian Refugee Women in (Re)settlement: Gender Relations and Social Mobility', *Feminist Review*, 73, 86–104.

French, D. 2005. *Military Identities: The Regimental System, the British Army, and the British People, c.1870–2000*. Oxford: Oxford University Press.

French, C., Dandekar, C., Birtles, C. and Wesseley, S. 2005. 'The Family and Military as "Greedy Institutions": Negotiating a Work–Life Balance in the British Armed Forces', Economic and Social Research Council presentation available at http://www.kcl.ac.uk/kcmhr/publications/assetfiles/veterans/French2005-familyandmilitary.pdf

Gibson, S. and Abell, J. 2004. 'For Queen and Country? National Frames of Reference in the Talk of Soldiers in England', *Human Relations*, 57, 871–91.

Gifford, B. 2006. 'The Camouflaged Safety Net: The U.S. Armed Forces as Welfare State Institution', *Social Politics: International Studies in Gender, State and Society*, 13, 372–99.

Gillem, M. L. 2007. *America Town: Building the Outposts of Empire*. Minneapolis: University of Minnesota Press.

Gilroy, P. 1993. *The Black Atlantic: Modernity and Double Consciousness*. London: Verso.

Goffman, E. 1961. *Asylums: Essays on the Social Situation of Mental Patients and Other Inmates*. Harmondsworth: Penguin Books.

Gonzalez, R. J. 2010. *Militarizing Culture: Essays on the Warfare State*. Walnut Creek, CA: Left Coast Press.

Goodell, J. and Hearn, J. 2011. *Shade it Black: Death and After in Iraq*. Newbury, Casemate.

Gordon, A. 1997. *Ghostly Matters: Haunting and the Sociological Imagination*. Minneapolis: University of Minnesota Press.

Gordon, L. 2008. 'The Shell Ladies' Project: Making and Remaking Home'. In A. Coles and A. M. Fechter (eds), *Gender and Family among Transnational Professionals*. New York and London: Routledge.

Graham, S. 2009. 'Cities as Battlespace: The New Military Urbanism', *City – Analysis of Urban Trends Culture Theory Policy and Action*, 13, 383–402.

Gray, H. 2016a. 'Domestic Abuse and the Public/Private Divide in the British Military', *Gender, Place and Culture*, 23(6), 912–25.

Gray, H. 2016b. The Geopolitics of Intimacy and the Intimacies of Geopolitics: Combat Deployment, Post-Traumatic Stress Disorder, and Domestic Abuse in the British Military', *Feminist Studies*, 42(1), 138–65.

Gray, H. R. C. 2017. 'Domestic Abuse and the Reproduction of the Idealised "Military Wife"'. In R. Woodward and C. Duncanson (eds), *Palgrave International Handbook of Gender and the Military*. London: Palgrave Macmillan, 227–40.

Gray, H. 2022. 'The Power of Love: How Love Obscures Domestic Labour and Shuts Down Space for Critique of Militarism in the Autobiographical Accounts of British Military Wives', *Critical Military Studies*. DOI: 10.1080/23337486.2022.2033915.

Greene, T., Buckman, J., Dandekar, C. and Greenberg, N. 2010. 'How Communication with Families Can Both Help and Hinder Service Members' Mental Health and Occupational Effectiveness on Deployment', *Military Medicine*, 175, 745–9.

Grewal, I. 2006. '"Security Moms" in the Early Twentieth-century United States: The Gender of Security in Neoliberalism', *Women's Studies Quarterly*, 34, 25–39.

Hardt, M. 1999. 'Affective Labor', *boundary 2*, 26, 89–100.

Harrell, M. C. 2000. *Invisible Women: Junior Enlisted Army Wives*. Arlington: RAND.

Harrell, M. C. 2001. 'Army Officers' Spouses: Have the White Gloves Been Mothballed?', *Armed Forces and Society*, 28, 55–75.

Harvey, D. 2001. *Spaces of Capital: Towards a Critical Geography*. Edinburgh: Edinburgh University Press.

Harvey, S. B., Stephani, L., Hatch, M. J. Hull, L., Jones, N., Greenberg, N., Dandekar, C., Fear, N. and Wesseley, S. 2012. 'The Long-term Consequences of Military Deployment: A 5-Year Cohort Study of United Kingdom Reservists Deployed to Iraq in 2003', *American Journal Epidemiology*, 176, 1177–84.

Hawkins, J. P. 2001. *Army of Hope, Army of Alienation: Culture and Contradiction in the American Army Communities of Cold War Germany.* Westport: Praeger.

Henry, M. 2012. 'Peacexploitation? Interrogating Labor Hierarchies and Global Sisterhood among Indian and Uruguayan Female Peacekeepers', *Globalizations*, 9(1), 15–33.

Higate, P. 2003. '"Soft Clerks" and "Hard Civvies": Pluralizing Military Masculinities'. In P. Higate (ed.), *Military Masculinities.* Westport: Praeger, 22–42.

Higate, P. 2012. 'Drinking Vodka from the "Butt-Crack"', *International Feminist Journal of Politics*, 14, 450–69.

Higate, P. and Cameron, A. 2004. 'Looking Back: Military Partners' Reflections on the Traditional Military', *Journal of Political and Military Sociology*, 32, 207–18.

Higate, P. and Cameron, A. 2006. 'Reflexivity and Researching the Military', *Armed Forces and Society*, 32, 219–33.

Higate, P. and Henry, M. 2009. *Insecure Spaces: Peacekeeping, Power and Performance in Haiti, Kosovo and Liberia.* London: Zed.

Higate, P. and Henry, M. 2011. 'Militarising Spaces: A Geographical Exploration of Cyprus'. In S. Kirsch and C. Flint (eds), *Reconstructing Conflict: Integrating War and Post-War Geographies. Critical Geopolitics.* London: Routledge, 133–55.

Hill Collins, P. 2004. 'Learning from the Outsider Within: The Sociological Significance of Black Feminist Thought'. In S. G. Harding (ed.), *The Feminist Standpoint Theory Reader: Intellectual and Political Controversies.* New York and London: Routledge, 103–26.

Hindman, H. 2008. 'Shopping for Hypernational Home: How Expatriate Women in Kathmandu Labour to Assuage Fear'. In A. Coles and A.-M. Fechter (eds), *Gender and Family among Transnational Professionals.* New York and London: Routledge, 43–63.

Hochschild, A. R. 1983. *The Managed Heart: Commercialization of Human Feeling.* Berkeley: University of California Press.

Hockey, J. 1986. *Squaddies: Portrait of a Subculture.* Exeter: Exeter University Publications.

Hogan, P. F. and Furst Seifart, R. 2009. 'Marriage and the Military: Evidence That Those Who Serve Marry Earlier and Divorce Earlier', *Armed Forces and Society*, 36, 420–38.

Hollan, S. L. 2009. 'The Enigmatic Lynndie England: Gendered Explanations for the Crisis at Abu Ghraib', *Communication and Critical/ Cultural Studies*, 6, 246–64.

Holyfield, L., Cobb, M, Herford, S. and Ogle, K. 2019. 'Masculinity under Attack: Melodramatic Resistance to Women in Combat', *Critical Military Studies*, 5(2), 168–88.

hooks, b. 1996. 'The Oppositional Gaze: Black Female Spectators'. In hooks, *Reel to Real: Race, Sex, and Class at the Movies*. New York: Routledge, 253–74.

Howell, A. 2018. 'Forget "Militarization": Race, Disability and the "Martial Politics" of the Police and of the University', *International Feminist Journal of Politics*, 20(2), 117–36.

Hurley, M. 2018. 'The "Genderman": (Re)negotiating Militarized Masculinities When "Doing Gender" at NATO', *Critical Military Studies*, 4(1), 72–91.

Hutnyk, J. 2010. 'Hybridity'. In K. Knott and S. N. McLoughlin (eds), *Diasporas: Concepts, Intersections, Identities*. London: Zed.

Hyde, A. 2014. 'Omissions and Admissions: Poetic Writing, Feminist Ethnography and Empathetic Violence', *Journal of Narrative Politics*, 1(1), 24–40.

Iskra, D., Trainor, S., Leithauser, M. and Segal, M. W. 2002. 'Women's Participation in Armed Forces Cross-Nationally: Expanding Segal's Model', *Current Sociology*, 50, 771–97.

Jenkings, K. N., Megoran, N., Woodward, R. and Bos, D. 2012. 'Wootton Bassett and the Political Spaces of Remembrance and Mourning', *Area*, 44, 356–63.

Jervis, S. 2008. 'Moving Experiences: Responses to Relocation among British Military Wives'. In A. Coles and A.-M. Fechter, *Gender and Family among Transnational Professionals*. New York and London: Routledge.

Jervis, S. 2011. *Relocation, Gender, and Emotion: A Psycho-Social Perspective on the Experiences of Military Wives*. London: Karnac Books.

Johnston, P. 2019. *British Forces in Germany: The Lived Experience*. London: Profile Editions.

Kandiyoti, D. 1988. 'Bargaining with Patriarchy', *Gender and Society*, 2, 274–90.

Kaplan, A. 2003. 'Homeland Insecurities: Some Reflections on Language and Space', *Radical History Review*, 85 (Winter), 82–93.

Kaplan, D. and Ben-Ari, E. 2000. 'Brothers and Others in Arms: Managing Gay Identity in Combat Units of the Israeli Army', *Journal of Contemporary Ethnography*, 29(4), 396–432.

Katz, C. 2006. 'Banal Terrorism, Spatial Fetishism and Everyday Insecurity'. In D. Gregory and A. Pred (eds), *Violent Geographies: Fear, Terror and Political Violence*. London: Routledge, 349–62.

King, A. 2006. 'The Word of Command: Communication and Cohesion in the Military', *Armed Forces and Society*, 32, 493–512.

King, A. 2007. 'The Existence of Group Cohesion in the Armed Forces: A Response to Guy Siebold'. *Armed Forces and Society*, 33, 638–45.

King, A. 2009. 'Unity is Strength: Staff College and the British Officer Corps', *The British Journal of Sociology*, 60, 123–44.

Kirke, C. 2009. 'Group Cohesion, Culture, and Practice'. *Armed Forces and Society*, 35, 745–53.

Kirke, C. and York, J. 2005. 'Postmodernist Command: A Contradiction in Terms for the British Army?', *Defence Studies*, 5, 305–22.

Kurotani, S. 2007. 'Middle-class Japanese Housewives and the Experience of Transnational Mobility'. In V. Amit (ed.), *Going First Class? New Approaches to Privileged Travel and Movement*. New York: Berghahn Books.

Kuus, M. 2009. 'Cosmopolitan militarism? Spaces of NATO Expansion', *Environment and Planning – Part A*, 41, 545–62.

Lather, P. 2007. *Getting Lost: Feminist Efforts Toward a Double(d) Science*. Albany: State University of New York Press.

Le Gamin au vélo. 2011 [film], dir. Luc Dardenne and Jean-Pierre Dardenne. France: Diaphana Films.

Lefebvre, H. [1961] 2008. *Critique of Everyday Life Volume Two*. London: Verso.

Lewis, R. 1996. *Gendering Orientalism: Race, Femininity, and Representation*. London: Routledge.

Little, R. D. and Hisnanick, J. J. 2007. 'The Earnings of Tied-Migrant Military Husbands', *Armed Forces and Society*, 33, 547–70.

Lobasz, J. K. 2008. 'The Woman in Peril and the Ruined Woman: Representations of Female Soldiers in the Iraq War', *Politics and Policy*, 29, 305–34.

Lomsky-Feder, E.; Gazit, N. and Ben-Ari, E. 2007. 'Reserve Soldiers as Transmigrants: Moving between the Civilian and Military Worlds', *Armed Forces and Society*, 34, 593–614.

Lomsky-Feder, E. and Rapoport, T. 2003. 'Juggling Models of Masculinity: Russian-Jewish Immigrants in the Israeli Army', *Sociological Inquiry*, 73(1), 114–37.

Long, E. 2019. 'The spirit of community, the Army family, and the impact on formal and informal support mechanisms. In R. Moelker, M. Andres, and N. Rones (eds), *The Politics of Military Families: State, Work Organizations, and the Rise of the Negotiation Household*, London: Routledge, 184–97.

Long, E. 2022. 'Living Liminal Lives: Army Partners' Spatiotemporal Experiences of Deployment', *Armed Forces and Society*, 48(3), 589–608.

Lundborg, T. 2012. *Politics of the Event: Time, Movement, Becoming.* London: Routledge.

Lutz, C. A. 2001. *Homefront: A Military City and the American Twentieth Century.* Boston, MA: Beacon Press.

Lutz, C. 2002. 'Making War at Home in the United States: Militarization and the Current Crisis', *American Anthropologist*, 104, 723–35.

Lutz, C. 2009. *The Bases of Empire: The Global Struggle Against U.S. Military Posts.* London: Pluto Press.

McClintock, A. 1995. *Imperial Leather: Race, Gender and Sexuality in the Colonial Contest.* New York: Routledge.

McClintock, A. 1993. 'Family Feuds: Gender, Nationalism and the Family', *Feminist Review*, 44, 61–80.

McInnis, V. 2017. *Women of Empire: Nineteenth-century Army Officers' Wives in India and the U.S. West.* Norman: University of Oklahoma Press.

MacDonald, K. 2004. 'Black Mafia, Loggies and Going for the Stars: The Military Elite Revisited'. *The Sociological Review*, 52, 106–35.

MacLeish, K. T. 2013. *Making War at Fort Hood: Life and Uncertainty in a Military Community.* Princeton: Princeton University Press.

Madhok, S., Phillips, A. and Wilson, K. 2013. *Gender, Agency, and Coercion.* Basingstoke: Palgrave Macmillan.

Madison, D. S. 2005. *Critical Ethnography: Method, Ethics, and Performance.* Thousand Oaks and London: Sage.

Mansfield, N. 2016. *Soldiers as Workers: Class, Employment, Conflict and the Nineteenth-century Military.* Liverpool: Liverpool University Press.

Massey, D. B. 1994. *Space, Place and Gender.* Cambridge: Polity.

Matarazzo, A. and Baines, E. (2021). 'Becoming Family: Futurity and the Soldier-Father', *Critical Military Studies*, 7(3), 278–95.

Merriman, P., Peters, K., Adey, P., Cresswell, T., Forsyth, I. and Woodward, R. (2017). 'Interventions on Military Mobilities', *Political Geography*, 56, 44–52.

Mies, M. 1983. 'Towards a Methodology for Feminist Research'. In G. Bowles and R. Duelli Klein (eds), *Theories of Women's Studies.* London: Routledge.

Millett, K. et al. 2016. *Sexual Politics*, Foreword by Catharine A. MacKinnon; Afterword by Rebecca Mead. New York: Columbia University Press.

Ministry of Defence 2011a. *The Armed Forces Covenant* https://www.gov.uk/government/uploads/system/uploads/attachment_data/file/49469/the_armed_forces_covenant.pdf

Ministry of Defence. 2011b. *Tri-Service Families Continuous Attitude Survey (FAMCAS)* Report 2011 https://www.gov.uk/government/uploads/system/uploads/attachment_data/file/280433/2011.pdf

Ministry of Defence. 2012. MOD Personnel Location Statistics https://www.gov.uk/government/uploads/system/uploads/attachment_data/file/280069/1_january_2012.pdf

Ministry of Defence. 2021. *Future Soldier Guide* https://www.gov.uk/government/publications/future-soldier-transforming-the-british-army

Moelker, R., Andres, M., Bowen, G. and Manigart, P. 2015. *Military Families and War in the 21st Century*. London: Routledge.

Moelker, R., Rones, N. and Andres, M. 2019. *The Politics of Military Families: State, Work Organizations, and the Rise of the Negotiation Household*. London: Routledge.

Moelker, R. and Van Der Kloet, I. 2006. 'Military Families and the Armed Forces'. In G. Caforio (ed.), *Handbook of the Sociology of the Military*. New York: Springer, 201–23.

Moon, K. H. S. 1997. *Sex among Allies: Military Prostitution in U.S.– Korea Relations*. New York: Columbia University Press.

Morgan, M. J. 2006. 'American Empire and the American Military', *Armed Forces and Society*, 32, 202–19.

Moskos, C. and Wood, F. 1989. *The Military: More Than Just a Job?* Washington, DC: Pergamon Brassey's.

Mulligan, K., Jones, N., Davies, M., McAllister, P., Fear, N. T., Wesseley, S. and Greenberg, N. 2012. 'Effects of Home on the Mental Health of British forces Serving in Iraq and Afghanistan', *British Journal of Psychiatry*, 201(3), 193–8.

Mulvey, L. 1975. 'Visual Pleasure and Narrative Cinema', *Screen*, 16(3), 6–18.

Murray, W. 1999. 'Does Military Culture Matter?', *Orbis*, 43, 27–42.

Myers, J. C. 2001. 'Performing the Voyage Out: Victorian Female Emigration and the Class Dynamics of Displacement', *Victorian Literature and Culture*, 29(1), 129–46.

O'Brien, T. 1998. 'How to Tell a True War Story', in P. Geyh et al. (eds), *Postmodern American Fiction: A Norton Anthology*. New York: W. W. Norton, 174–83.

Okros, A. and Scott, D. 2015. 'Gender Identity in the Canadian Forces: A Review of Possible Impacts on Operational Effectiveness', *Armed Forces and Society*, 41(2), 243–56

Ong, A. 1999. *Flexible Citizenship: The Cultural Logics of Transnationality*. Durham, NC: Duke University Press.

O'Reilly, K. 2005. *Ethnographic Methods*. London and New York: Routledge.

Pateman, C. 1988. *The Sexual Contract*. Cambridge: Polity.

Pearsall, J. (ed.) 1998. *The New Oxford Dictionary of English*. Oxford: Oxford University Press.

Peteet, J. 1994. 'Male Gender and Rituals of Resistance in the Palestinian Intifada: A Cultural Politics of Violence', *American Ethnologist*, 21, 31–49.

Peterson, V. S. 2002. 'Rewriting (Global) Political Economy as Reproductive, Productive, and Virtual (Foucauldian) Economies'. *International Feminist Journal of Politics*, 4, 1–30.

Pratt, G. and Yeoh, B. 2003. 'Transnational (Counter) Topographies', *Gender, Place and Culture*, 10, 159–66.

Ray, S. 2013. 'The Nonmartial Origins of the "Martial Races": Ethnicity and Military Service in Ex-British Colonies', *Armed Forces and Society*, 39(3), 560–75.

Razack, S. 2000. 'From the "Clean Snows of Petawawa": The Violence of Canadian Peacekeepers in Somalia, *Cultural Anthropology*, 15(1), 127–63.

Rethinking Military Spouses: Critical Research Group. 2021. [Report] 'Bringing the Homefront to the Forefront: UK perspectives on critical research with military spouses'. Post-Webinar Full Report, University of York.

Rich, A. 2001. *Arts of the Possible*. New York: Norton.

Robbins, B. 1998. 'Introduction Part I: Actually Existing Cosmopolitanism'. In P Cheah and B. Robbins (eds), *Cosmopolitics: Thinking and Feeling beyond the Nation*. Minneapolis: University of Minnesota Press.

Salih, R. 2003. *Gender in Transnationalism: Home, Longing and Belonging among Moroccan Migrant Women*. London, Routledge.

Sandars, C. T. 1999. *America's Overseas Garrisons: The Leasehold Empire*. Oxford and New York, Oxford University Press.

Savage, M. 2015. *Social Class in the 21st Century*. London: Pelican.

Scott, J. C. 1985. *Weapons of the Weak: Everyday Forms of Peasant Resistance*. New Haven and London: Yale University Press.

Scott, S. 2011. *Total Institutions and Reinvented Identities*. New York: Palgrave Macmillan.

Segal, M. W. 1986. 'The Military and the Family as Greedy Institutions', *Armed Forces and Society*, 13, 9–38.

Sheringham, M. 2006. *Everyday Life: Theories and Practices from Surrealism to the Present.* Oxford, Oxford University Press.

Siebold, G. L. 2007. 'The Essence of Military Group Cohesion'. *Armed Forces and Society*, 33, 286–5.

Silva, C. R. 2017. 'Military Families: Life, Social Organization and Remote Basing Experiences for Brazilian Military Families'. In R. Woodward and C. Duncanson (eds), *Palgrave International Handbook of Gender and the Military.* London: Palgrave Macmillan, 211–26.

Sjoberg, L. 2007. 'Agency, Militarized Femininity and Enemy Others: Observations From the War In Iraq', *International Feminist Journal of Politics*, 9, 82–101.

Skeggs, B. 1997. *Formations of Class and Gender: Becoming Respectable.* London: Sage.

Skeggs, B. 2004. *Class, Self, Culture.* London: Routledge.

Smart, C. 2009. 'Shifting Horizons: Reflections on Qualitative Methods', *Feminist Theory*, 10, 295–308.

Smirl, L. 2008. 'Building the Other, Constructing Ourselves: Spatial Dimensions of International Humanitarian Response', *International Political Sociology*, 2, 236–53.

Soeters, J., Winslow, D. and Weibull, A. 2006. 'Military Culture'. In G. Caforio (ed.), *Handbook of the Sociology of the Military.* New York: Springer, 237–54.

Spivak, G. C. 1988. 'Can the Subaltern Speak?'. In C. Nelson and L. Grossberg (eds), *Marxism and the Interpretation of Culture.* Basingstoke: MacMillan Education, 271–313.

Stanford, F. 2011. *Don't Say Goodbye: Our Heroes and the Families They Leave Behind.* London: Hodder & Stoughton.

Stanley, L. 1992. *The Auto/Biographical I: The Theory and Practice of Feminist Auto/Biography.* Manchester: Manchester University Press.

Stavrianakis, A. and Selby, J. 2013. *Militarism and International Relations: Political Economy, Security, Theory.* Abingdon and New York: Routledge.

Stern, M. and Zalewski, M. 2009. 'Feminist Fatigue(s): Reflections on Feminism and Familiar Fables of Militarisation', *Review of International Studies*, 35, 611–30.

Strategic Command Germany Enabling Office. 2023. 'LEC HR'. https://bfgnet.de/employment/lec-hr

Taber, N. 2011. '"You better not get pregnant while you're here": Tensions between Masculinities and Femininities in Military Communities of Practice'. *International Journal of Lifelong Education*, 30, 331–48.

Taussig, M. T. 2011. *I Swear I Saw This: Drawings in Fieldwork Notebooks, Namely My Own*. Chicago: University of Chicago Press.

Thomas, L. 2012. 'Working-class Whiteness from Within and Without: An Auto-Ethnographic Response to Avtar Brah's "The Scent of Memory"', *Feminist Review*, 100(1), 106–23.

Thornborrow, T. and Brown, A. D. 2009. 'Being Regimented: Aspiration, Discipline and Identity Work in the British Parachute Regiment'. *Organization Studies*, 30, 355–76.

Throsby, K. 2013. '"If I go in like a cranky sea lion, I come out like a smiling dolphin": Marathon Swimming and the Unexpected Pleasures of Being a Body in Water', *Feminist Review*, 103, 5–22.

Tidy, J. 2015. 'Forces Sauces and Eggs for Soldiers: Food, Nostalgia, and the Rehabilitation of the British Military', *Critical Military Studies*, 1(3), 220–32.

Titunik, R. F. 2008. 'The Myth of the Macho Military', *Polity*, 40, 137–63.

UK HM Government. 2010. *Strategic Defence and Security Review* https://www.gov.uk/government/uploads/system/uploads/attachment_data/file/62482/strategic-defence-security-review.pdf

Valentine, D. 2007. *Imagining Transgender: An Ethnography of a Category*. Durham, NC: Duke University Press.

Venning, A. 2005. *Following the Drum: The Lives of Army Wives and Daughters, Past and Present*. London: Headline.

Vertovec, S. 2010. 'Cosmopolitanism'. In K. Knott and S. N. McLoughlin (eds), *Diasporas: Concepts, Intersections, Identities*. London, Zed, 63–8.

Vinitzky-Seroussi, V. and Ben-Ari, E. 2000. '"A Knock on the Door": Managing Death in the Israeli Defense Forces', *Sociological Quarterly*, 41, 391–411.

Vuga, J. and Juvan, J. 2013. 'Work–Family Conflict between Two Greedy Institutions – the Family and the Military', *Current Sociology*, 61, 1058–77.

Walsh. K. 2008. 'Travelling Together? Work, Intimacy and Home among British Expatriate Couples in Dubai'. In A. Coles and A.-M. Fechter (eds), *Gender and Family among Transnational Professionals*. New York and London: Routledge.

Ware, V. 2010. 'Whiteness in the Glare of War: Soldiers, Migrants and Citizenship: Intersecting Whiteness, Interdisciplinary Debates', *Ethnicities*, 10(3), 313–30.

Ware, V. 2012. *Military Migrants: Fighting for YOUR Country*. Basingstoke: Palgrave Macmillan.

Westhuis, D. J., Fafara, R. J. and Ouellette, P. 2006. 'Does Ethnicity Affect the Coping of Military Spouses?', *Armed Forces and Society*, 32, 584–603.

Wilcox, L. 2013. 'Explosive Bodies and Bounded States', *International Feminist Journal of Politics*, 16, 66–85.

Winslow, D. 2009. 'Misplaced Loyalties: The Role of Military Culture in the Breakdown of Discipline in Two Peace Operations', *Journal of Military and Strategic Studies*, 6, 1–19.

Woodward, R. 1998. '"It's a man's life!": Soldiers, Masculinity and the Countryside'. *Gender, Place and Culture – A Journal of Feminist Geography*, 5(3), 277–300.

Woodward, R. 2004. *Military Geographies*. Malden, MA: Blackwell.

Woodward, R. 2008. '"Not for Queen and Country or any of that shit . . .": Reflections on Citizenship and Military Participation in Contemporary British Soldier Narratives'. In E. Gilbert and D. Cowan (eds), *War, Citizenship, Territory*. London: Routledge.

Woodward R., Jenkings K. N. and Williams, A. 2017. 'Militarisation, Universities and the University Armed Service Units', *Political Geography*, 60, 203–12.

Woodward, R. and Winter, P. 2006. 'Gender and the Limits to Diversity in the Contemporary British Army', *Gender, Work and Organization*, 13, 45–67.

Woodward, R., and Jenkings, N. 2018. *Bringing War to Book: Writing and Producing the Military Memoir*. London: Palgrave Macmillan.

Wool, Z. H. 2013. 'On Movement: The Matter of US Soldiers' Being after Combat', *Ethnos: Journal of Anthropology*, 78, 403–33.

Wool, Z. H. 2015a. *After War: The Weight of Life at Walter Reed*. Durham, CT: Duke University Press.

Wool, Z. H. 2015b. 'Critical Military Studies, Queer Theory, and the Possibilities of Critique: The Case of Suicide and Family Caregiving in the US Military', *Critical Military Studies*, 1 (1), 23–37.

Yeoh, B. and Willis, K. 2004. 'Constructing Masculinities in Transnational Space: Singapore Men on the "Regional Beat"'. In P. Jackson, P. Crang, P. and C. Dwyer (eds), *Transnational Spaces*. London and New York: Routledge, 147–63.

Yuval-Davis, N. 1997. *Gender and Nation*. London: Sage.

Zimmerman, S. 2020. *Militarizing Marriage: West African Soldiers' Conjugal Traditions in Modern French Empire*. Columbus: Ohio University Press.

EU Authorised Representative:

Easy Access System Europe Mustamäe tee 50, 10621 Tallinn, Estonia

gpsr.requests@easproject.com

Printed and bound by CPI Group (UK) Ltd, Croydon, CR0 4YY

25/02/2026

02060092-0003